EVERYTHING
ABOUT
HOCKEY

J. Alexander Poulton

OVER
TIME
BOOKS

The Publisher: Overtime Books

Website: www.overtimebooks.com

Library and Archives Canada Cataloguing in Publication

Poulton, J. Alexander (Jay Alexander), 1977–
      Everything about hockey / J. Alexander Poulton.

Includes bibliographical references.
ISBN 978-1-897277-71-3

      1. Hockey. 2. Hockey—Miscellanea. I. Title.

GV847.P685 2012   796.962   C2012-903365-0

Project Director: Faye Boer
Project Editor: Jordan Allan
Cover Photo Credits: photo of ice and boards—top left corner: © Sparkia I Dreamstime.com; photo of puck and stick on red—4th row from top, center: © Jupiter Images; all other photos: © Photos.com
Photo Credits: Photos courtesy of Janina Kürschner (p. 242, 243, 269, 280, 361, 400, 409, 412); all other photos: © Photos.com

We acknowledge the financial support of the Government of Canada through the Canada Book Fund (CBF) for our publishing activities.

Canadian Patrimoine
Heritage canadien

PC: 5

Dedication
To FF, MD, NR, VH, CB, CP and JR

Introduction

"A fast body-contact game played by men with clubs in their hands and knives laced to their feet."

–Paul Gallico

In the world of hockey, there are enough facts, stats, trivia and history to fill countless volumes. Since the early days of the game until today, the athletes—both the pros and the beer leaguers—the fans and those in the business have made the sport of hockey into a global phenomenon. From the frozen pond in your backyard to the gold medal game at the Olympics, I have included the most important aspects of hockey and its history into one book. For the sake of space, I could not include all the names of the players who ever played in the professional ranks, but I have diligently tried to include all the major events that have shaped the game. There is no doubt that I have probably omitted a few, but I believe I have managed to capture a breadth of history and facts that will give the reader a detailed overview of all that is hockey. It is a single volume that you can open up and discover something new each time. For the hardcore hockey fan or for those with a growing interest, this book takes you from the letter "A" sewn onto a player's jersey all the way to explaining the various "Zones" on the ice.

A: The letter found on the jersey of the player designated the team's alternate captain or, as they are more informally referred to, "assistant" captain. Teams are only allowed to appoint two alternate captains, and should there be no captain on the team, teams cannot appoint a third alternate captain. In the Ontario Hockey League (OHL), Québec Major Junior Hockey League (QMJHL), Western Hockey League (WHL) and minor leagues under the jurisdiction of Hockey Canada, however, teams are permitted to have up to three alternate captains.

AHL (American Hockey League): A minor hockey league founded in 1940. It is one of the NHL's primary leagues for developing players. Currently 30 teams are on the roster of the AHL, and its league offices are located in Springfield, Massachusetts. The annual champion of the American Hockey League is awarded the Calder Cup. Although the majority of the teams in the league are from the United States, four teams have arenas in Canada: the St. John's Ice Caps, the Abbotsford Heat, the Toronto Marlies and the Hamilton Bulldogs. Each AHL team is affiliated with an NHL team and acts as their junior farm team.

See Calder Cup

ALH (Asia League Ice Hockey): A professional ice hockey league based in East Asia currently with seven teams from Japan, China and South Korea, with the league head-quartered in Japan. The ALH was formed in 2003 after the failure of the Japan Ice Hockey League and the folding of the Korea Ice Hockey League. The goal of the league was to promote hockey in Asia, to bring increased awareness to the developing of national hockey programs and in return hopefully to build better national teams for the Olympics. In the first season in 2003–04, four Japanese teams and one Korean team participated. That year, the Nippon Paper Cranes won the championship. In the following seasons, teams from China and Russia were added to the league. As of 2011, only teams from China, Japan and South Korea remain in the league. Several NHL players have played in the Asia League, including Esa Tikkanen, Jamie McLennan, Wade Flaherty, Tyson Nash and Claude Lemieux.

Asia League Champions

2003–04	Nippon Paper Cranes
2004–05	Seibu Prince Rabbits
2005–06	Seibu Prince Rabbits
2006–07	Nippon Paper Cranes
2007–08	Oji Eagles
2008–09	Nippon Paper Cranes
2009–10	Anyang Halla
2010–11*	Tohoku Free Blades and Anyang Halla

During the 2010–11 playoffs, the Tohoku Free Blades were set to face off against the Anyang Halla when a 9.0 earthquake struck off the coast of Japan near Tohoku, forcing the league to cancel the remaining playoff games and declare both the Free Blades and Halla the champions because of the extremely unsafe circumstances.

Adams Division: The NHL's Adams Division was formed in 1974 as part of the Prince of Wales Conference. Named in honour of Charles Adams, founder of the Boston Bruins, it lasted until 1993. When originally formed, it comprised the Boston Bruins, Buffalo Sabres, California Golden Seals and Toronto Maple Leafs, and in its final year in 1993, it included the Boston Bruins, Buffalo Sabres, Hartford Whalers, Montréal Canadiens, Ottawa Senators and Québec Nordiques. The division was changed in 1993 to reflect the more regional character of the new NHL to appeal to the new emerging markets in the United States. The Bruins won the most division titles from 1974 to 1993 with nine, followed by the Montréal Canadiens with five.

See Northeast Division

Air Canada Centre (ACC): The current home arena of the Toronto Maple Leafs. Built in 1999, this building replaced the iconic Maple Leaf Gardens that was constructed in 1931 and where so many historic moments had occurred. But as the NHL's teams opened bigger and more modern facilities across the league, so too did the Maple Leafs have to follow suit to keep up. Construction on the Air Canada Centre was actually undertaken for the sole purpose of housing the NBA's Toronto Raptors while the Leafs considered opening their own separate facility. However, while construction was underway, Maple Leaf Sports and Entertainment Group (owner of the Leafs) purchased the Raptors along with their partially completed building and altered the ACC's designs to suit the needs of an NHL team. The building seats 18,819 fans for hockey games and is home to the Maple Leafs, the Raptors and the Toronto Rock of the National Lacrosse League. When the building opened in 1999, Air

Canada purchased the naming rights for the building for a period of 20 years.

See Toronto Maple Leafs

Alberta Oilers: The original name of the Edmonton Oilers during the first World Hockey Association (WHA) season of 1972–73.

See Edmonton Oilers

Allan Cup: Trophy awarded annually to the winner of the national senior men's amateur hockey championships in Canada. The Allan Cup was created in 1909 by Montréal businessman and president of the Montréal Amateur Athletic Association, Sir Hugh Montagu Allan, to be presented to the amateur champions of Canada. At first, the trophy began as a challenge cup, but due to the difficulties of organizing amateur tournaments across a country the size of Canada, it moved to a champion-based system where the winner was decided after a full season and playoffs. The first winners of the Allan Cup were the Ottawa Cliffsides.

Starting in 1920, the Allan Cup championship team was selected to represent Canada in amateur play at the Olympics and at the World Championships. This practise was stopped in the 1960s when Canada formed a men's national team. Although the Allan Cup no longer holds the prestige it once did, it remains an important part of Canadian hockey history. The city of Thunder Bay holds the most championships with 10. The original Allan Cup sits in the Hockey Hall of Fame while a replica is given to the championship team.

All-Montréal: Major pro team in the Canadian Hockey Association (CHA), 1909–10.

All-Star Game: Although the first official "All-Star" game was held midway through the 1947–48 season, several earlier games that were touted as All-Star games deserve mention. The first game to call itself "All-Star" occurred on January 2, 1908, between the Montréal Wanderers and a team of All-Stars from the Eastern Canada Amateur Hockey Association (ECAHA). The game was set up as a benefit for the family of Montréal Wanderers defenceman Hod Stuart, who died in a diving accident in 1907 just three months after his club had won the Stanley Cup. The game pulled in $2000, all of which went to help Stuart's family.

The NHL's first All-Star game occurred on February 14, 1934. This game was held as a result of an incident that happened on December 12, 1933, during a game between the Boston Bruins and Toronto Maple Leafs. During the game, Toronto's King Clancy tripped Boston's Eddie Shore,

sending him crashing to the ice. Not seeing who had tripped him, Shore took out his anger on the nearest Maple Leaf, which happened to be Ace Bailey. Shore hit Bailey from behind, flipping him over. Bailey's head hit the ice, splitting it open and sending him to the hospital, where doctors called in a priest to perform last rites for him. Fortunately, Bailey recovered, but he was never able to play hockey again.

To help pay his medical bills and help the Bailey family, the NHL held its first All-Star game between the Toronto Maple Leafs and an All-Star team made up of players from the seven other NHL teams. The most memorable moment came when Bailey shook Eddie Shore's hand in a gesture of forgiveness. The Montréal Canadiens also held an All-Star benefit game in honour of the late Howie Morenz after he died as a result of injuries suffered during a game. The game was held November 3, 1937, between the Montréal Canadiens and a team of NHL All-Stars.

The annual All-Star game was not in place until 1947–48. It was held at Maple Leaf Gardens on October 13, 1947. The format pitted the defending Stanley Cup champions against a team of NHL All-Stars. The All-Stars won the game 4–3 over the defending cup champion Toronto Maple Leafs. From 1947 to 1966, the All-Star game was played prior to the start of the season, but when the league expanded in 1967, two All-Star teams were selected to play against each other.

Gordie Howe made the most appearances at All-Star games with a record 23 times, while Ray Bourque appeared in 19 games and Wayne Gretzky in 18. Wayne Gretzky leads the all-time scoring at the All-Star game with 13 goals and

12 assists for 25 points, while Mario Lemieux scored 13 goals and 10 assists for 23 points in just 10 appearances.

Altercation: A polite word for a fight or a pushing match. "The two players involved in the altercation were sent to the sin bin [penalty box]for five minutes to cool down."

See Penalty Box

Amateur Draft: Established in 1963, the draft was the system under which the NHL teams would claim the rights to players from the junior levels of hockey. This meant that any amateur player under the age of 20 was eligible for selection. The Amateur Draft changed its name to the NHL Entry Draft in 1979. Starting in 1980, the rules were changed to allow players who had previously played professionally

to be drafted. This rule change was made to facilitate the absorption of players from the defunct World Hockey Association (WHA).

See Entry Draft

American Airlines Center (AAC): Current home of the Dallas Stars. First opened on September 1, 1999, the AAC was built to replace the aging Reunion Arena, which had outlived its usefulness. The arena seats up to 18,584 fans for hockey games. The AAC hosted the 55th NHL All-Star game on January 24, 2007.

See Dallas Stars

Anaheim Ducks: Founded under the name of the Mighty Ducks of Anaheim in 1993 by the Walt Disney Company, at first many people looked at the team as sort of a joke. They were after all named after a youth-oriented movie from 1992 staring Emilio Estevez called *The Mighty Ducks*. The logo of the team was taken straight from the movie, a stylized goaltender mask in the shape of a duck bill with two crossed hockey sticks on a black and green background.

The Ducks moved into the Arrowhead Pond—now the Honda Center—located a short distance from Disneyland, the same year they were scheduled to begin playing. The Ducks hired Ron Wilson as their coach, selected Paul Kariya fourth overall in the 1993 NHL Entry Draft and put together a solid team of rookies and veterans in the Expansion Draft for the start of the season.

The franchise's first game was played at home on October 8, 1993, against the Detroit Red Wings. The game showed the fans that their team still had a long way to go before becoming

A

one of the dominant franchises, losing by a painful score of 7–2. The Ducks lost their next two games before finally winning their first-ever NHL game against the Edmonton Oilers on October 13, 1993, by a 4–3 score. The first few seasons in the league were tough for the Ducks, who lost more games than they won and missed out on the postseason. Fans, however, stood by their team and were finally rewarded with some action at the end of the 1996–97 season, when they made the playoffs for the first time. Not only did they make the playoffs, but they ended up winning in the first round against the Phoenix Coyotes. Unfortunately, the Ducks were stopped abruptly by the Detroit Red Wings in the second-round in a four-game sweep.

Over the next few years, the Detroit Red Wings consistently spoiled the Ducks' postseason aspirations whenever they managed enough points to make it into the playoffs. It wasn't until the turn of the century that the Ducks' fortunes began to turn around. Although the Ducks were one of the worst teams in the league from 2000 to 2002, the 2002–03 season saw the team make a complete 180. The main reason was the hiring of head coach Mike Babcock. A master motivator and strategist, Babcock turned the Ducks from a 13th-place team in the Western Conference to a 7th-place team in just one year, good enough for a spot in the playoffs. Unfortunately, they were up against the Detroit Red Wings. This time, the Ducks shocked the hockey world by sweeping the defending Stanley Cup champions.

In the second round, they faced off against the equally menacing Dallas Stars. The first game ended up being the fourth longest game in NHL history, going into a fifth overtime period before forward Petr Sykora scored to give the Ducks the win. The Ducks went on the beat the Stars to make it into the Western Conference finals for the first time in franchise history and were matched up against the sixth seeded Minnesota Wild. Ducks goaltender Jean-Sébastien Giguère was the hero of the series, stringing together three consecutive shutouts and allowing only one goal in the fourth game to sweep the Wild and move into the Stanley Cup finals against the New Jersey Devils.

The finals proved to be one of the more exciting match-ups despite both teams being known for their excessively defensive systems. Both teams won all their games on home ice, meaning the Ducks were behind one game after game five, needing to win game six to hold on. The most memorable moment in game six came when Devils defenceman Scott Stevens knocked out Ducks star Paul Kariya with a vicious check on the Devils blue line. Kariya lay on the ice a few seconds before waking up in a cloud. Most thought he was done for the night, even done for the series, but in the second period, Kariya returned and scored as the Ducks went

A

on to win the game 5–2. Unfortunately, the Ducks could not close out the series with a pivotal game seven win, losing a hard-fought match to the Devils 3–0. Although the Conn Smythe Trophy is generally handed out to a player on the winning team, that year it was given to Giguère for his brilliant play (he accepted the honour rather reluctantly). The following year, the Ducks, likely still reeling from the loss in the finals, plummeted in the standings and missed the playoffs altogether.

In 2004, as the spectre of an NHL lockout loomed, the Walt Disney Company put the Mighty Ducks of Anaheim up for sale, and in 2005, as a full season went by with no hockey, the Broadcom company bought out Disney for $75 million. Their first order of business was to change the name of the team to the Anaheim Ducks and to hire former Vancouver Canucks general manager Brian Burke as GM and executive vice-president. Burke's first order of business was to hire former defenceman Randy Carlyle as his head coach and steal away Scott Niedermayer from the Devils.

When hockey finally returned for the 2005–06 season, the Ducks added rookies Ryan Getzlaf, Corey Perry and Chris Kunitz to the fold, helping their offensive output and putting wins on the board. They finished the season with a 43–27–12 record. Into the playoffs, it was goaltender Ilya Bryzgalov's turn to shine as he helped finish off the Calgary Flames in the first round in a tough seven-game series and then swept the Colorado Avalanche in the next round. The Ducks ultimately lost to the Edmonton Oilers in the Western Conference finals in five games. However, the Ducks had proven they were a team of the future, with solid rookies and experienced veterans.

During the off-season, the Ducks made one massive acquisition that changed their postseason fate. Word that defenceman Chris Pronger was unhappy in Edmonton spread like wildfire around the league, and the Ducks eventually won the sweepstakes. With all the elements of success in place, the Ducks finished the 2006–07 season first in their division with a record of 48–20–14 for 110 points.

Into the playoffs, the Ducks finally looked to be the team to beat. They squashed the Minnesota Wild in five games, did the same to the Vancouver Canucks and beat the Detroit Red Wings in six games to advance into the Cup finals for just the second time, this time against the Ottawa Senators. The Senators were tired from a long, hard-fought Eastern Conference battle, managing only one win against the Ducks, who lifted the Stanley Cup at home in front of their fans. The Ducks became the first West Coast team to win the Stanley Cup since the Victoria Cougars in 1925.

Since that first Stanley Cup victory, the Ducks have had a few up-and-down seasons, losing veterans like Pronger and Niedermayer, but they have always remained competitive and keep the fans coming back to the Honda Center for more high-flying action.

Anaheim Ducks Records

Most goals in a season: Teemu Selänne, 52 (1997–98)

Most goals in a season, defenceman:
    Lubomir Visnovsky, 18 (2010–11)

Most goals in a season, rookie: Bobby Ryan, 31 (2008–09)

Most assists in a season: Ryan Getzlaf, 66 (2008–09)

Most assists in a season, defenceman:
    Scott Niedermayer, 54 (2006–07)

Anaheim Ducks Records (continued)

Most points in a season: Teemu Selänne, 109 (1996–97)

Most points in a season, defenceman:
Scott Niedermayer, 69 (2006–07)

Most points in a season, rookie: Bobby Ryan, 57 (2008–09)

Most penalty minutes in a season: Todd Ewen, 285
(1995–96)

Most wins in a season: Jean-Sébastien Giguère, 36
(2006–07)

Most shutouts in a season:
Jean-Sébastien Giguère, 8 (2002–03)

See Honda Center

Arena: The name for a building in which hockey is played. When hockey first began, games were played on outdoor rinks and were subject to the whims of the weather, but gradually, hockey began to move indoors and the hockey arena was born. However, as many hockey moms and dads can attest, it is sometimes colder in the arena than it is outside. The first organized indoor hockey game took place on March 3, 1875, at the Victoria Skating Rink in Montréal, Québec. The Victoria Rink was also where the first Stanley Cup finals game was played on March 22, 1894, between the Montréal Hockey Club and the Ottawa Hockey Club. Montréal won the game 3–1.

See Rink

Arena Cup: The Arena Corporation of Montréal presented the Arena Championship Cup during the brief existence of the Eastern Canada Amateur Hockey Association from 1905 to 1909. The Ottawa Hockey Club and the Montréal

Wanderers shared the inaugural championship in 1906 because they finished the season with the same record. The Wanderers won the 1907 and 1908 titles, while the Ottawa Hockey Club won the last Arena Cup in 1909 before the league was disbanded.

Armour: The foam-and-plastic protection worn by players under their jerseys. When players first started wearing padding for protection, it was nothing more than dense foam and leather, but as the game got faster and the players got bigger, the padding became more rigid and armour-like. The chest protectors that goaltenders wear even look somewhat like bulletproof armour.

Around-the-world Glove Save: When a goaltender swings his arm in a circular motion and snags the puck out of midair. Patrick Roy was the best at exaggerating this little piece of goaltender magic.

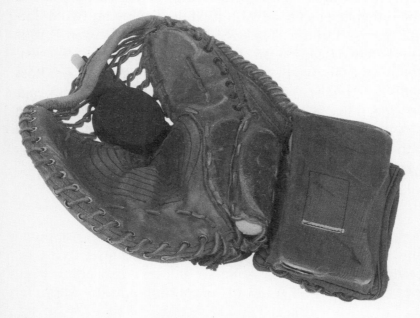

Arrowhead Pond: Former name of the Honda Center, where the Anaheim Ducks play their home games.

See Honda Center

Art Ross Trophy: NHL trophy awarded to the player who leads the league in scoring points at the end of the regular season. Former player, general manager and head coach Art Ross donated the trophy to the NHL; he was a legendary figure in the world of hockey in the early 20th century. It was first awarded at the conclusion of the 1947–48 season to Elmer Lach of the Montréal Canadiens.

Wayne Gretzky has won the Art Ross Trophy the most times, with a record 10 wins. Gordie Howe and Mario Lemieux each won the trophy six times, and Phil Esposito and Jaromir Jagr each have five. Gretzky is the only player to have won the trophy with two different teams (Edmonton Oilers and the Los Angeles Kings), and Joe Thornton is the only player to have won it while playing on two different teams in one season (first half with the Boston Bruins before a mid-season trade sent him to the San Jose Sharks). From 1980 to 2001, only three players won the Art Ross Trophy: Gretzky (10 times), Lemieux (6 times) and Jagr (5 times). The streak of wins was only broken in 2002 when Calgary Flames forward Jarome Iginla won the title. In 2009, Sidney Crosby became the youngest to win the trophy when at the age of 19 he scored 120 points.

In case of a tie at the end of the season, NHL rules have a series of tiebreakers: 1) Player with the most goals; 2) Player with fewer games played; and 3) Player scoring first goal of the season. Scoring ties have only occurred

A

three times in NHL history, and the winner in each case was decided by the first tiebreaker rule.

Artificial Ice: When hockey first began, it was purely a winter sport played outdoors on frozen ponds and rivers. As the game grew in popularity, some rinks were moved indoors, but the surface was still at the mercy of the elements. It wasn't until the late 19th century that a great leap in technology allowed hockey to move indoors permanently. The first artificial ice surface was opened to the public not in Canada, but in jolly old England in 1876. The ice surface was designed and constructed by Professor Gamgee. The professor built the 100-square foot surface over a network of copper pipes containing a mixture of glycerin and water that was circulated through the pipes after being chilled by ether. The freezing cold pipes were then covered with water, and the first artificial ice rink was born.

Canada was slow to clue into this new technology despite the demand for indoor artificial ice. Canada's first indoor rink finally opened in 1911 in Vancouver, British Columbia. The project was spearheaded by brothers Lester and Frank Patrick because, in order to play hockey in the temperate rainforest climate of BC, one needed artificial ice. One year later, Eastern Canada followed suit and opened its first artificial ice rink in Toronto. By 1920, there were still only four artificial ice rinks in Canada, but today that number would be too great to count. The principal of making a sheet of ice is still the same today, but the technology has gotten a lot better.

Asian Cup: A hockey tournament that lasted from 1992 to 1995 and featured teams from Kazakhstan, Japan, China and South Korea. Japan won the tournament in 1992 and 1993. There was a break in the tournament in 1994 and then Kazakhstan won in 1995. The tournament was eventually cancelled due to lack of interest.

Assist: In most cases, when a goal is scored, a point is awarded to the teammates who last touched the puck before the goal was scored. A maximum of two assists is awarded per goal.

Atlanta Flames: In the early 1970s, a group of Georgia executives led by Tom Cousins backed a successful bid to bring an NHL franchise to Atlanta. The 1972–73 NHL season saw the Atlanta Flames and New York Islanders added to the list of teams. The new hockey club made the 15,000-seat Omni Coliseum their home rink. The team's name was plucked from history to commemorate the burning of Atlanta during the American Civil War.

Cliff Fletcher was the first general manager of the team and former Montréal Canadiens legend Bernie Geoffrion was named the team's head coach. The hope in the Flames inaugural season was to put together a successful team, but expansion franchises have a notorious history of bad luck in their first seasons. The team played their first regular season game on October 7, 1972, against fellow expansion team the New York Islanders. The Flames managed to win the game by a score of 3–2. Morris Stefaniw scored the franchise's first goal shorthanded at 12:48 of the first period. The Flames finished their inaugural season with a respectable record of 25–38–15, but missed out on the playoffs.

The Atlanta Flames had better success in the 1973–74 season, finishing with a record of 30–34–14 and for the first time made it to the playoffs. Unfortunately for the young franchise, they faced off against the eventual Stanley Cup champion Philadelphia Flyers and were soundly beaten in four straight games. Although the team did not win any trophies, forward Eric Vail took home the Calder Trophy as rookie of the year, finishing the season with 39 goals and 21 assists.

The 1974–75 season saw the Flames post a winning record for the first time (34–31–15) but just missed out on a playoff spot that year. Again the team went home without a trophy, but another rookie stood out: Willie Plett scored 33 goals and 23 assists to win the Flames another Calder Trophy. The 1975–76 season saw the Flames again finish with a mediocre record going into the playoffs and once again getting eliminated in the first round.

Although the team scored 264 goals during the 1976–77 season, they surrendered 265 goals to their opponents, making for an up-and-down season. They again managed

A

to just make the playoffs but again were defeated in the first round. The 1977–78 season saw the team improve on the ice, but the number of fans in the stands began to dwindle. When the club started in 1972, they had an average attendance of around 13,000 fans, but by the end of the 1978 season, the Flames could only pull in around 10,000 fans per game and on some nights even less. The team needed a push in the playoffs to get the fans back, but unfortunately their run in the playoffs that year ended in the first round again.

In the 1978–79 season, the team posted their best record (41–31–8), but again the team could not find success in the playoffs, losing in the first round to the Toronto Maple Leafs. For the 1979–80 season, the Atlanta Flames posted yet another middle-of-the-road season with a record of 35–32–13 and yet again another early exit from the playoffs. With a shrinking fan base and a lack of postseason revenue to make up for losses, the owners of the Atlanta Flames quietly began shopping the team around. The team played its last game at the Omni Coliseum on April 12, 1980, losing to the New York Rangers 5–2. The Atlanta Flames owners found a willing group in the city of Calgary, and during the off-season, sold and shipped the team north, where they became the Calgary Flames.

See Calgary Flames

Atlanta Thrashers: In its last major round of expansion, the NHL returned to the city of Atlanta (formerly the Atlanta Flames) along with new franchises in Nashville, Columbus and Minnesota. Atlanta was awarded a franchise on June 25, 1997, and immediately began preparations to start the 1999–2000 season.

The team was named after Georgia's state bird, the brown thrasher. The owners named Don Waddell as the team's general manager and hired coach Curt Fraser to lead the expansion team through its opening years. The team's first order of business was selecting Patrick Stefan first overall at the 1999 Entry Draft and acquiring veteran Kelly Buchberger as the new franchise's first captain.

The Thrashers played their first game on October 2, 1999, posting a 4–1 loss to the New Jersey Devils. Captain Buchberger scored the team's first-ever goal that night. As was expected of an expansion franchise, the club did not perform very well in their first season, ending with a record of 14–61–7. With a bad season comes a high draft choice, and the Thrashers used their 2000 first-round draft selection to take Dany Heatley, who became one of the team's best players. After another poor campaign in 2000–01, the Thrashers selected Russian superstar Ilya Kovalchuk in the 2001 Entry Draft.

After just three years, Time Warner, initial owners of the Thrashers, sold the team to Atlanta Spirit LLC, a group made up of Atlanta businessmen, in 2003. As the executives worked out the sale of the team before the start of the 2003–04 season, tragedy struck the organization when Dany Heatley crashed his Ferrari, seriously injuring himself and fatally wounding fellow teammate Dan Snyder. Heatley received three years probation for reckless driving causing death.

The 2003–04 season saw the Thrashers start to turn their team to the winning side, moving up to second in their division, but once again they missed out on the playoffs. After the lockout season in 2004–05, the Thrashers returned to

A

the ice and began winning games. Newly acquired veterans Peter Bondra, Bobby Holik and Scott Mellanby gave the team the offensive punch it needed, and for the first time, they finished with a winning percentage above .500. They did trade Dany Heatley to the Ottawa Senators, but in return they received exciting forward Marian Hossa, who added his own offensive talents to the Thrasher arsenal. Despite the improvements, the Thrashers missed out on the 2005–06 Stanley Cup playoffs.

The 2006–07 season saw the Thrashers lose their second-best scorer Marc Savard when he signed with the Bruins, but they added Steve Rucchin, Niko Kapanen and Jon Sim. Along with goaltender Kari Lehtonen and both Hossa and Kovalchuk having a great year, the Thrashers were able to make the playoffs for the first time in the franchise history. However, the euphoria of making the playoffs was quickly extinguished when the New York Rangers swept the Thrashers in the opening round.

After their brief taste of the playoffs, the Thrashers struggled through the next few seasons, missing the playoffs for four straight years. After so long without winning games, the Thrashers organization was losing fans to the point where only a few thousand filled the stands for regular season games. As a result, the franchise was hemorrhaging money. They tried to save some money by trading high-priced Kovalchuk to the New Jersey Devils, but the franchise was already too far gone.

By the end of the 2009–10 season, the rumours of the team folding operations and moving to another city became rampant. Cities vying for the team included Kansas City, Québec City, Hamilton and Winnipeg. By January 2011, the Thrashers ownership group released a statement saying they had lost $130 million over the last six years. The writing was on the wall. At the end of the season, the sale of the franchise to True North Sports and Entertainment in Winnipeg, Manitoba, was approved by the NHL, ushering in the return of the Winnipeg Jets.

Atlanta Thrashers Records

Most goals in a season: Ilya Kovalchuk, 52 (2005–06, 2007–08)

Most goals in a season, defenceman: Dustin Byfuglien, 20 (2010–11)

Most goals in a season, rookie: Ilya Kovalchuk, 29 (2001–02)

Most assists in a season: Marc Savard, 69 (2005–06)

Most assists in a season, rookie: Dany Heatley, 41 (2001–02)

Most points in a season: Marian Hossa, 100 (2006–07)

Atlanta Thrashers Records (continued)

Most points in a season, defenseman: Dustin Byfuglien, 53 (2010–11)

Most points in a season, rookie: Dany Heatley, 67 (2001–02)

Most penalty minutes in a season: Jeff Odgers, 226 (2000–01)

Most wins in a season: Kari Lehtonen, 34 (2006–07)

See Winnipeg Jets

Atlantic Division: Formed in 1993 as part of the Eastern Conference, the Atlantic Division was formerly known as the Patrick Division. Currently, the division is made up of the New Jersey Devils, New York Islanders, New York Rangers, Philadelphia Flyers and Pittsburgh Penguins.

See Patrick Division

Attacking Zone: The area of the ice in which one team is on defence and the other is on offence looking to score.

Avco Cup: Championship trophy of the World Hockey Association (WHA) from 1972 to 1979. The trophy was named after the Avco Corporation, who bought the naming rights to the Cup in 1972 when the WHA was formed. Although the trophy never reached the level of significance of the Stanley Cup, the trophy itself was praised for its looks (especially the free-floating globe in the stem of the cup). There are three trophies in existence: one in the Hockey Hall of Fame, one in Winnipeg and the other in Halifax.

The WHA had been in such a rush to start their first season in 1972–73 that they had not prepared a championship trophy. When it was finally decided to go with the Avco Cup and have it made, it wasn't ready when the New England Whalers won the inaugural championship in 1973. Instead the Whalers paraded around the ice with their divisional championship trophy instead, leaving a few players feeling a little strange and making the WHA bosses look foolish. The Avco Cup was retired in 1979 when the WHA folded.

See Hockey Hall of Fame; WHA

B

BCHL (British Columbia Hockey League): The Junior A league is made up of 16 teams divided into the Coastal Conference and Interior Conference. Part of the Canadian Junior Hockey League, the BCHL has produced some players of note including Brett Hull, Carey Price, Glenn Anderson, Chuck Kobasew, Mark Recchi and Scott Gomez. The champions of the BCHL are awarded the Fred Page Cup.

Babe Pratt Trophy: Annual trophy given to the best defenceman on the Vancouver Canucks. Named in honour of legendary defenceman Babe Pratt, who played for the New York Rangers, Toronto Maple Leafs and Boston Bruins from 1935 to 1952. Although he never played a professional hockey game in Vancouver, Babe Pratt became a fixture in the city, calling the Canucks games on *Hockey Night in Canada* and later serving as a goodwill ambassador for the club.

Baby Leafs: The nickname of the St. John's Maple Leafs, the Toronto Maple Leafs former American Hockey League (AHL) farm team.

Back Checking: When one team loses the puck in the opponent's zone and the forwards must hurry back to their end to stop the other team from scoring.

B

Back Door: When a team is in the offensive zone, the back door is the area at the side of the net behind the defence-men. A player is said to be "sneaking in the back door" when he gets in behind the defence and is left alone in front of the goaltender.

Backstop: The goaltender.

Back-up Goaltender: All professional hockey teams have two goaltenders on their roster: one who plays in the game, and one who sits on the bench in the event that the starting goaltender is injured or is pulled by the coach. On a team, you have one goaltender that plays more often and is given the title of the number one goalie, while a back-up goaltender is given the number-two designation.

Backyard Rink: There is nothing more iconic or more Canadian than the homemade backyard rink. Across the frozen North, many young children learn to skate on the ice of the backyard rink. Many of today's NHL players took their first steps toward the professional ranks on the rinks built by their parents behind their homes, the most famous of them being the Great One himself, Wayne Gretzky. The story of how young Wayne Gretzky got from his backyard rink in Brantford, Ontario, to the top of professional hockey is part of hockey lore and a large part of how Canadians identify with the game.

Built in large part so that Wayne's dad, Walter, would not have to freeze to death down at the local rink, "Wally's Coliseum," as it was known, served the young protégé well. According to Wayne, "I used to go out after school for an hour and a half, and then I'd come in to eat dinner, and when it came time to go out again, I'd be sitting there and he'd say, 'You didn't do any shooting or practicing.' And I'd say, 'I didn't feel like it.' And he'd say, 'Well, someday, you may have to get up at 6:30 and go to work from seven to five, and you'd better feel like it.' Little things like that would give me the motivation."

Hockey parents across the country build these rinks with the hopes that their kids will one day grow up to be just like Wayne Gretzky, keeping the tradition of the backyard rink alive for generations to come.

Badgering: Referees everywhere are very familiar with badgering. When a player disagrees with a call a referee has made, the player will often argue with the ref until play has resumed. This incessant arguing is called badgering.

B

Balcony: Colloquial term for the upper arena seats at a hockey game.

Bandy: The game of bandy was one of the first stick-and-ball games played on ice and is still played today (mainly in Europe). Bandy pre-dates hockey and is often thought of as one of the sports that led to the development of ice hockey.

The rules of bandy are similar to those of soccer. The game is played on a rectangular sheet of ice the same size as a soccer field and has 11 players plus one goaltender. The game is divided into two halves of 45 minutes each and employs a similar offside rule to regulation soccer games. But this is where the similarities to soccer end and the ones to hockey begin.

The most obvious similarities are the speed and physical nature of both hockey and bandy. In both sports, players are allowed and encouraged to intimidate and to physically hit their opponents to get them off the ball or puck. Bandy players use equipment similar to modern hockey players and are only allowed to hit the ball with their bandy sticks. Like hockey, the game is known for being fast paced and physical.

Historical records indicate games similar to bandy being played in around the 10th century, but the sport only became popular around the 1700s in Europe and Russia. Russians consider themselves the creators of bandy. Bandy, in Russian, means "Russian Hockey." Bandy had become so popular in Europe that, in 1853, the British Royal Family got involved in a game that was played at Windsor Castle, with Prince Albert acting as goaltender.

The Bandy World Championships were first held in 1957 and are still played every two years. Currently there are

13 countries that participate in the championships. With 20, Russia holds the most gold medals since the tournament began. Canada has never won.

Although bandy was a demonstration sport at the 1952 Winter Olympics in Oslo, Norway, it has never become an official Olympic medal sport. Only Finland, Norway and Sweden participated in the 1952 Games.

See Hockey; Hurling; Hurly-on-ice

Banana Blade: When the curved stick was first introduced into the NHL in the 1960s, the curve in the blade was so

B

pronounced that it resembled a banana; made famous, or infamous, by Bobby Hull of the Chicago Blackhawks.

BankAtlantic Center: Home arena of the Florida Panthers. Formerly known as the Broward County Civic Arena, the National Car Rental Center and the Office Depot Center. It opened on October 3, 1998; with a seating capacity of 17,040 for hockey games.

See Florida Panthers

Battle of Alberta: Take two cities in one province that generally don't like each other, add sports to the mix and

you have a battle. In the province of Alberta, the Edmonton Oilers and the Calgary Flames hold a special place in the hearts of their respective fans. Both are passionate about their teams, and that passion in the stands has trickled down to the players on the ice and led to one of the best rivalries in NHL hockey (of course, this mutual hatred continues into the Canadian Football League, the National Lacrosse League and all university-related sports). The battle for Alberta hockey supremacy began in 1980 when the Atlanta Flames folded, and the team moved to Calgary. The Edmonton Oilers had until then enjoyed just one season as the province's only NHL team.

The rivalry was made all the more potent as the Oilers completely dominated the NHL, led by Wayne Gretzky, Mark Messier and Paul Coffey among others. By the mid to late 1980s, with a few years of aggression built up, the Calgary Flames had finally shaken off their expansion-losing ways to become one of the league's top-tier teams, just like the Oilers. While the regular season match-ups between the teams were heated, it was during the playoffs that the true hatred developed. Unfortunately, the Flames were on the losing end of most encounters. The Oilers defeated the Flames in the playoffs in 1983, 1984, 1988 and 1991.

The Flames did have one shining moment in the Battle of Alberta when they came out on top in the 1986 playoffs. The infamous series was decided when rookie Oiler defenceman Steve Smith accidentally scored the tie-breaking goal on his own net in the seventh game of the series, thereby giving the Flames the goal they needed to move on in the playoffs. The Flames ultimately lost in the Stanley Cup finals to the Montréal Canadiens.

B

The rivalry cooled during the 1990s, and while games between the two clubs are a little more physical and contemptuous than against other teams, the Battle of Alberta has not seen much in the way of causalities for years.

See Calgary Flames; Edmonton Oilers

Battle of Ontario: When hockey first began to take roots in Canada, it was the rivalries between provincial cities that brought fans to the seats and helped to create the passion for the game we love today. Long before the founding of the NHL and even before the creation of the Stanley Cup, teams from Ottawa and Toronto played spirited hockey games that often involved more fighting than hockey. But as hockey began to grow and leagues began to form, the rivalry became a little more dignified, but the rivalry remained.

In the early years, the Ottawa Hockey Club (also called the Ottawa Silver Seven and Ottawa Senators) was the toast of the hockey world. They boasted some of the greatest players in the history of the game and dominated all challengers. When the NHL came into existence, Ottawa and the Toronto Arenas (later the Maple Leafs) were one of a handful of teams in the league, so naturally a fierce rivalry grew. Unfortunately for Toronto hockey fans, their club came out on the losing side of most matches. In the playoffs, Toronto only managed to beat the Senators just once in two meetings in the postseason, while Ottawa made the playoffs on numerous occasions and even won a handful of championships.

The rivalry completely died when the Ottawa Senators folded operations in 1934. The Toronto Maple Leafs focused all of their aggression on the Montréal Canadiens while the Senators were away. However, in 1992, the Ottawa Senators

B

returned to the nation's capital and reignited the Battle of Ontario.

The two teams rarely played each other, however, as they were in different conferences up until 1998, when the league was realigned and Toronto was brought into the Eastern Conference. By that time, the Senators had shaken off their expansion woes, and the Leafs were looking the best they had in decades under the captaincy of Mats Sundin.

The teams have met three times in the playoffs since the Senators' return to the NHL, and although the Senators have often been ranked higher than the Leafs going into those playoffs, the Leafs came out winners in all three battles (unfortunately, the Leafs did not make it to the Stanley Cup finals in those seasons). Despite the Senators coming out on the losing end of those series, they fought hard in each one and more than a little blood was shed between the two teams. With career bad guys Darcy Tucker on the Leafs and Chris Neil on the Senators, and let's not forget Tie Domi of the Leafs, there were plenty of on-ice fights and cheap shots to rile the crowd and renew the passions in the Battle of Ontario.

Then came the stick incident of 2004. During a game between the Toronto Maple Leafs and Nashville Predators, Leafs captain Mats Sundin's stick broke on a shot, and he threw the stick away in frustration. Being so light, the stick went a little farther than Sundin expected and flew up into the crowd. For his lack of discipline, Sundin was given a one game suspension. Of course, the one game that he missed just happened to be against the Ottawa Senators. During that game in Toronto, Senators captain Daniel Alfredsson

B

just happened to break his stick, and instead of dropping it to the ice, Alfredsson faked a toss of his stick into the crowd. To make the incident even more hurtful, the Leafs lost that game to the Senators 7–1.

Although the teams have not met in the playoffs for several years and on-ice incidents in games have been minimal, regular season games between the two clubs always guarantee a heated affair both from the players and the fans. Season-to-season battles may be won, but the war will rage on.

See Ottawa Senators; Toronto Maple Leafs

Battle of Québec: The battle of Québec began during the 1979–80 season when the Québec Nordiques joined the NHL. Initially the rivalry was not that intense because the Nordiques spent the first two seasons in a different division, but passions began to rise in 1982 when the Montréal Canadiens moved into the Nordiques' division and they met in the playoffs for the first time. This series was ground zero for their rivalry. After losing the opening game, the Nordiques won the next two games, putting them in a good spot to clinch the best-of-five series. But the Canadiens came storming back in the fourth game, winning by a 6–2 margin. It was in this fourth game that things got a little violent. In the game, the referee handed out 251 minutes in penalties, 159 minutes in a first period incident alone. In the fifth and deciding game, the two teams battled hard, but it was the Nordiques that came out on top when Dale Hunter scored 22 seconds into the overtime period to send the Canadiens packing.

The rivalry reached epic proportions in 1984 when the two teams met in the playoffs for a second time in what would

B

come to be known as the "Good Friday Brawl." By game six of the series, Montréal had taken a 3–2 series lead and were hoping to move on with a win before a home crowd. Game six was held in Montréal on April 20, 1984, and the Canadiens got their wish, winning the game by a score of 5–3 and moving onto the next round. However, the game is best remembered for the multiple brawls that started as the second period was coming to a close. Nordiques forward Dale Hunter pinned Canadiens forward Guy Carbonneau to the ice, starting a bench-clearing brawl. Even the goalies got involved! Referees could do little as players paired up and traded punches. Order was eventually restored, and players were sent to their dressing rooms while referees figured out the penalties.

The teams returned to the ice for the start of the third period, and before the puck even dropped, another brawl broke out again in an attempt to settle accounts from the second period. Players piled on top of players, sucker punches were thrown and players hunted each other looking to settle the score. In all, 10 players were thrown out of the game and over 250 minutes on penalties were handed out. The brawl most likely favoured the Canadiens as they were still down in the game at the start of the third period, and after things were settled and the game continued, they finished the game off with a 5–3 win.

The teams met again in the 1985 playoffs, but things were remarkably civil in comparison to previous years. The Nordiques ended up winning that series in game seven on a goal by Peter Stastny. The Canadiens won the next time in the 1987 playoffs and in 1993, the year they won the Cup. The rivalry died in 1995 when the Québec Nordiques folded

B

operations and moved to Denver to become the Colorado Avalanche.

See Bench-clearing Brawl; Montréal Canadiens; Québec Nordiques

Bauer: Founded in 1927 by the Bauer family in Kitchener, Ontario, owners of the Western Shoe Company, the Bauer hockey equipment company was the first to produce hockey skates with the blade permanently attached to the boot. Bauer actually just made the boot and bought the blades from the Starr Manufacturing Company of Nova Scotia. The skates only became popular when the company signed Bobby Hull to an endorsement deal. By 1975, Bauer skates and their other brands had 95 percent of the market share. In 1994, Nike saw the potential profits to be made in the industry and bought out the Bauer name and company. Now all hockey equipment is produced under the name

B

Nike Bauer. Players today that still wear Nike Bauer equipment are Evgeni Malkin, Steven Stamkos and goaltender Tim Thomas.

Beer Leagues: An organized sports venue in which participants focus their efforts on both the event at hand and the post- and pre-game activities that include consumption of a large amount of alcoholic beverages.

Bell Centre: Current home of the Montréal Canadiens, formerly known as the Molson Centre. Construction on the site began just two weeks after the Montréal Canadiens defeated the Los Angeles Kings in the 1993 Stanley Cup finals. Since 1926, the Canadiens played their home games at the historic Montréal Forum, where so many legendary players had skated and so many Stanley Cups had been won. But as the league expanded and more teams built modern facilities with luxury boxes and club seats, the old Forum just could not accommodate the Canadiens' future needs. So it was decided that the team should move. The new arena took three years to complete and officially opened for business in March 1996.

Located in Montréal's downtown district on the corner of Avenue des Canadiens-de-Montréal and Rue de la Montagne, the new arena seats 21,273 fans, making it the largest in the NHL. With so many fans in the arena, it is one of the loudest in the league (that is, when the Canadiens are winning) with noise levels reaching as high as 135 decibels, which is comparable to the sound of a jet engine or a gun blast.

B

Retired jersey numbers hanging in the rafters at the Bell Centre:

7   Howie Morenz (C) November 2, 1937

9   Maurice Richard (RW) October 6, 1960

4   Jean Beliveau (C) October 9, 1971

16 Henri Richard (C) December 10, 1975

10 Guy Lafleur (RW) February 16, 1985

1   Jacques Plante (G) October 7, 1995

2   Doug Harvey (D) October 26, 1995

12 Dickie Moore (LW) November 12, 2005

12 Yvan Cournoyer (RW) November 12, 2005

5   Bernie Geoffrion (RW) March 11, 2006

18 Serge Savard (D) November 18, 2006

29 Ken Dryden (G) January 29, 2007

19 Larry Robinson (D) November 19, 2007

23 Bob Gainey (C) February 23, 2008

33 Patrick Roy (G) November 22, 2008

3   Emile Bouchard (D) December 4, 2009

16 Elmer Lach (C) December 4, 2009

See Montréal Canadiens

Bench-clearing Brawl: The least common type of brawl in hockey—when everybody on the ice and on the benches gets involved in one large fight extravaganza. To avoid such brawls, the NHL imposes heavy fines and penalties for any player leaving the bench to join a fight on the ice. One of the most famous bench-clearing brawls occurred between the Québec Nordiques and Montréal Canadiens on April 20, 1984—referred to as the "Good Friday Brawl". The rivalry between the two teams had been building for years and finally exploded during the playoffs after Dale Hunter instigated the brawl with a vicious hit to Guy Carbonneau. Both teams' benches cleared instantly, and referees had a difficult time restoring order and picking up all the equipment littering the ice.

See Battle of Québec

Bench Minor: A penalty given to either a coach, player or trainer for the use of offensive language towards the officials, for throwing objects onto the ice or for interfering with the progress of the game. A player is selected by the coaching staff to serve a two-minute penalty for the infraction.

List of Bench Minor Penalties

Abuse of officials

Delay of game

Deliberate illegal substitution

Faceoff violation

Illegal substitution

Improper starting lineup

Interference from players' or penalty bench

Interference with an official

Leaving bench at end of period

Refusing to start play

Stepping onto ice during period (coach)

Throwing objects onto ice

Too many men on the ice

List of Bench Minor Penalties (continued)

B

Unsportsmanlike conduct

Unsustained request for measurement

Between the Pipes: When hockey was first played on the ponds of rural Canada, the only objects that could be found to mark the goal area were usually large rocks. Eventually, as the game became more organized, rocks were no longer considered appropriate to demarcate the goal and were replaced by metal pipes. So today, a goaltender standing in his crease is said to be standing "between the pipes."

Bickell Cup: Toronto Maple Leafs team trophy presented to an individual player or person within the organization "for a tremendous feat, one season of spectacular play or remarkable service over the years." It is not always given out every year if no player or member of the organization is felt to deserve it. Named after Jack Bickell, who purchased the former Toronto Arenas in 1919 and changed their name to the St. Patricks. He remained part shareholder of the club when it was sold to Conn Smythe in 1927. He remained connected with the franchise until his death in 1951.

Bill Masterton Memorial Trophy: Trophy awarded annually to the NHL player who best exemplifies the qualities of perseverance, sportsmanship and dedication to hockey through the season. The Professional Hockey Writers' Association (PHWA) selects the winner after each team nominates one player for the award. It is often given to a player who makes a comeback from an injury or illness.

The trophy is named in honour of the late Bill Masterton, a Minnesota North Stars player who died on January 15, 1968, after hitting his helmet-less head on the ice during a game.

Biscuit: Colloquial term for the puck.

Biscuit in the Basket: While biscuit is another term for puck, basket is another term for the hockey net. Putting biscuits in the basket simply means to score goals.

Blades: Refers to the sharp steel under the boot of the skate, but the term is also commonly used to describe the whole skate.

Blades of Steel: One of the first popular hockey video games. First developed by Konami for the arcade in 1987 then ported out to the Nintendo Entertainment System in 1988. All teams were fictional but based out of real North American cities.

Blast: A very hard slapshot aimed at the goaltender.

See Slapshot

B

Bleu, Blanc, Rouge: French nickname for the Montréal Canadiens, referring to the colours of the team jersey. Many references to this nickname often erroneously write it as Bleu, Blanc et Rouge.

Blind Pass: When a player passes the puck to a teammate without looking. This does not always work in the professional ranks, but when it does, the play will certainly make the highlight reels.

Blocker: One of the later additions to the world of hockey, the blocker is now an essential piece of equipment in the goaltenders' war on the puck. However, when it was first introduced, some NHL coaches vehemently protested its use. In the early days of hockey, goaltenders had to make do with gloves that were almost identical to those of the forwards and defencemen. Old black-and-white photos of early NHL goaltenders such as Clint Benedict, Georges Hainsworth and Lorne Chabot show slightly modified players' gloves with added padding over the hands for protection. Remarkably, it wasn't until the 1947–48 NHL regular season that one innovative goaltender decided to try something new.

Like a kid improvising equipment for a street hockey game, Chicago Blackhawks goaltender Emile "the Cat" Francis wanted to increase the protection on his stick hand, so he decided to tape an outer layer of dense sponge rubber to his glove. This gave Francis the extra protection he was looking for, and it reduced the amount of open net for the shooter. The league quickly approved it, and soon all the goaltenders had added this weapon to their arsenal.

See Trapper

Blue Line: Two thick blue painted lines that divide an ice rink into three parts, the neutral zone and two defensive zones where the goaltenders are located. Linesmen use the blue lines to judge whether a player is offside, when an attacking player crosses the blue line before the puck.

See Defensive Zone; Neutral Zone; Offside

Blue Liner: A defenceman. Defencemen were dubbed blue liners because they spend most of their time on the ice standing on the blue line.

Boarding: When a player violently pushes an opponent into the boards. Boarding normally occurs when a player is pushed headfirst from behind into the boards. Either a major or a minor penalty can be called for boarding, and

B

the penalty is called at the discretion of the referee and depends on whether the victim has been injured on the play. When a major penalty is assessed, the offending player receives an automatic fine of $100 and might have to appear before the disciplinary judge for possible suspension.

See Major Penalty; Minor Penalty

Board of Governors: The board of governors of the NHL establish policies for the league and uphold its constitutions and bylaws. Every NHL club appoints a governor and an alternate each of whom have the full power and authority to represent their club in meetings and decisions and bind it by vote. There are normally two Board of Governors meetings per year where matters of the NHL are discussed. A Chairman of the Board is selected from amongst the board of governors.

Body Check: When one player uses his body to hit another player. One of the most devastating checkers in recent history was former New Jersey Devils defenceman Scott Stevens. Throughout his career, he legally hit many players, often with cringe-worthy results.

Bolts: Nickname for the Tampa Bay Lightning.

Boots: Another colloquial term for skates.

Boston Bruins: The first American team in the United States, the Boston Bruins got their start in 1924 when Boston grocery tycoon Charles Adams convinced the NHL to expand south of the border. The NHL agreed, and on December 1, 1924, the new Boston Bruins played their first game against the Montréal Maroons at Boston Arena, which the Bruins won by a score of 2–1. Despite the good start, the

B

Bruins only won 6 games that season and lost 24, putting them in last place overall. Their losing ways didn't last long. Just two seasons later, they made the 1927 playoffs and made it all the way to the Stanley Cup finals before losing to the Ottawa Senators in a best of five series. Boston had the players, the coach (Art Ross) and the physical stature to last against the more talented teams in the league; all they were missing was a franchise goaltender to take them one step further. They got their wish when Tiny Thompson joined the club for the 1928–29 season.

Backstopped by Thompson and led by defenceman Eddie Shore and forwards Harry Oliver and Dutch Gainor, the Bruins put in the second best record for the season and entered the playoffs as heavy favourites behind the Montréal Canadiens. However, it was Boston that defied expectations by defeating the Canadiens in the opening round before finishing off the New York Rangers in the Stanley Cup finals to win the franchise's first Stanley Cup.

The next season, the Bruins posted an even better regular season performance, but in the playoffs, the Montréal Canadiens got their revenge by beating Boston in the finals. The Bruins were one of the better teams in the 1930s, leading the charge with legends like Shore, Thompson, Dit Clapper, Babe Siebert and Cooney Weiland, sitting at the top of the league five times during the '30s. The power in the league shifted often in those days and no one team was able to dominate, with seven different teams trading the Stanley Cup championship in those 10 years.

The Bruins did manage to leave the decade with a Stanley Cup of their own when backstopped by another rookie goaltender named Frank Brimsek during the 1939 playoffs.

B

The Bruins' "Kraut Line" of Bobby Bauer, Milt Schmidt and Woody Dumart were just beginning to gel on the ice offensively, and backed by Brimsek, the Bruins were hard to beat. After finishing the season atop the standings, the Bruins powered their way through the New York Rangers in the first round and easily beat the Toronto Maple Leafs in the Stanley Cup finals to win their second championship.

Riding the success of their young stars up front and the solid goaltending of Brimsek, the Bruins led the league again in the 1939–40 season but were unceremoniously dumped from the playoffs by the eventual Cup champions New York Rangers in the opening round. The Bruins returned for the 1940–41 season to put in an even better season with a record of 27–8–13. They carried their winning ways into the playoffs where they narrowly escaped defeat by the Toronto Maple Leafs in the opening round after a tough seven game series and then went on to defeat the Detroit Red Wings in the final in four straight games for their third Stanley Cup.

After the Bruins finished celebrating their win, they lost many of their star players like Frank Brimsek, Milt Schmidt and Bobby Bauer when those men joined the army to fight

B

in World War II. With the departures of these star players, Boston slowly began to slip in the overall standings, and by 1944, they missed out on the playoffs altogether. There were a few good seasons after that, but the Bruins had no luck in the playoffs, always facing teams such as Detroit, Toronto and Montréal when they were at their peaks. Despite having players like Bronco Horvath, Johnny Bucyk and Vic Stasiuk, the Bruins spent much of the 1940s and '50s as perennial bridesmaids but never the brides in the playoffs. As for the 1960s, it was a decade that the Bruins would rather forget, spending the majority of those 10 years at the bottom of the league. It wasn't until the late '60s that the Bruins finally began turning things around when a defenceman named Bobby Orr joined the team.

Talk of an impressive young defenceman out of Parry Sound, Ontario, began in the early 1960s, and the Boston Bruins were the lucky team to get their hands on Bobby Orr. For several years, Bruins fans watched and waited for the young Orr to develop and be old enough to enter into the NHL. This put a lot of pressure on Orr's shoulders, but the young defenceman could take the heat. Playing his first game in a Bruins sweater on October 19, 1966, against the Detroit Red Wings, Bobby Orr made his first appearance and from that day changed the face of hockey forever.

No one had ever played the position quite like Orr before. In the history of the game to that point, most defenceman were content to sit back in their own zone and not challenge the opposition, preferring simply to move the puck up to the forwards. But Orr changed all that. With incredible speed and amazing vision on the ice, Orr moved the puck up the ice with such speed, fluidity and skill like no one had

B

ever seen before. In his first year in the league, Orr won the Calder Trophy as the rookie of the year and followed it up the next season with his first Norris Trophy as the league's best defenceman. Bobby Orr not only improved with each passing year, but the fortunes of the Bruins also followed him. The Bruins were a last place team in 1966–67 when he joined, and just two years later, the Bruins were at the top of the league, challenging the dominance of the power-house Montréal Canadiens.

The Bruins added other ingredients for success—Phil Esposito, Ken Hodge, Wayne Cashman and goaltender Gerry Cheevers—making the Bruins one of the best teams in the league. Only a few seasons back, talk was of just making the playoffs, but with Orr, Esposito and Cheevers, Bruins fans had the Stanley Cup on their tips of their tongues again.

The 1969–70 season saw the Bruins finish tied for first over-all with the Chicago Blackhawks and had Bobby Orr leading the league in scoring with 120 points, which was the first time in league history that a defenceman took that title. The Bruins beat the New York Rangers, Chicago Black-hawks and St. Louis Blues to win their first Cup since 1941. Bobby Orr scored his most famous goal in the fourth and final game of the Stanley Cup final against the St. Louis Blues, potting the overtime winner before he was immor-talized by a cameraman who caught him celebrating his goal while flying through the air.

The Bruins' 1970–71 season was even better than the previous year, finishing first overall with 121 points and with Esposito, Orr, Bucyk and Hodge finishing one through four as top scorers in the league. The Bruins met the Montréal

B

Canadiens in the first round. The Canadiens had an average season, but in the playoffs, they placed rookie netminder Ken Dryden in goal and played absolutely outstanding hockey. The Bruins could not solve Dryden as they had every other goaltender that season, and though they managed to take the series to a seventh game, the Canadiens ended up winning.

With the taste of defeat still fresh in their mouths, the Bruins roared back for the 1971–72 season, taking sole possession of first place overall and winning the Cup in the final against the New York Rangers, with Bobby Orr again winning the Conn Smythe trophy as most valuable player in the playoffs.

While Boston remained one of the better teams in the league, the '70s saw the rise of the Philadelphia Flyers and the resurgence of the Montréal Canadiens back to the top of the league. The Bruins managed to make the Stanley Cup finals a few times during that decade, but they always lost out in the end. As the decade progressed, the Bruins' core of players that brought them success in the early part of the decade began to retire or were lost through trades. They were replaced with quality players such as Raymond Bourque, Rick Middleton, Barry Pederson and Cam Neely, and they remained a top-tier team, but these players could never take the club all the way. In the 1980s, the Bruins fell to powerhouses like the New York Islanders and Edmonton Oilers.

It was a credit to the organization for managing to ice a competitive team through the decades, but the Bruins were never able to win the Cup. The era of Raymond Bourque came and went, Adam Oates moved on, Cam Neely retired and Joe Thorton briefly shone in Beantown,

B

but they could not regain their former glory. That is, until the 2010–11 season, when the likes of defenceman Zdeno Chara, goaltender Tim Thomas and forwards Milan Lucic, Nathan Horton and Brad Marchand took the Bruins to the Stanley Cup finals for the first time since 1990 and beat out a skilled Vancouver Canucks team to win the franchise's sixth Stanley Cup. With a similar lineup, the Bruins fell short of defending their Cup champion status in 2011–12, losing to the Washington Capitals in the first round.

Boston Bruins Records

Most goals in a season: Phil Esposito, 76 (1970–71)

Most assists in a season: Bobby Orr, 102 (1970–71)

Most points in a season: Phil Esposito, 152 (1970–71)

Most points in a season, defenceman: Bobby Orr, 139 (1970–71)

Most points in a season, rookie: Joe Juneau, 102 (1992–93)

Most penalty minutes in a season: Jay Miller, 304 (1987–88)

Most points per game in a season: Bill Cowley, 1.97 (1943–44)

Lowest goals against average in a season: Frank Brimsek, 1.56, (1938–39)

Most wins in a season: Pete Peeters, 40 (1982–83)

Most shutouts in a season: Hal Winkler, 15 (1927–28)

See TD Garden

Boston Garden: Built in 1928, the Boston Garden was the iconic home of the Boston Bruins until 1995. Designed by Tex Rickard, who also helmed the third rebuild of New

York's Madison Square Garden, Boston Garden was built mainly as a boxing arena and proper dimensions for hockey were a secondary consideration. Rickard wanted boxing fans to be able to get the best view of a fight from all locations, and so he built the seats extremely close to the action. For hockey games, this put the fans in the centre of the action and gave the rink a unique atmosphere. But the building did have its problems.

The rink was undersized compared to most other arenas, being nine feet shorter in length and two feet narrower in width. This was because when the building was constructed the league had not yet instituted standard rink sizing. This was an advantage for the Bruins as opposing teams had difficulty adapting to the smaller rink size. The building also had no air conditioning, making the arena hot and prone to fogging over, and twice during the Stanley Cup finals in 1988 and 1990, games were disrupted by power outages.

The last official NHL game held at the Garden was game five of the Eastern Conference quarterfinals against the New Jersey Devils on May 14, 1995. The Devils closed out Boston Garden's illustrious history by beating the Bruins by a score of 3–2 and eliminating them from the playoffs. The Bruins and Montréal Canadiens played an exhibition game on September 28, 1995, at the Garden, and in a special ceremony, legends from both teams removed the banners from the rafters. The banners were raised a few months later in their new modern home at the TD Garden.

See TD Garden

Bread Line: The New York Rangers top line from the 1930s to the 1940s was so named because of their importance to

B

the team's goal-per-game output. The line consisted of Mac Colville, Neil Colville and Alex Shibicky.

Brain Bucket: Colloquial term for a helmet.

Branch: An old term for a hockey stick. It's a fitting reference since when hockey sticks were first made, they were carved out of a single piece of wood usually taken from the branch of a hardwood tree.

See Stick

Brawl: Hockey players fight, but they don't often brawl. In a brawl, everybody on the ice is involved in the fight. Brawls

B

have been a part of hockey since the game began and hockey is not likely to ever be without them. Even the goaltenders get in on the action when there is a brawl. Because goaltenders are less mobile, they usually choose to fight each other to even the odds.

See Bench-clearing Brawl

Brendan Byrne Arena: Former name of the New Jersey Devils home arena from 1982 to 1996. The arena changed its name to Continental Airlines Arena from 1996 to 2007 before the team moved to the Prudential Center. The building has since been renamed the Izod Center.

See Izod Center; Prudential Center

Breakaway: A breakaway occurs when a player gets the puck and has an open run at the goaltender—something that's always guaranteed to get fans on their feet. Along with the penalty shot, a breakaway is one of the most exciting moments in hockey. Maurice Richard was one of the best breakaway players in the game. When asked what the fondest memory of his hockey career was, Toronto Maple Leafs goaltender Johnny Bower said, "The day the Rocket retired!"

Breakout: When a team gains control of the puck in their defensive end, they try to "breakout" of their zone and go on the attack. Most teams have established breakout plays to accomplish this important aspect of the game.

Break the Ice: When a team scores the first goal in a game, they are said to have "broken the ice."

B

Break-shins: This term alludes to the violent nature of the early form of the game. There were many early accounts of "hurley-on-ice" leading to broken teeth, cut lips and bruised shins. In an era before proper padding, calling the game "break-shins" seemed like a natural evolution after so many boys returned home from the pond with bruises all over their legs.

Brick Wall: What every goaltender aspires to be. The "brick wall" is the elusive quality that some goaltenders have, seemingly able to stop every shot as if a brick wall had been constructed on the goal line of the net. Terry Sawchuk was the best bricklayer in NHL history, putting up a wall in front of his net for 103 career shutouts. Goaltender Nikolai Khabibulin was so successful at stopping pucks early in his career that he earned himself the nickname the "Bulin Wall."

Bridgestone Arena: Current home of the Nashville Predators. Originally known as Nashville Arena, Gaylord Entertainment Center and Sommet Center, the arena opened in 1994 and seats 17,113 for hockey games. It is also used as a basketball arena and concert hall.

See Nashville Predators

Broad Street Bullies: Nickname for the 1970s incarnation of the Philadelphia Flyers, so named by Jack Chevalier and Pete Cafone of the Philadelphia Bulletin on January 3, 1973. They came up with the name after a particularly rough game between the Flyers and the Atlanta Flames. The rough-and-tumble style of hockey became the trademark of the Flyers in the early 1970s and was instituted by their head coach Fred Shero. The team philosophy was probably best summed up by Flyers forward Bobby Clarke when he said, "We take the shortest route to the puck and arrive in ill humour."

The physical intimidation style of play worked well for the Flyers, led by tough guy Dave "The Hammer" Schultz. The players did not just hit hard; they could also score goals, leading the Flyers to back-to-back Stanley Cup wins in 1974 and 1975.

See Philadelphia Flyers

61

B

Broadway Blueshirts: Nickname for the New York Rangers.

Brooklyn Americans: *See* New York Americans.

Buds: Nickname for the Toronto Maple Leafs.

Buffalo Sabres: Along with the Vancouver Canucks, the Buffalo Sabres joined the NHL for the start of the 1970–71 season. The team was first owned by Seymour Knox III and his brother Northrup Knox, who had both previously tried to get an NHL franchise when the league expanded in 1967. After a brief contest in the media, the name for the Sabres was chosen because the Knox brothers both thought the sabre was a weapon carried by a leader and was a symbol of strength.

Former Toronto Maple Leafs head coach Punch Imlach took the job as the Sabres general manager and head coach, and the Sabres began constructing a team. At the 1970 Amateur Draft, the Sabres chose first overall and selected Gilbert Perreault. The Sabres then cobbled together a team from other teams' cast-off players and began their inaugural season. It was a season the Sabres would rather forget, finishing well out of playoff contention, the only bright spot being Perreault's 38 goals and 34 assists to lead the team. His performance earned him the Calder Trophy as rookie of the year.

In the team's second season, they added another young French Canadian rookie named Rick Martin and also acquired René Robert from the Pittsburgh Penguins late in the 1971–72 season. While teams like Boston and Chicago were burning up the league, the Sabres were quietly building a deadly lineup of players led by Martin, Perreault and Robert, who became known as the "French Connection" line. The Sabres once again fell out of playoff contention, but the future looked promising for the young franchise.

The Sabres finally made the playoffs for the first time after the 1972–73 season but went up against the eventual Stanley Cup champions the Montréal Canadiens and lost the quarterfinal series in six games.

After a bad year, the Sabres bounced back for the 1974–75 regular season, finishing on top of the newly created Adams Division and tied for the league lead with Montréal and Philadelphia with 113 points and a record of 49–16–15. The Sabres surprised everyone in the playoffs, beating the Chicago Blackhawks in the opening round and then taking out the Montréal Canadiens to move into the Stanley Cup finals for the first time in the franchise's brief history to face the Broadstreet Bully Philadelphia Flyers. The series was marked by the memorable "Fog Game," when an unusual heat wave swept through Buffalo that May and, because of the lack of air conditioning in the building, created a layer of fog and water over the ice, making playing and seeing the game difficult. The game got even weirder when right before a faceoff, Sabres centre Jim Lorentz spotted a bat flying through the air, raised his stick and smacked it out of the air, killing it instantly. The fog was so bad at one point that players and referees even waved towels around the arena in an effort to disperse it. The Sabres won the game in overtime on a goal by René Robert, but ultimately could not solve the Flyers and lost the Stanley Cup finals in six games.

The Sabres line of Robert, Perreault and Martin continued to score prolifically through the late '70s, but the Sabres could never find success in the playoffs, a theme that began to haunt the team through the 1980s and into the mid-1990s.

B

They had bright moments in those years, like Pierre Turgeon, Dale Hawerchuk and Alexander Mogliny, but the Sabres fell flat in the playoffs, consistently bettered in the postseason by division rivals Montréal, Boston and Québec. Since 1970, the Sabres managed to ice competitive teams, but the one key ingredient they always seemed to lack was a top-notch goaltender, which they finally acquired when they signed Czech-born netminder Dominik Hasek.

The goaltender with the unconventional yet effective style finally brought some stability to the Sabres backend and helped propel them from a middle of the pack team to being a major competitor come playoff time. It took awhile, but in the 1999 playoffs, the Sabres finally made it back to the Stanley Cup finals.

To help set the stage, first a little back story. For the start of the 1998–99 season, the NHL wanted to crack down on players interfering with goaltenders in their crease. It was a simple wish by the league, but its implementation in professional play led to a season of slow video-reviewed goals, angry coaches and blown games.

The new rule stated that if any part of a player's body was found to be inside the blue paint in front of the goaltender when a goal was scored, then the goal was automatically called back. This rule was followed to the letter, meaning that even if a player was not found to be interfering with the goaltender but the tip of his skate touched the blue paint, then the goal was disallowed.

Fans, players and team owners all complained about the new rule, but the NHL was determined to see it through to the end of the season, including the playoffs. This is where

B

the Sabres come back into the story, when the rule exploded in the league's face during the Stanley Cup finals in which Buffalo faced off against the Dallas Stars. Even though both teams had some talented offensive players, the series was noted for its defensive play and low-scoring games. After playing five games, it was the Dallas Stars that came away with the advantage going into game six with a 3–2 series

B

lead. Buffalo head coach Lindy Ruff was relying on his number one goaltender Dominik Hasek to help force a game seven final, but the Stars came out fast in game six and looked like a team that wanted to win. But Hasek was up to the task and kept his teammates in the game, holding the Stars to two goals while the Sabres managed two of their own. The game was headed into sudden death overtime.

The game went into the third overtime period, where several Stars players managed to pile in front of Hasek's goal, just outside the crease. When a shot came in from the point, Hasek managed to get a piece of the puck, and it fell right in front of him. Dallas forward Brett Hull swatted the puck into the open side of the net and began to celebrate his Stanley Cup–winning moment. The Sabres immediately protested the goal to referee Terry Gregson because, as the replay clearly showed, Hull's skate was in the crease at the time the puck went into the net. Gregson made no effort to have the goal reviewed despite a full season of reviewed goals and allowed the Stars to continue with their Stanley Cup celebration. It was a bitter pill for the Sabres to swallow.

After that season, the Sabres fell into a dark period. Hasek missed most of the 1999–2000 season with injuries, and even the arrival of Doug Gilmour and the return of Hasek for the playoffs couldn't help the Sabres as they fell in the first round to the Philadelphia Flyers. The Sabres spent the next few seasons playing mediocre hockey and never made it anywhere in the playoffs. Hasek was eventually traded to the Detroit Red Wings, new players were added and subtracted, but still the Sabres could not find a winning combination. As the new millennium progressed, the Sabres had some good seasons, some bad, and not even the return to their old 1970s jerseys could help the Sabres find success

B

in the postseason. Even today, if they remain healthy and play long-time head coach Lindy Ruff's system, the Sabres have potential to go far.

Buffalo Sabres Records

Most goals in a season: Alexander Mogliny, 76 (1992–93)

Most assists in a season: Pat Lafontaine, 95 (1992–93)

Most points in a season: Pat Lafontaine, 148 (1992–93)

Most points by a defenceman: Phil Housley, 81 (1989–90)

Most penalty minutes in a season: Rob Ray, 354 (1991–92)

Most shutouts in a season: Dominik Hasek, 13 (1997–98)

Most wins in a season: Ryan Miller, 41 (2009–10)

See First Niagara Center

Bury the Puck: When the puck is shot hard into the back of the net. Often used when there is traffic in front of the goal, and the puck still manages to find its way into the net.

Bush League: Common term used by players for the low-level minor leagues. Players will often use the term to refer to a poorly managed league.

Butterfly Goaltending: The term "butterfly" refers to a style of goaltending in which the goaltender drops to his knees on the ice and extends his legs parallel to the goal line to take away the bottom of the net from the shooter; the goaltender's legs are extended like the wings of a butterfly. As to why it was called butterfly and not something more masculine is a mystery. Since 70 percent of all shots on goal are aimed at the lower half of the net, butterfly goaltending has become the prevailing style used by NHL goaltenders.

B

The style was developed in the 1960s by goaltending legend Glenn Hall. During the era when goaltenders did not wear masks, it was dangerous for the goalie to crouch low in the net and expose his face to the puck. At first, Hall was lauded for his courage to drop to his knees to make saves, exposing himself to injury, but Hall insisted that he developed the style to avoid injuries. By using the butter-fly position, Hall did not have to dive after stray pucks and put his face in a vulnerable position. The butterfly allowed him to cover the width of the net without relying on acrobatic and potentially dangerous saves. Hall was not without his share of facial injuries, but the butterfly style probably saved him from some of the over 400 stitches that his contemporary, Terry Sawchuk, received to his face over the course of his career.

The goaltender that truly popularized the butterfly style, and the main reason it is practised so widely in the NHL today, was Patrick Roy. Almost every save Roy made was in the butterfly position, and because he used it so effectively, it was copied by most of his colleagues in the NHL and all the way down to the peewee goaltending schools. Few have been able to equal his effectiveness with the style, but it still remains the dominant style in goaltending circles.

See Hybrid Style; Stand-up Style

Butt-ending: Similar to spearing, a player uses the end of the shaft of the stick to jab another player, earning an automatic penalty. The same penalty rules for spearing apply to butt-ending.

See Spearing

Buzzer: The siren that sounds at the end of each period. Some arenas use loud horns instead of a buzzer-type sound.

Buzzer Beater: A goal that is scored with only a few seconds remaining in the period; also, when a team that is trailing by a goal near the end of a game scores the tying goal.

B

C: The letter found on the jersey of the player designated as the team captain. The captaincy is usually given to the senior member of the team who best displays leadership qualities to other players.

According to NHL rules, the captain is the only player allowed to speak with the referees about on-ice rules, or if the captain is not on the ice, the alternate captains may speak with the referee. Although not an official part of the captaincy, the captain often assumes the role of the dressing room leader and will also be the voice of his team's concerns with the management. The captain is also called upon to perform special ceremonial on-ice functions, and if lucky enough to win the Stanley Cup, the captain is the first one to receive the Cup from the commissioner.

Steve Yzerman holds the record for the longest serving captain at 1303 games. The youngest permanent captain in the NHL is Sidney Crosby of the Pittsburgh Penguins, who became captain at the age of 19 years and 297 days. Brian Bellows holds the record for youngest at 19 years and 131 days, but he was only captain for the Minnesota North Stars on an interim basis in 1984.

In NHL history, there have been only six official goaltender captains: John Ross Roach of the Toronto St. Patricks in the 1924–25 season, George Hainsworth of the Montréal Canadiens in the 1932–33 season, Roy Worters of the New York Americans during the 1932–33 season, Alex Connell of the Ottawa Senators in the 1932–33 season, Charlie Gardiner of the Chicago Blackhawks in the 1933–34 season and Bill Durnan of the Montréal Canadiens during the 1947–48 season. The NHL changed the rulebook following the 1947–48 season, prohibiting goaltenders from serving as captains or alternates after opponents of the Montréal Canadiens complained to the league that Bill Durnan left his crease all the time to argue with the referees. Although the Canucks named goaltender Roberto Luongo as their captain, he was captain in name only, with Willie Mitchell acting as on-ice captain for all official matters. Luongo gave up his captaincy in 2010 to Henrik Sedin.

CAHA (Canadian Amateur Hockey Association): From 1914 until 1994, the CAHA served as the governing body of all amateur ice hockey in Canada. After 1994, the CAHA merged with another governing body, the Canadian Hockey Association or Hockey Canada.

The CAHA was formed in 1914 in Ottawa when the trustees of the Allan Cup decided that an association was needed to oversee the organization of the annual Allan Cup tournament and all inter-league play. Later, the CAHA took on the responsibility of organization of international teams to play in the Olympics, the World Juniors and other tournaments.

See Allan Cup

C

CBA: Abbreviation for Collective Bargaining Agreement.

See Collective Bargaining Agreement

CCM: The Canada Cycle & Motor Company began in 1899 producing bicycles and, for a brief period, working on automobiles. Looking to diversify, the company began manufacturing hockey skates in 1905 using the scrap steel that was left over from their bicycle and auto factories. Their line of hockey skates were widely popular across Canada but fell out of favour in the 1980s when other brands began flooding the market, and the original company went bankrupt in 1983. Over the years, the company was bought and sold by various concerns until 2004, when it was bought out by Reebok.

CH: The letters that make up the logo of the Montréal Canadiens. They stand for *"Club de Hockey"* and not Canadiens or Habs as most people think.

See Habitants; Montréal Canadiens

CHL (Canadian Hockey League): It is the larger body that represents the three Canadian-based major junior ice hockey leagues for players between the ages of 16 and 20. The three member leagues are the Western Hockey League (WHL), Ontario Hockey League (OHL) and Québec Major Junior Hockey League (QMJHL). There are 59 teams in the league in nine provinces as well as four American states.

While the individual leagues play for their own championships, the CHL schedule ends with the Memorial Cup tournament that sees each of the three league champions and a host team play for the right to be named national champion. The CHL also hosts the CHL Top Prospects game and the Subway Super Series, a six game All-Star exhibition against a team of All-Star Russian juniors.

See Memorial Cup; OHL; QMJHL; WHL

CHL (Central Hockey League): A now-defunct minor professional league that existed from 1963 to 1984 in the United States. The original members of the league were the Omaha Knights, Minneapolis Bruins, St. Paul Rangers, St. Louis Braves and Cincinnati Wings. The CHL's championship trophy was the Adams Cup. The first president of the league was legendary hockey man Jack Adams, who served until his death in 1968. The league folded in 1984 due to financial problems.

CPHL (Canadian Professional Hockey League): A minor professional hockey league that was founded in 1926. After three seasons, it became known as the International Hockey League in 1929. The inaugural members of the league were

the Hamilton Tigers, Stratford Nationals, Windsor Hornets, Niagara Falls Cataracts and London Panthers.

CWHL (Canadian Women's Hockey League): Founded in 2007, the league consists of six teams, three in Ontario, one in Québec, one in Alberta and one in Boston. The Montréal Stars have won four out of five of the league championships. The league boasts such Olympic stars as Jayna Hefford, Kim St. Pierre, Jennifer Botterill and Angela James.

Cage: Colloquial hockey term that can mean several things. Most commonly used in reference to the goal net, it can also refer to the penalty box (a "cage" for the guilty). Sometimes it is also used in reference to the goaltenders' metal grill on their masks.

Calder Cup: The American Hockey League championship cup. Named after Frank Calder, the first president of the NHL, the trophy was first handed out in 1937 to the Syracuse Stars. The Hershey Bears have won the Cup the most, with 11 victories in their franchise history. The Cleveland Barons come in second with nine wins, and the Springfield Indians/Kings are third with seven championships.

Calder Memorial Trophy: The rookie of the year award. Annual award given to the player selected as the most proficient or talented in his first year or rookie season in the NHL. Voting is conducted among the members of the Professional Hockey Writers' Association (PHWA) at the end of the regular season.

The trophy is named in honour of former league president from 1917 to 1943 Frank Calder. Although rookie of the year honours began at the end of the 1932–33 season, it wasn't until the conclusion of the 1936–37 season that the players received an actual trophy.

The first player awarded the rookie of the year honour was Detroit Red Wings centre Carl Voss in 1933. The first player to receive the actual trophy was Toronto Maple Leafs centre Syl Apps in 1937. The oldest player to win the trophy was Calgary Flames forward Sergei Makarov, who was 31 when he won in 1990 even though he had played "unofficial" but still professional hockey for the Red Army team in Russia. After that season, the NHL changed the rules regarding age, stating that only a player 26 years old or younger was eligible to win the rookie award. Bobby Orr, Dale Hawerchuk and Jeff Skinner are the only 18 year olds to win the trophy.

Calgary Corral: Original home arena of the Calgary Flames from 1980 to 1983. It was also known as the Stampede Corral.

Calgary Flames: When the Atlanta Flames franchise failed and moved to Calgary in 1980, hockey fans in the city finally had a team of their own to take on their provincial rivals, the Edmonton Oilers.

After the move from Atlanta had been finalized, the Flames moved from their former home in the Patrick Division to the Smythe Division for their second season in Calgary. The Atlanta Flames had been around for several years and had established a respectable team, so when the Calgary Flames opened for business, the club didn't have to suffer through several losing seasons as most expansion clubs do. In their first season, the Flames posted a 39–27–14 record and got into the playoffs for the first time as well. The city was a buzz, as the Flames easily beat the Chicago Blackhawks in the preliminary round, then surprised everyone with a tough seven game series win over the Philadelphia Flyers to make it into the semifinals against the Minnesota North Stars, one step away from the Stanley Cup finals. But the dream season ended when the North Stars beat the Flames in six games.

The Flames followed up that miracle season with a disappointing sophomore effort. The losing ways of the team were a wake-up call for general manager Cliff Fletcher, who knew some changes needed to be made to the club if they ever wanted to get close to the successes of their neighbours to the north in Edmonton.

Before the start of the 1982–83 season, head coach Bob Johnson was replaced by Al MacNeil and the drafting of quality players became a priority, selecting future stars such as Joel Otto and later Joe Nieuwendyk. They also added one of the most recognizable figures in hockey, a moustachioed forward from the Colorado Rockies named Lanny McDonald. The Flames slowly began to turn their team around and finished off the season with a berth in the playoffs. After defeating Vancouver in the opening round, the Flames lost in the division finals to their provincial rivals. This became a familiar occurrence in the next few postseasons for the Flames, losing in the playoffs to the eventual Stanley Cup winner. Over the next few seasons, GM Cliff Fletcher added players like Doug Risebrough, Al MacInnis, Hakan Loob and goaltender Mike Vernon.

By the 1985–86 season, the Flames were a solid, physical team that could score goals, but the reality was that Wayne Gretzky and the Oilers were far better and were dominating the league and all the teams in their division. Into the 1986 playoffs, the Flames got past the Winnipeg Jets in the first round and again met the Oilers in the division finals, but this time the Flames came out of the series as the winner, thanks to a little luck. The Flames took the series into a seventh and deciding game and won it late in the third when Oilers defenceman Steve Smith accidently scored on his own net to give the Flames a 3–2 lead. The Flames held on, and the Oilers' quest for a third straight Stanley Cup was scuttled. The Flames then made it past the St. Louis Blues in the conference finals to face the Montréal Canadiens in the Stanley Cup final. The Flames ultimately lost the Cup to the Canadiens, but they would get their revenge soon enough.

After two more successful seasons with early exits from the playoffs, the Flames returned to the playoffs again in 1989 with a renewed sense of now or never. The team had a good mix of veterans and young players and needed to seize the moment while they were still on top. The Flames did not have to face Edmonton this time around because the Los Angeles Kings, with Gretzky on their side, had done them a favour. Calgary dispatched Vancouver in the opening round, followed by the Kings and the Chicago Blackhawks before facing the Montréal Canadiens for a Stanley Cup rematch. This time, it was the Flames who prevailed, beating the Habs in six games to win the franchise's first Stanley Cup.

Unfortunately, the Cup and the playoffs seemed to pass Calgary by for the next few years as the club struggled to find the chemistry and consistency that made them strong in the 1980s. The club just barely made it into the play-offs in the early 1990s and, starting in 1997, missed out on the postseason all together for seven years in a row. But all of that was forgotten in 2004 when the Flames managed to squeak into the playoffs and went on a run that electrified the city and all of Canada (except Edmonton).

The Flames, led by Jarome Ignila and goaltender Miikka Kiprusoff, charged past the Vancouver Canucks, defeated the highly skilled Detroit Red Wings, then stymied the Pacific Division champion San Jose Sharks to make it into the Stanley Cup finals for the first time since 1989. It was a Cinderella story that united hockey fans across Canada who were hoping to see the Cup back in the north for the first time since Montréal won in 1993. But the fairy tale did not end well when the Tampa Bay Lightning won the series in the seventh game to take the Cup away from Calgary.

Since that heart-breaking loss, the Flames have had a few up-and-down seasons but have not made any significant waves in the postseason since the '04 Cup run.

Calgary Flames Records

Most points in a season: Kent Nilsson, 131 (1980–81)

Most goals in a season: Lanny McDonald, 66 (1982–83)

Most assists in a season: Kent Nilsson, 82 (1980–81)

Most penalty minutes in a season: Tim Hunter, 375 (1988–89)

Most wins in a season: Miikka Kiprusoff, 42 (2005–06)

Most losses in a season: Mike Vernon, 30 (1991–91)

See Scotiabank Saddledome

California Golden Seals: *See* Oakland Seals

Campbell Conference: Now known as the Western Conference, the Clarence Campbell Conference was created in 1974 when the NHL decided to realign its teams into two conferences and four divisions. The NHL was in the habit of naming its conferences and divisions based on geographical location (Canadian Division and American Division), but since the integration of several new teams in the late '60s and early '70s, geographical location had little to do with division names. The Campbell Conference remained until 1993, when Campbell was changed to the Western Conference to help new hockey fans better understand the game and its divisions.

Before 1993, the Campbell Conference consisted of the Norris and Smythe divisions. The winner of the Western Conference

C

finals in the playoffs is still to this day awarded the Clarence S. Campbell Bowl. The conference and the Bowl are named after former league president Clarence Campbell, who served as head of the NHL from 1946 to 1977.

See Western Conference

Campbell Bowl (also Clarence S. Campbell Bowl): The trophy awarded to the winner of the Campbell Conference (now called the Western Conference). It was first awarded in the 1968 playoffs, a year after the league expanded from six teams to 12. The first winner of the trophy was the Philadelphia Flyers. The Clarence S. Campbell Bowl is still awarded to this day to the winner of the Western Conference.

See Prince of Wales Trophy

Canada Cup: The Canada Cup was an international hockey tournament held five times between 1976 and 1991. The tournament was created to meet the demand of international hockey fans to have a true world championship style tournament that allowed the best players from all

nations to compete regardless of amateur or professional status, as was the case in the Summit Series of 1972 between Canada and the Soviet Union.

Taking place during the NHL off-season, Canada was joined by the Soviet Union, Czechoslovakia, Finland, Sweden and the United States (West Germany played in one tournament in 1984, replacing Finland). All tournaments were held in Canadian cities. Of the five Canada Cup tournaments, Canada won four while the Soviet Union won one in 1981.

Canada beat Czechoslovakia in the 1976 inaugural tournament, with the Leafs' Darryl Sittler scoring the championship goal in overtime. Five years later, the Soviets won in a 8–1 romp over Canada in the final. Canada won in 1984 with a win over Sweden in the final. The most memorable tournament moment came in 1987 when Mario Lemieux and Wayne Gretzky teamed up to lead the Canadian team to another victory, with Lemieux scoring the championship winning goal on a two-on-one pass from Gretzky in the final minutes of the game against the Soviets. The final Canada Cup was held in 1991, with Canada taking the championship over the United States. Five years later, the Canada Cup was replaced by the World Cup of Hockey in 1996.

See World Cup of Hockey

Year	Champion	Runner Up	Most Valuable Player
1976	Canada	Czechoslovakia	Bobby Orr
1981	Soviet Union	Canada	Vladislav Tretiak
1984	Canada	Sweden	John Tonelli
1987	Canada	Soviet Union	Wayne Gretzky
1991	Canada	United States	Bill Ranford

C

Canadian Airlines Saddledome: Name of the home arena of the Calgary Flames between 1996 and 2000. Previously known as the Olympic Saddledome and afterwards the Pengrowth Saddledome, it is now called the Scotiabank Saddledome.

See Scotiabank Saddledome

Canadian Division: One of the two divisions in the NHL that lasted between 1926 and 1938 after the NHL opened up franchises in the United States. Despite its name, the Canadian Division was not exclusively Canadian as the New York Americans and St. Louis Eagles were part of the division.

Canadien: Brand of hockey stick that was manufactured by CCM, who were best known for their wooden sticks.

Canes: Nickname for the Carolina Hurricanes.

Cannon: Common word used to refer to a very hard slapshot.

See Slapshot

Capital Center: Home arena of the Washington Capitals from 1974 to 1997. Built in Landover, Maryland, the arena was the home of the NBA's Washington Bullets and the College Georgetown Hoyas. The average seating for a hockey game was 18,200 spectators. The arena played host to the classic game seven Easter epic battle between the Capitals and New York Islanders on April 18, 1987, in the Patrick Division semifinals. After three periods of regulation play, the game was tied at two goals apiece, but it wasn't until the fourth overtime period that Pat Lafontaine of the Islanders scored the game-winning goal. The game ended at 1:58 AM local time, 6 hours and 18 minutes after the opening faceoff. Capitals goaltender Bob Mason let in the winning goal while Islanders goaltender Kelly Hrudey stopped a record 73 shots. The Capital Center was demolished in 2002 to make way for a shopping mall.

See Verizon Center

Caps: Nickname for the Washington Capitals.

Carlton the Bear: Official mascot of the Toronto Maple Leafs. The six-foot-four polar bear made his first appearance on October 10, 1995, at the Leafs home opener in Toronto against the New York Islanders.

Carlton's name and number is taken from the address of the Leafs fabled old home arena, the Maple Leaf Gardens, located at 60 Carlton Street in Toronto. The Maple Leaf Gardens was the Leafs home arena from 1931 to 1999.

Carolina Hurricanes: Hartford was never a city that could support an NHL franchise for very long. Small market teams are difficult to manage, and after almost three decades in the league, the Hartford Whalers had not won a Cup and had missed out on the playoffs from 1993 until 1997. At the end of the 1996–97 season, it was announced that the Whalers would move to Raleigh, North Carolina, and become the Carolina Hurricanes.

Due to the short time frame of the move, the new arena that was proposed was not yet ready, so the team was forced to play their home games in Greensboro, a 90-minute drive away from the more populated Raleigh. It took two years before the new arena in Raleigh was ready, and in the meantime, the teams' attendance numbers suffered. Despite having one of the larger arenas in the league with 21,000 seats, the Hurricanes averaged only 10,000 fans per game because fans did not want to drive from Raleigh and hockey fans in Greensboro were still upset that the arrival of the NHL in North Carolina forced the eviction of the minor league Greensboro Monarchs. While the Hurricanes suffered through those first two years with mediocre attendance and a mediocre team, things finally began to turn around, led by Ron Francis and Gary Roberts. By the 1998–99 season, the Hurricanes had made their first appearance in the playoffs. Unfortunately, the Hurricanes lost in the first round to the Boston Bruins, but the future did not look so dim for the franchise that some in the media had dubbed the "natural disasters."

The club's move to the new Entertainment and Sports Arena in 1999–2000 did not give the season the spark the franchise needed, missing out on the postseason yet again. In 2000–01, the Hurricanes managed to turn things around and make their way into the playoffs. Although they lost to the New Jersey Devils in six games, more and more people in Raleigh started to believe in the future of the club.

The fan's patience with the Canes paid off in 2001–02 when they finished first in the Southeast division and rode the experience of veterans Ron Francis, Jeff O'Neil and some inspired goaltending by Arturs Irbe into the Stanley Cup finals. The Canes lost the finals to the Detroit Red Wings in five games. The impressive showing in the finals gave their fans some hope, but the Hurricanes did not gain any momentum from their Cup finals appearance, missing out on the playoffs in 2002–03 and again in 2003–04. The one positive from the failed seasons was that the Hurricanes got to select Eric Staal in the 2003 Entry Draft.

No one in the hockey world would have expected the Hurricanes to come out of the NHL lockout season as one of the league's best clubs, but that's just what they did, finishing the 2005–06 season with a franchise record 112 points, good for fourth overall in the NHL. The Hurricanes opened the playoffs with a come-from-behind win over the Montréal Canadiens that saw their number one goaltender replaced in favour of rookie Cam Ward. Riding the success of their rookie goalie, the Hurricanes blew by Montréal, the New Jersey Devils, then beat the Buffalo Sabres to make it into the Stanley Cup finals for a second time in their brief history. Up against the Edmonton Oilers, this was the first time two former WHA franchises had met in the NHL Stanley Cup finals. The series was a classic Stanley Cup series, both hardworking, forechecking, tough teams. Naturally, the series went to a seventh and deciding game, where the Canes won in the end by a score of 3–1. Several veteran Hurricanes got to hoist

the Stanley Cup for the first time, including Rod Brind'Amour, Bret Hedican and Glen Wesley.

After the Cup win, the Hurricanes put together another disastrous season, finishing 11th in the conference and becoming the first club since the 1939 Chicago Blackhawks to miss the playoffs after winning the Stanley Cup the previous season. In order to turn the club's fortunes around, several players were traded and coaches were fired, but the team could only achieve minor successes. But as in the past, when the club suffered through a few bad seasons and acquired Eric Staal, the Canes new troubles netted them Jeff Skinner in 2010.

Skinner joined the club at just 18 years of age for the 2010–11 season but had an incredible year, winning the Calder Trophy as rookie of the year. Skinner was the lone bright spot for the Hurricanes that season as they again finished out of the playoffs. During the 2011–12 season, the Hurricanes decided to take a new direction by hiring head coach Kirk Muller, and although they missed the playoffs, the club managed to turn things around in the last half of the season, promising a future that could see the team once again rise to the top.

Carolina Hurricanes Records
(including Hartford Whalers Records)

Most goals in a season: Blaine Stoughton, 56 (1979–80)

Most assists in a season: Ron Francis, 69 (1989–90)

Most points in a season: Mike Rogers, 105 (1979–80, 1980–81)

Most points in a season, defenceman: Mark Howe, 80 (1979–80)

Most points in a season, rookie: Sylvain Turgeon, 72 (1983–84)

Fastest hat trick: Ray Whitney, 1 min 40 sec, February 8, 2007 vs. Boston Bruins

Most hat tricks in a season: Eric Staal, 4 (2008–09)

Most penalty minutes in a season: Torrie Robertson, 358 (1985–86)

Most wins in a season: Cam Ward, 39 (2008–09)

See Hartford Whalers; PNC Arena

Carom: When the puck rebounds or ricochets off the boards or any other object on the ice, players included.

Central Division: Division created in 1993 when the league restructured all division because of the addition of several new teams. The current teams in the Central Division are the Chicago Blackhawks, Columbus Blue Jackets, Detroit Red Wings, Nashville Predators and St. Louis Blues. The Detroit Red Wings have won the Central Division championship 13 times since 1993.

See Norris Division

Central Registry: The NHL's repository of data regarding all player affairs, including contracts, transactions, draft eligibility and other specific operations involving players. It tracks a player from the time he is drafted to the end of his career as a player.

Central Scouting Bureau: Department with the NHL that is responsible for ranking young prospects for the NHL Entry Draft. Hockey executive Jack Button founded the Bureau in 1975 to aid teams in the player selection process. The department, located in Toronto, consists of a basic office staff and a group of North American and European scouts that send in reports on players progress several times during a given hockey season.

Centreman: Of the three forwards in hockey, there are two wingmen (left and right) and a centreman. The centre usually takes the faceoffs. Their general purpose on the ice is to move the puck into the area in front of the net and to lead the play up the ice on attacking rushes.

Centre Bell: Current name of the home arena of the Montréal Canadiens. It opened on March 16, 1996, after three years of construction that began following the Canadiens Stanley Cup win in 1993. The Montréal Canadiens opened the building with a game against the New York Rangers, and Vincent Damphousse scored the first goal in the new building. For a hockey game, the Centre Bell seats 21,273 fans and is the largest in the league. Located in the downtown core of Montréal, the Centre Bell also hosts concerts, special shows and other sporting events.

See Bell Centre; Montréal Canadiens

Centre Molson: Former name of the Montréal Canadiens home arena from 1996 to 2002.

See Centre Bell

Challenge Cup: When the Stanley Cup was first created, it did not belong to any league as it now belongs to the NHL. Lord Stanley wanted to celebrate hockey all across the country and have the Stanley Cup as its symbol, therefore the Cup could not belong to anyone league or team. In order to make the process of awarding the Cup clear, the Stanley Cup trustees outlined specific rules to follow in the Challenge Cup era. They were:

The Cup is automatically awarded to the team that wins the title of the previous Cup champion's league, without the need for any other special contest.

Challengers for the Cup must be from senior hockey associations and must have won their league championship. Challengers will be recognized in the order in which their request is received.

The challenge games (where the Cup could change leagues) are to be decided either in a one-game affair, a two-game total goals affair or a best-of-three series, to the benefit of both teams involved. All matches take place on the home ice of the champions, although specific dates and times would have to be approved by the trustees.

This meant that if the Ottawa Hockey Club held the Stanley Cup in 1905, they could indeed be challenged for the trophy by any team from a reputable league. This led to interesting contests such as the 1905 Dawson City Challenge and

C

offered marginal teams a shot at hockey immortality. Before 1912, these challenges could take place at any time, given the condition of the ice and the weather, thus leading the current Cup holders having to defend their title several times in one year. After 1912, the trustees of the Cup decided that trophy only had to be defended at the end of the champion team's regular season.

During this era, all the leagues had no annual formal play-offs system to decide their own league championships and whoever finished first in the standings was declared the champion. The Challenge Cup era ended in 1914 when the Pacific Coast Hockey Association and the National Hockey Association came to an agreement that their respective champions would face off against each other to decide the Stanley Cup champion. Other teams could no longer issue challenges for Lord Stanley's mug. The Cup only became sole property of the NHL in 1926.

See Stanley Cup

Date	Winning Team	Losing Team	Playoff Format	Score
March 17, 1893	Montréal Hockey Club	1893 AHAC Champions, No challengers		
March 22, 1894	Montréal Hockey Club	Ottawa Hockey Club	Single elimination	3–1
March 8, 1895	Montréal Victorias	1895 AHAC Champion		
March 9, 1895	Montréal Hockey Club	Queen's University	Single elimination	5–1
February 14, 1896	Winnipeg Victorias	Montréal Victorias	Single elimination	2–0
February 29, 1896	Winnipeg Victorias	1896 MHA Champion		

Challenge Cup (continued)

Date	Winning Team	Losing Team	Playoff Format	Score
December 30, 1896	Montréal Victorias	Winnipeg Victorias	Single elimination	6–5
March 6, 1897	Montréal Victorias	1897 AHAC Champion		
December 27, 1897	Montréal Victorias	Ottawa Capitals	Single elimination	15–2
March 5, 1898	Montréal Victorias	1898 AHAC Champion		
February 15–18, 1899	Montréal Victorias	Winnipeg Victorias	Two-game Total goals	5–3
March 4, 1899	Montréal Shamrocks	1899 CAHL Champion		
March 14, 1899	Montréal Shamrocks	Queen's University	Single elimination	6–2
February 12–15, 1900	Montréal Shamrocks	Winnipeg Victorias	Best of Three	2–1
March 7, 1900	Montréal Shamrocks	Halifax Cresents	Best of Three	2–0
March 10, 1900	Montréal Shamrocks	1900 CAHL Champion		
January 29–31, 1901	Winnipeg Victorias	Montréal Shamrocks	Best of Three	2–0
February 19, 1901	Winnipeg Victorias	Winnipeg Hockey Club	Single elimination	4–3
January 21–23, 1902	Winnipeg Victorias	Toronto Wellingtons	Best of Three	2–0
March 1902	Winnipeg Victorias	1902 MHA Champion		
March 15–17, 1902	Montréal Hockey Club	Winnipeg Victorias	Best of Three	2–1
January 29–31, February 2–4, 1903	Montréal Hockey Club	Winnipeg Victorias	Best of Three	2–1

Challenge Cup (continued)

Date	Winning Team	Losing Team	Playoff Format	Score
March 7–10, 1903	Ottawa Hockey Club	Montréal Victorias	Two-game Total goals	9–1
March 12–14, 1903	Ottawa Hockey Club	Rat Portage Thistles	Best of Three	2–1
Dec 30, 1903, January 1–4, 1904	Ottawa Hockey Club	Winnipeg Rowing Club	Best of Three	2–1
February 23–25, 1904	Ottawa Hockey Club	Toronto Marlboros	Best of Three	2–0
March 2, 1904	Ottawa Hockey Club	Montréal Wanderers	Two-game Total goals	7–2
March 9–11, 1904	Ottawa Hockey Club	Brandon Wheat Cities	Best of Three	2–0
January 13–16, 1905	Ottawa Hockey Club	Dawson City Nuggets	Best of Three	2–0
March 3, 1905	Ottawa Hockey Club	1905 FAHL Champion		
March 7–11, 1905	Ottawa Hockey Club	Rat Portage Thistles	Best of Three	2–1
February 27–28, 1906	Ottawa Hockey Club	Queen's University	Best of Three	2–0
March 6–8, 1906	Ottawa Hockey Club	Smith Falls	Best of Three	2–0
March 14–17, 1906	Montréal Wanderers	Ottawa Hockey Club	Two-game Total goals	12–10
December 27–29, 1906	Montréal Wanderers	New Glasgow Cubs	Two-game Total goals	17–5
January 21–23, 1907	Kenora Thistles	Montréal Wanderers	Two-game Total goals	12–8
March 16–18, 1907	Kenora Thistles	Brandon Wheat Cities	Best of Three	2–0
March 23–25, 1907	Montréal Wanderers	Kenora Thistles	Two-game Total goals	12–8
January 9–13, 1908	Montréal Wanderers	Ottawa Victorias	Two-game Total goals	22–4

Challenge Cup (continued)

Date	Winning Team	Losing Team	Playoff Format	Score
March 7, 1908	Montréal Wanderers	1908 ECAHA Champions		
March 10–12, 1908	Montréal Wanderers	Winnipeg Maple Leafs	Two-game Total goals	20–8
March 14, 1908	Montréal Wanderers	Toronto HC	Single elimination	6–4
December 28–30, 1908	Montréal Wanderers	Edmonton Hockey Club	Two-game Total goals	13–10
March 6, 1909	Ottawa Hockey Club	1909 ECAHA Champions		
January 5–7, 1910	Ottawa Hockey Club	Galt HC	Two-game Total goals	15–4
January 18–20, 1910	Ottawa Hockey Club	Edmonton Hockey Club	Two-game Total goals	21–11
March 9, 1910	Montréal Wanderers	1910 NHA Champions		
March 12, 1910	Montréal Wanderers	Berlin Dutchmen	Single elimination	7–3
March 10, 1911	Ottawa Hockey Club	1911 NHA Champions		
March 13, 1911	Ottawa Hockey Club	Galt HC	Single elimination	7–4
March 16, 1911	Ottawa Hockey Club	Port Arthur Bearcats	Single elimination	13–4
March 5, 1912	Québec Bulldogs	1912 NHA Champions		
March 11–13, 1912	Québec Bulldogs	Moncton Victorias	Best of Three	2–0
March 5, 1913	Québec Bulldogs	Sydney Millionaires	Two-game Total goals	20–5
March 7–11, 1914	Toronto hockey Club	Montréal Canadiens	Two-game Total goals	6–2
March 14–19, 1914	Toronto Hockey Club	Victoria Aristocrats	Best of Five	3–0

C

C

Chamonix: A small town located at the base of Mont Blanc in southeast France that played host to the first Winter Olympic Games and witnessed the Canadian national hockey team defeat the world to win gold.

Change-up: A shot that fools the goaltender. The term is borrowed from baseball. The goaltender thinks the puck will come in fast, but the shooter either doesn't get enough power behind the shot or else the puck deflects off another player along the way.

Changing on the Fly: The changing of players on the ice while the play continues. Changing on the fly never occurs when the opposing team is in control of the puck or when the puck is in the defensive zone, which would give the other team the advantage. When changing on the fly, the players must be careful to avoid putting too many men on the ice. Sometimes in the confusion of changing players, one extra player will remain on the ice, and if the referee notices the infraction, he will assess a two-minute minor penalty.

Charging: An infraction that occurs when a player takes three or more strides or leaves his feet before checking an opponent. A two-minute minor penalty is assessed.

Charleston Chiefs: Fictional team in the Hollywood movie *Slap Shot.*

   See Slap Shot (movie)

Cheap-shot Artist: The most hated of players in hockey circles. Cheap-shot artists hit, punch, jab, trip and injure other players, usually when the other guy is not looking, and are often the first to plead their innocence to the referees. One of the recent and most notorious cheap-shot artists was Bryan Marchment. Countless times during his career, Marchment intentionally went knee-on-knee with the top players of the NHL and was responsible for many players losing games to unnecessary injuries.

Cherry Picking: When a player remains near the opponent's attacking zone and waits for an outlet pass, hoping to get a breakaway on net.

Chest Protector: Since the puck was rarely shot above waist level in the early days of hockey, it was unnecessary for a goaltender to have any protection on his chest. But as players got better, shots became harder, and increasingly, goaltenders crouched lower to make saves, so they needed something to protect their chests. The first chest protectors were actually borrowed from baseball catchers and protected the chest and shoulder, with an extra flap to cover the groin area. The modern chest protector looks more like a bulletproof vest than a puck stopper, but because some players now can shoot the puck over 100 miles per hour, goaltenders need every piece of padding they can get.

Chicago Blackhawks: Hockey first came to the Windy City in the mid-1920s when brothers Frank and Lester Patrick, owners of the Western Hockey League (WHL), called up millionaire coffee baron Major Frederic McLaughlin. The WHL was in the process of disbanding as it could not keep up with the NHL. The Patricks offered McLaughlin the chance to buy the Portland Rosebuds team for the low price of $200,000. The Patricks convinced the coffee baron that the NHL would be willing to open another franchise in the U.S. as it had already welcomed Boston in 1924 and New York and Pittsburgh in 1925. McLaughlin agree to the terms and moved the Rosebuds to Chicago.

As a commander in World War I, the major belonged to the 85th Blackhawk Division, and as he remembered those days with affection, he named his new team the Chicago Blackhawks. McLaughlin was also aware that an infamous Native American of the Sauk tribe named Chief Blackhawk once roamed the plains of the Midwest. The team found a home in the Chicago Coliseum and was ready for the start of the 1926–27 season.

The Hawks first season was a mediocre one. Their first game was played on November 17, 1926, against the Toronto St. Patricks. They won the game, beating Toronto by a score of 4–1. Chicago ended up finishing the season in third place in the American Division with a record of 19–22–3. Making the playoffs for the first time as well, the Hawks went up against the Boston Bruins in the opening round and were promptly eliminated in the two-game total-goals series by a combined score of 10–5.

Following the end of the disappointing season, McLaughlin promptly fired old Rosebuds head coach Pete Muldoon.

According to Toronto sportswriter Jim Coleman of the *Toronto Globe and Mail*, when McLaughlin told Muldoon of his termination, Muldoon responded by yelling "Fire me, Major, and you'll never finish first. I'll put a curse on this team that will hoodoo it until the end of time." Thus the Curse of Muldoon was born, one of the first major curses in professional sports and not the last curse in Chicago sports history. While the Blackhawks would go on to win three championships in their first 40 years of existence, they did so without ever finishing first overall.

From 1927 to 1934, the Blackhawks had some good seasons and some bad, finishing with the worst record in the league in 1928–29 and going all the way to the Stanley Cup finals (and losing) in 1931. However in 1934, things finally fell into place for Chicago. Goaltender Charlie Gardiner was at the top of his game, and forwards Paul Thompson and Johnny Gottselig were scoring prolifically. In the 1934 play-offs, Chicago made it past the Canadiens in the opening round, then defeated the Montréal Maroons before besting the Detroit Red Wings in the Stanley Cup finals.

As happy as the Blackhawks were in winning their first Cup, something was not right in the locker room. Goaltender Charlie Gardiner was normally a light-hearted joker, but in the weeks leading up to the Stanley Cup final, he had become quiet and melancholy. There was much speculation as to why Gardiner had suddenly changed, but it all became clear when two months after winning the Cup Gardiner collapsed and died of a brain haemorrhage in his hometown of Winnipeg at the young age of 29.

Without Gardiner in goal, the Blackhawks were no longer a Stanley Cup contender, and after a disappointing early exit from the 1935 playoffs, Hawks owner McLaughlin again decided to change the make-up of his team. Seeing that the league was dominated by Canadian teams and Canadian players, the staunchly proud American owner decided he would employ Americans first as best he could. Managers around the league laughed at his attempts to Americanize the Hawks, and after two unsuccessful seasons, his experiment had seemed to fail. When the Hawks just made it into the playoffs after a dismal season in 1937–38 with a record of 14–25–9, no one expected the club to go far. But in the playoffs, Chicago's American goaltender Mike Karakas backstopped his team past the Montréal Canadiens in the first round with a dramatic overtime win in the

C

deciding game, then another close win over the New York Americans in the semifinals to place them in the Stanley Cup finals against the Toronto Maple Leafs.

But in the final game against the New York Americans, Karakas suffered a broken toe. This left the Hawks without their star goaltender for the Toronto series. Forced into a tough situation, the Hawks called up minor-league goaltender Alfie Moore. No one knew how he would perform, but in the first game, he helped the Hawks win 4–1. After losing the second game, Mike Karakas was able to return for game three and led the Hawks through the next two games to take their second franchise Stanley Cup. However, the Hawks' fortunes took a turn for the worse for the next two decades as the rise of Detroit, Toronto and Montréal pushed all other competitors to the side. From 1938 to 1960, the Hawks only made the Stanley Cup finals once (they were eliminated in four straight games). Over that time, they had great players like Max Bentley, Gaye Stewart, Gus Bodnar and Bill Mosienko, but they could not win the important hockey games. It wasn't until the arrival of goaltender Glenn Hall and a young forward named Bobby Hull that everything changed for the Hawks.

With the goaltending situation finally solved for the Hawks after so many years of changing goaltenders and with some new young offensive talent, the Hawks moved back into league prominence by the late '50s, and by the 1960–61 season were top contenders for the Stanley Cup. Going into the 1961 playoffs, the Hawks were able to dispose of the five-time Stanley Cup champion Montréal Canadiens and then defeat Gordie Howe and his Red Wings to win their first Cup since 1938. It was a great feeling for the young team, but unfortunately it was a feeling that would have to sustain them for a long time.

C

Through the 1960s and 1970s, while the Hawks were one of the premier teams with players like Hull, Pierre Pilote, Alex Delvecchio, Stan Mikita and Tony Esposito, the Hawks seemed cursed in the playoffs, countless times losing in heart-breaking fashion on their chance to bring the Cup home. Then through the 1980s, the Hawks had great skill up front with guys like Denis Savard and Steve Larmer, but the club lacked a goaltender to take them far into the play-offs. The Hawks best playoff performances came in 1982, 1983, 1985 and 1989, making it all the way to the conference finals but never further.

When Ed Belfour joined the team for the 1990–91 season, fans thought the team's playoffs woes were done once and for all, but even the Calder and Vezina trophy–winning goaltender could not take the Hawks past the dreaded conference finals; that is, until the 1992 playoffs when the team finally broke through into the Stanley Cup finals. After beating the Oilers in the conference finals, the Hawks moved on to face the defending Cup champion Pittsburgh Penguins. The Hawks tried but could not solve the Penguins, losing in four straight in their first Stanley Cup finals appearance since 1973.

The Hawks remained a competitive club through much of the 1990s but started to fall in the standings as the new millennium approached, losing much of their core from the 1980s and '90s to retirement, trades or free agency. In the new millennium, the Hawks could not find any consistency despite such standouts as Eric Daze, Tony Amonte and Alexei Zhamnov. From 1998 to 2008, the Hawks made it into the playoffs just once. However, there was a silver lining as they were able to select high in the NHL Entry Drafts, taking Jonathan Toews and Patrick Kane in 2006 and 2007. The two dynamic forwards soon formed the core of the club that led the Hawks back into contention.

By the 2009–10 season, the Hawks were once again one of the top teams in the league with a powerful offence and the goaltending of Antti Niemi to provide confidence on the defensive end. The team rode their success to their first Stanley Cup championship win in 49 years.

Chicago Blackhawks Records

Most seasons with the team: Stan Mikita, 22

Most goals scored in a season: Bobby Hull, 58 (1968–69)

Most assists in a season: Denis Savard, 87 (1987–88)

Most points in a season: Denis Savard, 131 (1987–88)

Most penalty minutes in a season: Mike Peluso, 408 (1991–92)

Most shutouts in a season: Tony Esposito, 15 (1969–70)

Most consecutive games played: Steve Larmer, 884

See United Center

Chicago Coliseum: Built in 1899, the Coliseum was Chicago's premiere arena for concerts, political rallies and events, but in 1926, it was retooled to suit the needs of the Chicago Blackhawks. Seating some 6000 fans, the arena was not suitable for professional hockey games, and once the Chicago Stadium was constructed, the Hawks changed venues. The Blackhawks played a few more games in the Coliseum because of disputes with the owners of Chicago

C

Stadium. They played their final game at the Coliseum on November 21, 1932, in a losing effort to the Montréal Canadiens.

Chicago Stadium: The iconic home of the Blackhawks from 1929 to 1994. Built at a cost of $9.5 million, Chicago Stadium was the world's largest sports arena at the time. It was built by sports promoter Paddy Harmon in the hopes of gaining control of the Blackhawks over Major McLaughlin, who was struggling with the Hawks in the smaller Chicago Coliseum. With seating for 15,000 fans, Harmon failed to gain control of the Hawks, he was eventually kicked off the Stadium's board and the Blackhawks took over control of the building permanently in 1929. It was also the first stadium with air conditioning. During the 1990s, most of the hockey clubs in the NHL were constructing new buildings to suit the needs of a modern club and the Chicago Stadium needed a serious update. The final hockey game at Chicago Stadium was played on April 28, 1994, when the Blackhawks lost to the Toronto Maple Leafs in the 1994 Stanley Cup playoffs. Mike Gartner of the Leafs scored the final goal in the building.

See United Center

Chiclets: A colloquial term for teeth.

Chip Shot: When a player passes the puck without any real control over the direction and without any power. Chipping the puck is considered a conservative style, as this type of shot makes it difficult to begin a formal rush towards the opposing team and it is likely that the other team will regain possession.

Chirping: When a player argues a penalty call with the referee, or when a player tries to get under the skin of an opposing player. Many expletives are typically used in chirping.

See Badgering

C

Chocolatetown: Nickname for the home of the AHL's Hershey Bears, where the famous Hershey Chocolate hails from.

Christian: American hockey stick manufacturer, founded by Dave Christian.

Circle the Wagons: When a player skates into the offensive zone, goes around the net avoiding all other players, and comes up the other side. It is not the most strategic move, but it can be effective if the opposing team takes the bait and pursues the player. However, what most often occurs is that the player loses the puck, resulting in a turnover.

Civic Arena: Former name of the Pittsburgh Penguins' old arena. First opened in September 1961, it was the first sports venue in the world with a retractable roof. It was originally constructed for use by the Pittsburgh Civic Light Opera, but it also hosted numerous concerts, religious and cultural affairs before it was handed over to the Pittsburgh Penguins in 1967. Because of its large dome shape, it was nicknamed "The Igloo" by the people of Pittsburgh. The arena closed in June 2010. The Penguins and Montréal Canadiens played the last game under its roof on May 12, 2010, a 5–2 victory for the Canadiens in game seven of the Eastern Conference semifinals.

See Consul Energy Center

Clarkson Cup: A trophy awarded to the top Canadian women's hockey team in Canada. It was created by and named after former Governor General Adrienne Clarkson. Though it was initially awarded in 2006 to the Canadian Women's National Ice Hockey Team, from 2006 to 2008 it was not awarded because of a number of rights issues

C

between Clarkson, Hockey Canada and the artist responsible for making the trophy. In 2009, all issues surrounding the Cup were resolved and the Cup was handed out to the Montréal Stars of the Canadian Women's Hockey League.

Cleveland Barons: (Formerly the Oakland/California Golden Seals) Member of the NHL from 1976 to 1978. After a failed attempt to bring another hockey franchise to Southern California, the California Golden Seals moved operations to Cleveland in 1976. The team was named in honour of the American Hockey League (AHL) team the Cleveland Barons that had been a part of the city from 1937 to 1973. The AHL Barons had enjoyed many years of success in the city, but despite several attempts, the city had never been awarded a franchise until the Golden Seals arrived in 1976. The new NHL Cleveland Barons' original arena was the Richfield Coliseum, which was also the home of the Cleveland Cavaliers and had the largest NHL seating capacity at the time with 18,544 seats. But the team never came close to filling those seats. The home opener on October 7, 1976, drew just 8900 fans.

Head coach Jack Evans did not have much to work with on his team and finished the 1976–77 season with a record of 25–42–13. General manager Harry Howell tried to fix his club through trades, but the following season was even worse, and the club finished with a record of 22–45–13.

Fearing that the Barons were about to go bankrupt, the NHL Board of Governors approved a merger with the equally struggling Minnesota North Stars. The merger continued under the North Stars name but assumed the Barons place in the Adams Division. The NHL did not return to the state of Ohio until 22 years later, when the Columbus Blue Jackets debuted in the fall of 2000.

Some notables players from the days of the Cleveland Barons are goaltender Gilles Meloche, forward J.P. Parise (father of New Jersey Devils Zach Parise), Denis Maruk and Al MacAdam.

See Minnesota North Stars; Oakland Seals

Clothesline: When one player sticks out his arms and strikes an unsuspecting player in the head, knocking him to the ground. Can sometimes result in an interference penalty.

See Interference

Club de Hockey Canadien: Corporate name of the Montréal Canadiens, established in 1909.

Clutch and Grab: A game in which either one or both teams are constantly hooking or holding the opposition in order to slow them down. This style of hockey is rarely seen today because of stricter enforcement of the rules.

Coach's Corner: Intermission television segment on the CBC's *Hockey Night in Canada* program featuring host Ron MacLean and the infamous Don Cherry.

Coast-to-coast: When a player starts with the puck in his own defensive end and skates all the way to the other end of the ice, never once passing the puck. Bobby Orr made this move famous.

See End-to-end

Collective Bargaining Agreement: Term for the contract between the NHL and the players that details the terms and conditions under which the league operates. It was a disagreement regarding the collective bargaining agreement that led to the 2004–05 lockout season.

C

All NHL clubs first recognized the National Hockey League Players Association (NHLPA) as the executive representatives of all players in June 1967. The first formal collective bargaining agreement was signed on May 4, 1976.

Colorado Avalanche: The Avalanche began their NHL franchise as the Québec Nordiques in 1972, but as time went on and the costs associated with operating a modern NHL franchise began to soar, many small-market teams like Québec and Winnipeg found it increasingly difficult to pay their

C

bills. Despite the Nordiques' success on the ice in the early 1990s, the team could no longer afford to stay in *la belle province*. Nordiques owner Marcel Aubut began shopping the club around, and in 1995, he found a buyer in the COM-SAT Entertainment Group in Denver, Colorado. On July 1, 1995, the deal became official, and just one month later, the Colorado Avalanche were presented to the media.

Unlike most new teams that enter into the NHL as expansion franchises and suffer through a few years of growing pains, the Nordiques team remained intact when they became the Avalanche, retaining the nucleus of players that had already spent several years together in the trenches.

On October 6, 1995, the Avalanche played their first home game against the Detroit Red Wings, winning by a score of 3–2. The stars on the team that year were Peter Forsberg, captain Joe Sakic, defenceman Adam Foote and, joining the team mid-season, goaltending phenom Patrick Roy, who had left the Montréal Canadiens after a public break-up with Canadiens coach Mario Tremblay and team president Ronald Corey. The Avalanche, or "Avs" as they were commonly called, finished their first season with a record of 47–25–10.

In the playoffs, the team made it past the Vancouver Canucks and Chicago Blackhawks in the opening two rounds before beating the Detroit Red Wings to win the Western Conference championship and a berth in the Stanley Cup finals against the Eastern Conference champion Florida Panthers. The finals were never in doubt for the Avs as they swept the Panthers in four straight to win the Stanley Cup in their first year in the league. Joe Sakic was named the MVP of the playoffs with 18 goals and 32 points, earning him the

Conn Smythe Trophy. The Stanley Cup victory was the first major professional sports championship for the city of Denver in their history—the NFL's Denver Broncos won the Super Bowl in 1997.

During their first few years in the league, the Avalanche were among the best teams. They consistently finished at the top of the league and were always a threat in the play-offs. During the 1996–97 season, the Avs finished with a record of 49–24–9, assuring themselves a spot in the play-offs. In the first round, they again disposed of the Chicago Blackhawks and then the Edmonton Oilers before meeting Detroit in the Western Conference finals. But this time, it was the Red Wings who came out on top, beating the Avs in six games.

Over the next few seasons, the team consistently placed near the top of their conference but always managed to come up short in the playoffs. Their luck began to change when the team decided to build a new arena, moving from the aging and cramped McNichols Sports Arena to the brand new Pepsi Center for the start of the 1999–2000 season. They played their home opener against the Boston Bruins on October 13, 1999, and won 2–1. The Avs finished the season with a record of 42–28–11–1.

Just prior to the end of the regular season, the club picked up veteran defenceman Ray Bourque from the Boston Bruins. Bourque, who had been with the Bruins since 1979, had requested a trade to a Stanley Cup contender in a last-ditch effort to win a Stanley Cup before he retired. The Avs did not win the Cup that year, losing in the Western Conference finals to the Dallas Stars, but in 2000–01, Ray

Bourque realized his lifelong dream when the Avalanche made it back into the Stanley Cup finals and defeated the New Jersey Devils to win their second Stanley Cup championship. When a team wins the Stanley Cup, the captain is usually the one who gets to hoist the Cup above his head first, but in this case, Avs captain Joe Sakic handed off the Cup to Ray Bourque, giving the NHL playoffs one of its most touching moments in years. After that emotional win, Ray Bourque retired from the NHL as a Stanley Cup champion.

The Avalanche continued to play good hockey for a few more years, but after the 2004–05 lockout season, the team's fortunes began to slide. In 2006–07, the team missed the playoffs for the first time in their history, and the core players that brought them their two Cups, Hall of Fame players like Joe Sakic and Patrick Roy, had either retired or were nearing the end of their careers. The drop in on-ice production began to translate into the number of fans in the stadium. The Avalanche set a record by selling out every game at McNichols Arena between November 9, 1995, and October 16, 2006, a total of 487 straight sell-outs. But since 2006, the team has been up and down in the standings and has missed the playoffs three times. Players have come and gone and so have the coaches, no combination seeming to translate to wins on the score sheet.

As of 2010, the Avs have added a few young players that bring hope for the future back to Denver. Young forward Matt Duchene continues to surprise with his sheer offensive talent and 2011 first-round draft pick Gabriel Landeskog looks to make his mark in the NHL as well.

Colorado Avalanche Records

Most goals in a season: Joe Sakic, 54 (2000–01)

Most game-winning goals in a season: Joe Sakic, 12 (2000–01)

Most assists in a season: Peter Forsberg, 86 (1995–96)

Most points in a season: Joe Sakic, 120 (1995–96)

Most points in a season, rookie: Paul Stastny, 78 (2006–07)

NHL record longest points streak, rookie: Paul Stastny, 20 games (2006–07)

Most penalty minutes in a season: Chris Simon, 250 (1995–96)

Best plus/minus in a season: Milan Hejduk, Peter Forsberg, +52 (2002–03)

Most wins in a season: Patrick Roy, 40 (2000–01)

Most shutouts in a season: Patrick Roy, 9 (2001–02)

Best goals-against average in a season: Patrick Roy, 1.94 (2001–02)

See Pepsi Center; Québec Nordiques

Colorado Rockies: Founded in 1976, the Colorado Rockies were the city of Denver's first franchise in the NHL. The team was born out of the demise of the Kansas City Scouts, who had lasted just two years in the league before selling

C

their controlling interest to a Denver-based group of executives headed by Jack Vickers. The only problem was that the Scouts were not a very good team, and the Rockies inherited the Scouts' losing streak for their inaugural season.

In the Rockies' six seasons in the league, they iced a wealth of talented players that included such NHL alumni as Lanny McDonald, Wilf Paiement, Rene Robert, Rob Ramage and Steve Tambellini, but the team never managed to find the right balance of chemistry and depth to take the franchise very far into the postseason. Their first season in the league was a complete disaster both on the ice and in the stands. The Rockies managed to win only 20 games, and with each game, McNichols Arena became progressively devoid of fans. During the 1977–78 season, the team only managed

to win 19 games, but with a little help from their horrible division, they made the playoffs for the first time. Despite the achievement, the Rockies squandered their playoff hopes, losing the best-of-three series in two straight games to the Philadelphia Flyers.

The team's management tried to bring in some semblance of a fighting spirit by hiring the infamous and flamboyant head coach Don Cherry in 1979. This led to the Rockies' unofficial motto for the 1979–80 season: "Come to the fights and see a Rockies game break out!" Even with all the added hype and testosterone, the Rockies still could not put numbers in the win column. At the end of the season, Don Cherry was fired. Despite the bad team, the true die-hard hockey fans kept showing up to the arena. The reason hockey did not last in Denver the first time was that no viable owner could be found to keep the team in place long term.

After two more seasons spent watching the playoffs from home, the owners sold the franchise to New Jersey shipping millionaire John McMullen and moved the team to the Meadowlands Arena, where the team was rechristened the New Jersey Devils for the start of the 1982–83 season.

See New Jersey Devils

Coloured Hockey League: This all-black hockey league was founded in 1894 and was popular in the Maritimes. With around a dozen teams in cities in Nova Scotia, New Brunswick and P.E.I., the league was known for its fast-paced high-scoring hockey, and as a result, it attracted many fans including Caucasians. With the rise of interest in the NHL, the league folded in 1925 because of financial issues. Some sports historians credited the coloured hockey league with being the first league to allow a goaltender to leave his feet to cover a puck, as it was illegal in all professional leagues and even in the NHL until 1919.

Columbus Blue Jackets: Based out of Columbus, Ohio, the Blue Jackets entered the NHL in 2000. The last hockey franchise in the state of Ohio was the Cleveland Barons, who left the NHL in 1978. Twenty-two years later, the Columbus Blue Jackets returned hockey to Ohio, joining the Minnesota Wild as the two expansion teams for the 2000–01 season. At the Expansion Draft in the summer before their inaugural season, the Blue Jackets general manager Doug MacLean amassed a talented group of veterans and journeymen players, including goaltender Rick Tabaracci, defenceman Lyle Odelein and forward Geoff Sanderson.

The Blue Jackets played their first regular season game under head coach Dave King on October 7, 2000, a 5–3 loss to the Chicago Blackhawks. It was a difficult season for the Blue Jackets, who finished with a record of 28–39–9–6 for 71 points, not good enough for a spot in the playoffs. The next season, they fared even worse as the team finished with just 57 points. Tragedy also struck the club when, during a home game on March 16, 2002, a shot by Blue Jackets Espen Knutsen was deflected by Calgary Flames' Derek Morris and flew up into the stands behind the net, striking 13-year-old Brittanie Cecil in the temple. She was taken to hospital but died as a result of a torn vertebral artery two days later. As a result of her death, the NHL made it mandatory for all NHL arenas to protect fans behind the goal with high protective netting.

C

At the 2002 Entry Draft, the Columbus Blue Jackets selected Rick Nash, who became the team's franchise player. With a top prospect and their horrible sophomore season behind them, the Columbus Blue Jackets started the 2002–03 season with promise, posting a record of 7–5–1–1 in the first 14 games, but the team struggled the remainder of the season and missed out on the playoffs again. Head coach Dave King was fired halfway through the season, but a change of coaches did not help them put wins up on the board.

The lone bright spot for the Blue Jackets in the 2003–04 season was forward Rick Nash, who finished the season with 41 goals, tying him with Jarome Ignila and Ilya Kovalchuk for the Maurice "Rocket" Richard Trophy, which is presented to the league leader in goals. (*See* Maurice "Rocket" Richard Trophy) After the lockout, things still did not get better for the Jackets. They tried new coaches, new general managers and new players, but the team lacked chemistry. Prior to the start of the 2007–08 season, the Blue Jackets organization, in an attempt to bring something fresh and exciting to the arena, bought a replica of a 1857 Napoleon cannon for Nationwide Arena and fired it whenever the team took the ice at the start of the game, when the Jackets scored a goal and when they won a game.

The Blue Jackets finally achieved some success in the 2008–09 season when they qualified for the playoffs for the first time in their history. However, the happiness was very short lived as their first-round opponents, the Detroit Red Wings, defeated them in four straight games. The Blue Jackets have not made the playoffs again.

Columbus Blue Jackets Records

Most goals in a season: Rick Nash, 41 (2003–04)

Most game-winning goals in a season: Rick Nash (2003–04) and Geoff Sanderson (2000–01), 7

Most assists in a season: Ray Whitney, 52 (2002–03)

Most points in a season: Rick Nash, 79 (2008–09)

Most points in a season, defenceman: Jaroslav Spacek, 45 (2002–03)

Most points in a season, rookie: Rick Nash, 39 (2002–03)

Most penalty minutes in a season: Jody Shelley, 249 (2002–03)

Highest plus/minus in a season: Jan Hejda, +23 (2008–09)

Most wins in a season: Steve Mason, 31 (2008–09)

Most shutouts in a season: Steve Mason, 10 (2008–09)

Best goals-against average in a season: Pascal Leclaire, 2.25 (2007–08)

Best save percentage in a season: Pascal Leclaire, 0.919 (2007–08)

Most saves in a season: Marc Denis, 2172 (2002–03)

Longest shutout streak: Steve Mason, 199:19 (2008–09)

See Nationwide Arena

Commissioner: Prior to February 1, 1993, the NHL had always been run by a president. Gil Stein served as the league's final president when the NHL Board of Governors replaced him with Gary Bettman. The position of commissioner was created specifically for Bettman, whose mandate was to sell the game in the U.S. markets, end the labour unrest between the players and the owners and bring the NHL into the new century.

Under the NHL Constitution, Article VI, section 6.1, the commissioner's job is defined as follows:

6.1 Office of Commissioner, Election and Term of Office. The League shall employ a Commissioner selected by the Board of Governors. The Commissioner shall serve as the Chief Executive Officer of the League and is charged with protecting the integrity of the game of professional hockey and preserving public confidence in the League. The Board of Governors shall determine the term of office and compensation of the Commissioner. The Commissioner shall be elected by a majority of the Governors present and voting at a League meeting at which a quorum was present when it was convened.

Compact Center: Former name of the San Jose Sharks home rink.

See HP Pavilion

Composite Sticks: For over 100 years, hockey players relied on wooden sticks, which served them well, but by the

1980s, companies began experimenting with materials other than wood. In the late 1980s, Wayne Gretzky was the first to relinquish his reliable wooden stick for an aluminium one. The lighter stick allowed players to shoot quicker, and the stiffer nature of aluminium provided a better transfer of energy to the puck for harder shots. Another revolution in stick technology occurred at the end of the 20th century with the development of composite graphite and Kevlar sticks. Though the sticks weighed just 16.2 ounces (459 grams), players found that the combination of the strength of the shaft and its ability to flex increased the speed of their shots considerably, much to the chagrin of goaltenders around the league. The majority of NHL players have since made the switch to composite sticks, but there are still a few holdouts that have kept their wooden ones.

See Stick

Concussion: Taken from the Latin word *concutere*, meaning to shake violently, a concussion is the most common type of brain injury in hockey. It happens when the head or body is struck a vicious blow, and the brain literally bounces around inside the skull.

Concussions in hockey have become the number one topic in more recent years as more and more players are forced to miss considerable amounts of time because of this injury. Many players indeed have been forced to retire from the game because of repeated concussions.

Concussions cause a wide variety of physical, cognitive and emotional symptoms. Victims will often experience headaches, difficulty thinking, sensitivity to light, sudden

C

bursts of anger and depression. Treatment to date mainly consists of monitoring by doctors and long periods of rest.

Many players in the history of hockey have suffered from concussions, but none more famously and recently than superstar Sidney Crosby, who has battled the injury for almost two seasons and counting. After suffering the initial injury, Crosby spent several months away from the game. Upon his return, he played only a few games before his concussion symptoms recurred.

Given the high-profile status of a player like Sidney Crosby and the frequency with which players seem to be suffering concussions, it is currently one of hottest topics of discussion in the NHL today.

See Post-concussion Syndrome (PCS)

Conn Smythe Trophy: Awarded annually to the player judged most valuable to his team during the NHL Stanley Cup playoffs. Established in 1964, the trophy was named after former owner and general manager of the Toronto Maple Leafs, Conn Smythe. The design of the trophy depicts a scale model of Toronto's Maple Leaf Gardens and has a large maple leaf flaring up behind the building. The first winner of the award was Jean Beliveau of the Montréal Canadiens in 1965. Boston Bruin Bobby Orr was the first player to win the trophy twice. Goaltender Patrick Roy holds the record for the most Conn Smythe awards with three, winning twice with the Montréal Canadiens in 1986 and 1993 and once with the Colorado Avalanche in 2001. Dave Keon's win in 1967 made him the only member of the Toronto Maple Leafs to have ever won the award.

The trophy does not always go to the winner of the Stanley Cup. Five times in the history of the trophy, it has gone to a member of the losing team, including J.S. Giguère of the Anaheim Ducks in 2003, Philadelphia Flyers goaltender Ron Hextall in 1987, Flyers forward Reggie Leach in 1976, St. Louis Blues goaltender Glenn Hall in 1968 and Detroit Red Wings goaltender Roger Crozier in 1966.

Consol Energy Center: Current home of the Pittsburgh Penguins. Opened for the 2010–11 season, the Consul Center was built to replace the aging Mellon Arena (known as the Igloo). Consol Center is a modern facility that seats 18,387 fans for hockey and also serves as a basketball arena and a concert hall. The Penguins officially opened the arena on October 7, 2010, with a 3–2 loss to the Philadelphia Flyers.

See Pittsburgh Penguins

Constitution of the NHL: Document outlining the purposes and objectives of the NHL, which are:

- To perpetuate hockey as one of the national games of the United States and Canada.

- The promotion of the common interests of the members of the league, each member being an owner of a professional hockey club located in the U.S. or Canada.

- The promulgation of rules governing the conduct of play of hockey games between member clubs in the league, the relationships between players and member clubs, between member clubs and the league and between member clubs and other hockey clubs, to the end that the public may be assured of a high standard of skill and fair play, integrity and good sportsmanship.

- The arbitration and settlement of disputes between the member clubs and between member clubs and players.

- The education of the public, through advertising, radio and other media, to the end that professional hockey, as played according to the standards of the league, may gain popular support and acceptance as a wholesome entertainment.

- The development of youth in mind and body and the teaching of fair play and good sportsmanship through the medium of hockey.

121

Continental Airlines Arena: Former name of the home arena of the New Jersey Devils from 1996 to 2007. When New Jersey moved to the Prudential Center in 2007, the building became known as the Izod Center.

See Izod Center; Prudential Center

Cooperalls: A style of long hockey pant that was introduced in the 1980s. Instead of the normal half-pant protection hockey players had been wearing for ages, the Cooper hockey equipment company thought that full pants would be a good idea. While many junior leagues adopted the pants because they better protected their players, only the Hartford Whalers and Philadelphia Flyers decided to wear them at the NHL level during the 1982–83 season. The pants were universally mocked at the NHL level and did not last much longer in the junior leagues. At the end of the

season, the Flyers and Whalers decided to retire their pants and return to the half pants and socks. The NHL made a wise decision by enacting a regulation that all teams must provide their players with the traditional half pants.

CoreStates Center: Former name of the Philadelphia Flyers home arena from 1996–98.

See Wells Fargo Center

Corel Centre: Former name of the Ottawa Senators home arena from 1996 to 2006.

See Scotiabank Place

Corral the Puck: A colourful way of describing how a player accepts a hard pass. When a player shoots a hard pass to a teammate, the receiver must "corral the puck" on his stick.

Cover Point: A term used in the early days of hockey when seven men played on the ice. The defencemen played in two positions, cover point and point. The cover point was played in front of the point, acting as the first line of defence.

Cow Palace: Arena in San Francisco that was home to the San Jose Sharks from 1991 to 1993 while the San Jose Arena was under construction. Built in 1941, Cow Palace was originally constructed as a general all-purpose arena but was never intended as a professional hockey arena. For games, it only seated 11,000, whereas the NHL average was around 18,000. Interesting fact: the NHL had previously rejected the building as a home for the expansion California Golden Seals in 1967.

See HP Pavilion; Oakland Seals

C

Crosschecking: When a player lifts his stick off the ice, holds it in front of his body parallel to his shoulders and smashes it into an opposing player. A referee will not always call a crosschecking penalty when a player (typically a defenceman) lightly crosschecks a player in front of the goal crease. For obvious crosschecking offences, a minor or major penalty may be assessed on the player, depending on the end result of the check.

See Major Penalty; Minor Penalty

Crossover: A skating technique in which one foot is placed in front of the other, thereby crossing over it. Crossovers can be done while skating forward or backwards, and it is one of the essential skating techniques taught to children at a young age, helping them to negotiate corners at a higher speed.

Crumb Bum Award: Award handed out by the New York Rangers to the player who gives back to the youth community. An odd name since, in urban parlance, crumb bum usually means a person who acts the fool.

Cue: A slang term for a hockey stick borrowed from the game of pool.

Cupping: When a player illegally closes his hand around the puck. Results in a delay of game penalty. If a player cups his hand over the puck in the goal crease, it results in an automatic penalty shot for the opposing team.

See Penalty Shot

Curved Sticks: The curved stick was invented in the 1960s, when Chicago Blackhawk Stan Mikita cracked the blade of

C

his stick during a practise. Since it was just a practise and the tape still held the blade together, he kept playing with the stick and found that the puck did some strange things with his blade's new curve. The curve made the puck go in all different directions, spinning through the air and making it difficult for the goaltenders to follow.

Teammate Bobby Hull tried out the blade and decided he wanted one of his own, finding that his shot was much more unpredictable and a lot harder than normal. Overnight, Mikita and Hull bent their stick blades in water, and the banana blade was born. But after several years, the league stepped in and decided that the extra curve gave forwards an unfair advantage, so they made a new rule allowing a curve of no more than half an inch. During their days of playing with the curved sticks, Mikita and Hull remained at the top of the scoring leaders in the NHL.

See Illegal Curve

Cycle the Puck: When in the attacking zone, the offensive team will alternate possession of the puck in the corners, keeping the opposition on their toes. One player will swoop into the corner, while his teammate circles around to the other side and returns to the corner to get the puck again from his teammate.

Cyclone Taylor Trophy: Team award for the Vancouver Canucks' most valuable player during the regular season and the playoffs. Named after the legendary Cyclone Taylor, who played most of his career in British Columbia prior to the start of the NHL.

125

D

Dallas Stars: The Dallas Stars began life as the Minnesota North Stars in 1967, but because of the changing dynamics of the NHL, the small market teams could not survive. In 1993, the club was forced to leave its home in Bloomington, Minnesota, and head south to Dallas, Texas, where a big arena was waiting for them in a city numbering in the millions. The NHL was unsure of the viability of a franchise in such a southern American city, but after seeing the success of the Florida Panthers, the NHL decided to green light the move.

The Stars played their first game in Dallas on October 5, 1993, a 6–4 win over the Detroit Red Wings. Though hockey was an unknown commodity in the Texas city, word of the club quickly began to spread, and soon people were filling the seats every game. It helped that during the Stars' first year in Dallas, Mike Modano scored 50 goals and the team made it into the playoffs. They defeated the St. Louis Blues in four straight games in the first round, but lost in the second round to the Vancouver Canucks.

The strike shortened 1995–96 season was one of change for the club, as they acquired former Canadiens player Guy Carbonneau, Joe Nieuwendyk from the Calgary Flames and brought in Ken Hitchcock as head coach. But the changes disrupted the team's chemistry, and for the first time since moving to Dallas, the Stars missed out on the playoffs. In the offseason, general manager Bob Gainey made a few more adjustments to the team, bringing in Darryl Sydor and Sergei Zubov for the 1996–97 season. The new additions led the Stars to the franchise's first 100-point season. Despite the points, playoff success once again eluded them when they were upset by the Edmonton Oilers in the first round in dramatic fashion when Oilers forward Todd Marchant came speeding through the neutral zone in overtime of game seven and caught Stars defenceman Grant Ledyard flat-footed to score the series-winning goal on Andy Moog.

During the summer, the Stars signed goaltender Ed Belfour, and the team finally began to show signs of being one of the top teams in the league, finishing the 1997–98 season atop the standings. Entering the playoffs, the team suffered a major setback in the opening round when San Jose Sharks' Bryan Marchment injured Joe Nieuwendyk, taking him out of commission for the remainder of the playoffs. The Stars managed to make it past the Sharks and then the Edmonton Oilers, but the Detroit Red Wings were just too much to handle without Nieuwendyk, and the Stars were ousted from the Western Conference finals in six games.

If the Stars were going to go all the way to the Stanley Cup finals and have a hope of winning, they needed another top-scoring player to round out their team. To solve this deficiency, they added sniper Brett Hull from the St. Louis Blues, and in the 1998–99 season, the Dallas Stars were again the top team in the standings at the end of the season. In the playoffs, the Stars faced the Edmonton Oilers again and beat them in four straight games. The Stars next faced the St. Louis

Blues and dispatched them in six games, then lasted through a tough seven game series against the Colorado Avalanche before moving into the finals against the Buffalo Sabres.

The Stars gained the advantage in the series, going up three games to two on the Sabres, and looked to finish them off in the sixth game. The game became a marathon and went into a third overtime before Brett Hull potted the winning goal to give the Stars their first franchise championship. However, the win did not come without controversy.

The entire 1998–99 season had been plagued by the foot-in-the-crease rule that stated that no player is allowed within the blue paint in front of the net when a goal is scored, no matter the circumstances. The season was filled with video replays, goal callbacks and frustrated fans and players. When Brett Hull scored the Stanley Cup–winning goal, the Buffalo Sabres immediately called for a video replay, which clearly showed that Hull's skate was in the crease at the time of the goal, but the referees for some reason did not want to review the goal. The goal stood, and the Dallas Stars won their first Stanley Cup.

The Stars had an excellent follow-up season, finishing second in the Western Conference and made it all the way back to the Stanley Cup finals. Ultimately, luck was not on their side this time as the New Jersey Devils beat them in six games on a double-overtime goal by Devils forward Jason Arnott. The Stars had a few successes at the beginning of the new millennium, finishing with a strong record and good playoff position, but they failed to make it deep into the playoffs. Despite losing players like Ed Belfour, Darryl Sydor and Brett Hull, the Stars were able to replace them with quality players. But by the 2008–09 season, the Stars

D

were no longer the same team that had once excited southern Texas. They had strong seasons leading up to 2008, but each was followed by an early playoff exit. From 2008 to 2011, the Stars have failed to make the playoffs, losing veterans Mike Modano and Marty Turco in the process.

The three-year playoff drought and resulting loss of revenues put the Stars in deep financial trouble, and for the 2010–11 season, the team had to be financially managed by the NHL. That did not stop the Stars from declaring bankruptcy, leading to speculation that the team would be moved out of the city. However, Vancouver businessman and Kamloops Blazers owner Tom Gaglardi purchased the Stars in November 2011, and he pledged to keep the team in Dallas for the time being.

Dallas Stars Records
(including Minnesota North Stars Records)

Most goals in a season: Brian Bellows (1989–90) and Dino Ciccarelli (1981–82), 55

Most goals in a season, rookie: Neal Broten, 38 (1981–82)

Most assists in a season: Neal Broten, 76 (1985–86)

Most points in a season: Bobby Smith, 114 (1981–82)

Most points in a season, defenceman: Craig Hartsburg, 77 (1981–82)

Most points in a season, rookie: Neal Broten, 98 (1981–82)

Most penalty minutes in a season: Basil McRae, 378 (1987–88)

Most wins in a season: Marty Turco, 41 (2005–06)

Most shutouts in a season: Marty Turco, 9 (2003–04)

See American Airlines Center; Minnesota North Stars

Dance: When two players lovingly embrace, hold each other by the shoulders, move around the ice gracefully and rain bare-knuckle punches down on one another.

D

Dasher: The lower part of the boards that surround the rink. Different rinks have different coloured dashers. They are normally yellow or light blue.

Dawson City Nuggets: Yukon city team that played for the Stanley Cup in 1905. In the years before hockey turned professional, the Stanley Cup was known as a Challenge Cup, which meant that any team, pro or amateur, could offer up a challenge to the defending Stanley Cup champions and play them in a playoff series for the championship. Several people got together in Dawson City, formed the Dawson City Nuggets and issued a challenge to the reigning champions, the Ottawa Silver Seven. Ottawa accepted, and the Nuggets made the long, arduous journey through Canada's North, over the Rockies, across the Prairies, to finally reach the nation's capital.

Led by the legendary One-eyed Frank McGee, the Ottawa Silver Seven defeated the Nuggets in the first game of the two game, total-goal series by a score of 9–2 and in the second game by a whopping score of 23–2. In the second game, Frank McGee was responsible for 14 of the 23 goals, thereby establishing a Stanley Cup single-game scoring record that will likely never be broken. Although the Dawson City Nuggets lost the Stanley Cup, they returned north as heroes for having the guts to take on the best team in the world at the time.

    See Challenge Cup

Defenceman: A player whose primary purpose on the ice is to stay behind the forwards and to stop opponents from breaking in on the goaltender in their own zone. It is the position in hockey that has some of the highest pressure to perform and the least amount of glory when the job is executed properly. A team may have a forward line of some of the greatest scorers in the game, but without a solid defence to back them up, the team remains incomplete.

All the great teams in history have had legendary defenders to stand along the blue line. The early incarnation of the Ottawa Senators had defensive stalwarts Eddie Gerard and Harvey Pulford. The Boston Bruins of the late 1920s were feared simply because of one man, Eddie Shore. The Montréal Canadiens' domination during the 1950s was quarter-backed by the greatest defensive defenceman of all time, Doug Harvey. The Toronto Maple Leafs of the 1960s had the always-reliable Tim Horton. And the Canadiens of the 1970s had the greatest trio of defencemen in Larry Robinson, Guy Lapointe and Serge Savard.

D

Would the Edmonton Oilers of the 1980s have been the same without Paul Coffey and Randy Gregg? Would the Bruins of the 1970s have ever won two Stanley Cups without the incredible Bobby Orr? The answer is no! A good defenceman is invaluable. They must look at all aspects of the game and, with his defensive partner, must protect their end of the ice. They also provide the first breakout pass from the defensive zone on a rush, and without this, the forwards are left standing in the neutral zone with nowhere to go.

See Offensive Defenceman; Stay-at-home Defenceman

Defending Champions: The previous winner of the Stanley Cup in any given year.

Defensive Zone: The area behind the blue line becomes the defensive zone when a team must defend their goal from the attacking team.

Deflection: The redirection of a shot normally done on purpose by a player as a scoring tactic.

Deke: When the puck carrier fools another player or goaltender to get the puck past him.

Delayed Offside: If a player enters the attacking zone ahead of the puck but does not touch it, the play is offside even though no whistle is blown immediately. The linesman will raise his arms to signal the offside, and if the player does not leave the zone or touches the puck, the linesman will whistle the offside.

Delay of Game: Any action that the referee believes slows the progress of the game results in a delay of game minor penalty. The following cases are considered a delay of game:

- If a player or goaltender deliberately shoots or throws the puck over the boards

- If a player or goaltender intentionally pushes the net out of its normal position

- If a team delays putting the correct number of players on the ice for a faceoff

- If a player or goaltender stops the play to adjust their equipment

- If a player deliberately falls or gathers the puck underneath him

- If a player closes his hand on the puck

- If the puck is not kept in motion by a player or goaltender.

Denied: A player is denied a goal when a goalie makes a difficult save on the shooter. Usually the shooter will have an open net, and the goaltender somehow lunges across to miraculously stop the puck. Denied!

Desert Dogs: Nickname for the Phoenix Coyotes.

D

Detroit Cougars: Original name of the Detroit Red Wings franchise. Following the 1926 Stanley Cup playoffs, the Western Hockey League (WHL) found itself in dire financial straits and opted to cease operations. Looking to take advantage of a gap in the market, the NHL decided to consider applications for an expansion franchise, and on May 15, 1926, the league accepted the application from the Townsend-Seyburn group out of Detroit. Frank and Lester Patrick, owners of the WHL, made a deal with the Detroit executives to sell the WHL's players to the NHL. The Detroit franchise purchased the entire lineup of the defunct Victoria Cougars, who had won the Stanley Cup in 1925 and who had just lost the 1926 Cup finals to the Montréal Maroons. Thus, the new Detroit club opted to keep the Cougars name in their honour, giving birth to the Detroit Cougars.

Since no arena was ready in time for the start of the 1926–27 season, the Detroit Cougars played their home games on the other side of the Detroit River in Windsor, Ontario, at Border Cities Arena. In the new league, the Cougars finished the season with a record of 12–28–4 and missed out on the playoffs. For the 1927–28 season, the Cougars moved back across the river and into the new Detroit Olympia. The team was led by legendary hockeyman Jack Adams. The team improved slightly but again failed to make the playoffs. Although they made the playoffs in 1928–29, the Toronto Maple Leafs defeated them in the first round. In the 1929–30 season, they again failed to make the postseason. Management decided it was time to give the team a new image.

Detroit Falcons: After the Cougars failed to make any inroads into the upper echelons of the NHL, Detroit management thought that renaming the team might give the franchise new life. For the start of the 1930–31 season, the Detroit Cougars became the Detroit Falcons. The revamping did little to change their fortunes on the ice as they continued to finish near the bottom of the standings. The Falcons lasted just two years in the NHL before the franchise was bought by grain merchant James E. Norris.

Detroit Red Wings: When James Norris bought the Falcons in 1932, his first act as owner was to change their name to the Red Wings. Norris had previously played hockey for the Montréal Hockey Club, also known as the "Winged Wheelers," so he took that name and tweaked it a bit.

The change on the ice was immediate as the Red Wings made it into the playoffs and past the first round for the first time, but the celebrations were cut short when they were defeated in the semifinals by the New York Rangers. However, the club was headed in the right direction. In 1936, head coach Jack Adams, leading scorer Marty Barry and goaltender Normie Smith led the franchise to their first Stanley Cup victory over the Toronto Maple Leafs and repeated in 1937 with a win over the New York Rangers.

During the 1941–42 playoffs, Detroit had the bad luck of being on the wrong side of a league record when the Toronto Maple Leafs came back from a 3–0 series deficit in the Stanley Cup finals to win the Cup. While other teams have come back from 3–0 deficits at some point in the playoffs,

Detroit holds the dubious distinction of being the only team to completely fall apart in the final round.

In 1942, when the NHL reduced its numbers to just the original six teams, Detroit found themselves back in the Stanley Cup finals and this time managed to win a third championship by defeating the Boston Bruins in four straight games. Detroit's best players at the time were goaltender Johnny Mowers and forwards Syd Howe and Sid Abel.

In 1946, the Red Wings added a player that changed the history of the franchise and the game of hockey forever, when a young strapping right-winger from Saskatchewan named Gordie Howe joined the team. Although he only managed to score seven goals and amass 22 points in that first season, he went on to score plenty more. By the 1949–50 season, Howe, along with linemates Ted Lindsay and Sid Abel, were the most prolific goal-scoring players in the NHL, finishing as the top three scoring leaders. They scored so often that sportswriters dubbed them the "Production Line." With solid offence up front and the goaltending of Harry Lumley, the Red Wings won another Stanley Cup by defeating the New York Rangers in a tough seven-game series.

Led by Gordie Howe and backstopped by the legendary Terry Sawchuk, the Red Wings were considered the best team of the early 1950s, winning the Cup in 1952, 1954 and again in 1955. Despite having Gordie Howe, who went on to set and break every imaginable scoring record in the game, the great Red Wings of the early '50s were surpassed by the incredible Montréal Canadiens of the late '50s, who won five straight Stanley Cup championships.

Into the 1960s, the Red Wings excelled on an individual level with players such as Howe, Alex Delvecchio and Norm Ullman, but they could not find a way to win in the play-offs. While teams like Montréal, Toronto, Boston and eventually Philadelphia moved forward and traded turns hoisting the Stanley Cup, Detroit's fortunes dropped alongside the bottom dwellers of the league. This period is commonly known as the "Dead Wings" era. It wasn't until the arrival of a young rookie named Steve Yzerman that the fortunes of the Motor City team began to turn around, but it certainly took a long time.

It wasn't until legendary head coach and multiple Stanley Cup winner (with the Montréal Canadiens) Scotty Bowman took over behind the Red Wings bench that the fans of the team could finally see the light. Along with players like Yzerman, Nicklas Lidstrom, Brendan Shanahan, Sergei Fedorov and goaltender Mike Vernon, the Red Wings snapped their Stanley Cup curse in 1997, defeating the Philadelphia Flyers to win their first championship in 42 years. They repeated as Cup champions in 1998 and remained one of the most dominant teams in the league for the next decade, winning again in 2002 and 2008. To this day, the club remains at the top of the league and is always a threat going into the playoffs, something they have not missed since 1991.

Detroit Red Wings Records

Most goals in a season: Steve Yzerman, 65 (1988–89)

Most assists in a season: Steve Yzerman, 90 (1988–89)

Most points in a season: Steve Yzerman, 155 (1988–89)

Most points in a season, defenceman: Nicklas Lidstrom, 80 (2005–06)

137

D

Detroit Red Wings Records (continued)

Most points in a season, rookie: Steve Yzerman, 87 (1983–84)

Most penalty minutes in a season: Bob Probert, 398 (1987–88)

Most wins in a season: Terry Sawchuk, 44 (1950–51 and 1951–52)

Most shutouts in a season: Terry Sawchuk, 12 (1951–52, 1953–54, 1954–55)

Most shutouts in the playoffs: Dominik Hasek, 6 (2002)

See Joe Louis Arena

Dey's Arena: Also known as Dey Brothers Arena, The Arena and Dey's Skating Rink, it was a series of ice rinks located in Ottawa that originally opened their doors in 1884. The first incarnation of Dey's Arena was intended as an indoor, natural ice skating rink but was torn down in 1895 to make way for a railway station. The second arena was built in 1896 to be primarily used as a recreational skating rink, but as hockey began gaining popularity, the game of puck slowly took over. The first game at the arena was between the Ottawa Capitals and a team from Cornwall on December 19, 1896. The arena was also the location of the first Stanley Cup win by the Ottawa Hockey Club in 1903 and played host to the famous 1905 Stanley Cup that saw the Ottawa Silver Seven destroy the Dawson City Nuggets.

A third arena was built to accommodate the increased number of fans that wanted to see the Ottawa Senators play. The capacity was set at 7000 fans, at the time making it the largest arena in Canada. It was constructed on the north side of Laurier Avenue next to the Rideau Canal, which today is the location of Confederation Park across the street from Ottawa City Hall. The arena opened on January 11, 1908, for a game between Ottawa and the Montréal Wanderers. The last Senators game at Dey's Arena was played on March 10, 1923, after which the club moved to the Ottawa Auditorium. The third instalment of the arena was torn down for good in 1927.

Dig: When the puck gets caught in the corner of the rink and several players try to gain possession, they have to "dig" the puck out of the mess of players, skates and sticks.

Dipsy Doodle: The same as a fake-out or a deke, but the move is a lot fancier.

See Deke; Fake

Disallowed Goal: When a player scores a goal, but it is subsequently called back by the referee or the video goal judge because of an action contrary to the rules—for example, the puck is kicked in, the goaltender is interfered with or a player deflects the puck in with his stick above the cross bar.

Disk: Alternate name for a puck. Taken from its shape.

D

Dive: When a player intentionally falls to the ice to draw a penalty against an opposing player, he is said to be "taking a dive." In the early days of hockey, diving was known as "fainting." If the referee sees the infraction, he can issue a diving penalty.

Doorstep: The area directly in front of the goaltender. Announcers often will say that a player in front of the net is "right on the doorstep."

See In the Slot; Kitchen

Down Low: In the attacking zone, down low is the area behind the net and the goal line. It is essential for a team to be able to win the battles "down low" in the corners of the rink to come up with the puck and possibly get a chance to score.

Draw: A faceoff.

Draft Lottery: The draft lottery is a weighted system that ranks the bottom 14 teams and is used to determine the order of selection at the NHL Entry Draft for the first 14 picks. Teams may move up or down depending on the results of a randomized lottery system. The first draft lottery was implemented in 1995.

See Amateur Draft; Entry Draft

Drop Pass: When a player going forward passes the puck backwards, sometimes between their legs, without looking at the intended recipient.

Dump-in: When an attacking team shoots the puck into the corner of the opponent's zone instead of carrying the puck in and taking the chance of being stripped of the puck.

Dump-and-chase: A style of hockey in which a team consistently throws the puck into the opponent's end and attempts to gain control of the puck by sending one or more players into the corners. Not the most popular style of hockey, but it can prove effective against some teams.

Duquesne Gardens: Home arena of the NHL's Pittsburgh Pirates from 1925 to 1929. Built in 1890 as a storage facility for the city's trolleys, it was converted into an ice rink in 1895. The arena's 5000 seats suited the needs of the expansion franchise in 1925, but with the onset of the Great Depression, it became harder and harder to keep up with teams like New York, who had begun construction on the 18,000-seat Madison Square Garden. After the Pittsburgh Pirates folded, Duquesne Gardens continued operating as a hockey arena for the Pittsburgh Hornets of the AHL until the arena was demolished in 1956.

D

Dynamite Line: The Boston Bruins number one line in the late 1920s that featured Cooney Weiland, Dit Clapper and Dutch Gainor. The Dynamite Line's most productive season as a line came in 1929–30, when the league brought in new rule changes to increase scoring. The most important rule change was the allowance of forward passing in the offensive zone, when previously it had only been allowed in the neutral zone and the team's defensive zone. Boston Bruins head coach Art Ross schooled his players on how best to take advantage of the new rules, and the Dynamite Line paid attention. Cooney Weiland led the league with 43 goals and 73 points, while Dit Clapper potted 41 goals and 61 points and Gainor scored 18 goals and 49 points, all in a 44-game regular season.

ECAHA (Eastern Canada Amateur Hockey Association):
The ECAHA was first a men's amateur and later a professional hockey league that operated from 1905 to 1909. The teams in the league competed for the ECAHA championship trophy donated by the Montréal Arena company. Some of the teams that competed in the league were the Montréal Hockey Club, Montréal Shamrocks, Montréal Victorias, Montréal Wanderers, Ottawa Hockey Club and Québec Hockey Club. The Montréal Wanderers won the championship trophy from 1906 to 1908 and Ottawa Hockey Club won in 1909.

From the start of the league, professional players were allowed to play on teams. Unable to compete with the more skilled clubs, the purely amateur Montréal Victorias and Montréal Hockey Club left the league, making it a professionals-only league and therefore had to drop the "amateur" from its title to become the Eastern Canada Hockey Association (ECHA). In November 1909, the Montréal Wanderers also left the league over arguments between owners about a new arena and started the National Hockey Association (NHA). The Montréal Canadiens and the Toronto Arenas joined the new league. The remaining teams in the ECHA disbanded the league and formed the Canadian Hockey Association. That league lasted only two weeks before it fell apart, and the rest of the teams merged with the NHA.

East Division: Division of the NHL created in 1967 when it expanded from the original six teams to 12. The division lasted from 1967 to 1974 and included the Montréal Canadiens, New York Rangers, Boston Bruins, Chicago Blackhawks, Toronto Maple Leafs, Detroit Red Wings, Vancouver Canucks, New York Islanders and Buffalo Sabres.

Eastern Conference: One of two conferences in the NHL established in 1993, the other conference being the Western Conference. Previously known as the Prince of Wales Conference, or Wales Conference for short, the Eastern Conference was originally formed in 1974 after the NHL realigned the expanding number of teams into two conferences and four divisions. The Wales Conference was renamed in 1993 to reflect the new geographical make up of the divisions and to help new fans connect with the NHL since names like the Wales Conference were deemed confusing. In 1993, there were just two divisions in the Eastern Conference, the Northeast and the Atlantic, but the Southeast was added in 1998 to accommodate new teams from the southeastern United States like the Carolina Hurricanes and Florida Panthers. Winners of the Eastern Conference playoffs are awarded the Prince of Wales Trophy.

See Prince of Wales Conference; Prince of Wales Trophy

Eastern Rules Hockey: The now hockey-wide rule of having six players on the ice as opposed to the seven-player game played in the Western hockey leagues at the turn of the 20th century. Six-man hockey is played with three forwards, two defencemen and a goaltender. In seven-player hockey under Western rules, there was a goaltender, two defensive players that were known as the "point" and "cover point," the three forwards and an extra seventh player known as the "rover."

See Cover Point; Rover

Easton: Brand of hockey equipment originally founded in 1922.

Edmonton Coliseum: Former name of the arena where the Edmonton Oilers' played from 1995 to 1998.

See Rexall Place

Edmonton Eskimos: Established in 1905 as an amateur hockey team known as the Edmonton Hockey Club, the team changed their name to the Edmonton Eskimos in 1910. In 1908, the Edmonton Hockey Club challenged the Montréal Wanderers for the Stanley Cup but lost in a two-game, total-goal series by a combined score of 13–10. They challenged the Ottawa Hockey Club in 1910 but lost again in a two-game, total-goal series by a score of 21–11.

After the 1910 defeat, the Edmonton Hockey Club folded and reformed as the Eskimos. The Eskimos continued to play amateur hockey in the province until 1921, when they—along with the Calgary Tigers, Saskatoon Sheiks and Regina Capitals—formed the Western Canada Hockey League (WCHL). From 1921 to 1926, the Eskimos won three Western Canada championships and, in 1923, got their last shot at the Stanley Cup when they played the NHL's Ottawa Senators for the Cup. This was in a time before the NHL had exclusive rights to the Stanley Cup, and winners from the NHL's regular season and from the WCHL battled to be named hockey's overall champion in the Challenge Cup. The Stanley Cup became sole property of the NHL winning team after the 1926 Stanley Cup finals.

See Challenge Cup

Edmonton Oilers: Originally founded in 1972 as one of the 12 founding members of the World Hockey Association (WHA), the Oilers were the only Alberta-based team in the league. Bill Hunter, owner of the Edmonton Oil Kings junior franchise of the Canadian Major Junior Hockey League (CMJHL), started the franchise. Hunter had tried to secure an NHL franchise in the past but had been turned down, so when it was announced that a competing professional league was starting up, he joined the WHA instead. Hunter chose the name Oilers because it had been used as a nickname for his Oil Kings junior team. But they were to be called the Alberta Oilers and not the Edmonton Oilers.

The team's first game was played against the Ottawa Nationals, and they won 7–4. The Oilers were an average team and pulled in a decent number of fans, but despite successes during the regular season, the Oilers could never put together a championship team in the WHA. Along the way, the club entrenched itself in the city, renamed themselves the Edmonton Oilers and acquired one player that changed the face of hockey in the city and in North America for years to come.

For the 1978–79 WHA season, new owner Peter Pocklington acquired a young, skinny, scoring phenom named Wayne Gretzky from the recently folded Indianapolis Racers. With Gretzky on board, the Oilers finished atop the

WHA standings and went all the way to the Avco Cup Finals where they lost to the Winnipeg Jets.

When the WHA folded because of financial issues at the end of that season, the Edmonton Oilers were brought into the NHL along with the Hartford Whalers, Québec Nordiques and Winnipeg Jets. The Oilers lost many of their roster players during the reclamation draft used to integrate the WHA players when they joined the NHL, but within a few short years, general manager Glen Sather put together a young team that knew how to win and score goals, and lots of them. By 1983, Sather had added Mark Messier, Glenn Anderson, Jari Kurri, Paul Coffey, Kevin Lowe, Grant Fuhr and Andy Moog. Together, that team set new individual and team scoring records that may never be beaten.

E

E

With Gretzky leading the way with 212 points during the 1982–83 season, the Oilers managed to score 424 total goals during the season. The only other team to ever come close was the 1970–71 Boston Bruins, who scored 399 goals in one season (the Oilers having played just four games more in 1982–83). But while the records were great and provided the fans with something to cheer about during the regular season, the Oilers could not seem to translate that dominance into playoff success. They finally came close in 1983, making it all the way to the Stanley Cup finals against the three-time defending champion New York Islanders, but they lost in four straight. It was a tough lesson for the young team but a necessary one.

The Oilers had always been a team of offence with defence coming second; however, the loss to the Islanders taught the coaching staff and the players to refocus their strategy. With a new emphasis on defence combined with their ever-potent offence, the Oilers became the toughest team in the league to beat. They finished the 1983–84 season with a record goals scored of 446 and the most points in the league. In the playoffs, the Oilers ended up in the Stanley Cup finals, once again facing off against the New York Islanders, but this time the young players were ready. The Oilers won the series in five games, and Wayne Gretzky lifted the Oilers' first Stanley Cup.

The Oilers won the Stanley Cup again in 1985 but lost their bid for a third in heart-breaking fashion in 1986 when, in the division finals against the Calgary Flames, Oilers defenceman Steve Smith scored on his own net in game seven to give the Flames the goal they needed to win. But the Oilers were not yet done with their dynasty, winning two more Cups in 1987 and 1988.

During the summer of 1988 came the most shocking news to hit the hockey world in decades. Just a few months after helping the Oilers win their fourth Stanley Cup, the Oilers called a press conference and a teary-eyed Wayne Gretzky announced that he had been traded to the Los Angeles Kings, along with Marty McSorley and Mike Krushelnyski, in return for Jimmy Carson, Martin Gelinas and first-round draft picks in 1989, 1991 and 1993. While many thought the trade signified the end of the Oilers, they returned to the Stanley Cup finals in 1990 and, led by Mark Messier, took home the franchise's fifth Stanley Cup.

After the win, the franchise went into decline through the 1990s. With players leaving, poor drafting and constant financial troubles, the Oilers spent the decade moving up and down the standings but achieved little success in the playoffs. By the dawning of the 21st century, the Oilers had completely shed their old dynasty image and were now just another small-market team trying to survive. There were some high points—Todd Marchant scoring in overtime in game seven against the Dallas Stars in the conference quarterfinals to send them into next round. But the dream ended as quickly as it began when the Colorado Avalanche dumped the Oilers from the Stanley Cup chase in five games.

After the 2004–05 lockout season, the Oilers were able to attract some higher-priced talent because of the more reasonable Canadian dollar and brought in defenceman Chris Pronger and forward Michael Peca. While the team suffered a little inconsistency at the start of the 2005–06 season, they managed to just squeak into the playoffs. While the regular season might have been forgettable, the Oilers shone in the playoffs, defeating the strong Detroit Red Wings, San Jose Sharks and Anaheim Ducks to make it back into the Stanley

Cup finals for the first time since their 1990 championship. Up against the Carolina Hurricanes, the Oilers put in a valiant effort but came up just one win short, losing in game seven by a score of 3–1.

The Oilers spent the next several seasons at the bottom of the league, though the one positive that came out of this was the availability of high-quality draft picks, which the Oilers used to select players like Jordan Eberle, Taylor Hall and Ryan Nugent-Hopkins, who are currently tearing up the ice and making Oilers fans once again believe that the old dynasty could rise once again.

Edmonton Oilers Records

Most goals in a season: Wayne Gretzky, 92 (1981–82)

Most goals in a season, defenceman: Paul Coffey, 48 (1985–86)

Most goals in a season, rookie: Jason Arnott, 33 (1992–93)

Most assists in a season: Wayne Gretzky, 163 (1985–86)

Most assists in a season, rookie: Jari Kurri, 43 (1980–81)

Most points in a season: Wayne Gretzky, 215 (1985–86)

Most points in a season, defenceman: Paul Coffey, 138 (1985–86)

Most points in a season, rookie: Jari Kurri, 75 (1980–81)

Most penalty minutes in a season: Steve Smith, 286 (1987–88)

Most wins in a season: Grant Fuhr, 40 (1987–88)

Most shutouts in a season: Tommy Salo (2000–01) and Curtis Joseph (1997–98), 8

See Rexall Place

Edmonton Mercurys: This Senior A hockey team from Alberta played in the Canadian Amateur Hockey Association (CAHA) and was not well known outside Edmonton until the 1952 Winter Olympics in Oslo, Norway. The CAHA usually selected the winner of the Allan Cup to represent Canada, but the Western Senior League had turned semi-pro and the winner was thereby disqualified from participating in the Olympics. The Mercurys were an intermediate Senior A team that had a history of international competition, having won the World Ice Hockey Championships in 1950.

In the early years of hockey in the Olympics, Canada completely dominated. However, by 1952, international teams had caught up to Canada and were no longer the pushovers they once were. The Mercurys were able to win their three opening round games against the Germans, Finns and Poles rather easily by a combined score of 39–4. They had a little more trouble against the Swedes, only winning by a 3–2 score. Canada then followed that up with an 11–2 trouncing of the host country Norway before moving on to the final game of the tournament against the American squad.

The Americans played the same tight, defensive, physical hockey as the Canadians, and they battled them to a 3–3 tie. As the Canadians had won more games by a larger margin, Canada was awarded the gold medal. They were the last Canadian team to win Olympic gold until 50 years later, when the Canadian men's national team won gold at the 2002 Winter Olympics in Salt Lake City.

> ***Edmonton Mercurys 1952 Lineup:*** George Abel, John Davies, Billy Dawe, Robert Dickson, Donald Gauf, William Gibson, Ralph Hansch, Robert Meyers, David Miller, Eric Paterson, Thomas Pollock, Allan Purvis, Gordon Robertson, Louis Secco, Francis Sullivan and Bob Watt.

Elbowing: The name explains the infraction rather well. It occurs when a player uses his elbow to hit another player. A major penalty is usually assessed because use of the elbow is seen as intentional.

See Major Penalty

Elmer Ferguson Memorial Award: Annual award handed out by the Hockey Hall of Fame to newspapers reporters and columnists for their coverage of the sport. Named after sports journalist Elmer Ferguson who was sports editor for the *Montréal Herald* in 1913 and wrote columns for the *Montréal Star* until his death in 1972. Ferguson was inducted posthumously into the Hockey Hall of Fame in 1984 and the Ferguson Memorial Award was first handed out that same year.

Empty-net Goal: When a goaltender is pulled in favour of putting in an extra attacker, and the opposing team is able to put the puck into the empty net for a goal.

With just 45 seconds remaining in the game, the Boston Bruins have removed their goaltender and sent in an extra attacker. The Bruins need one goal to tie the Canadiens and send the game into overtime. The Bruins dump the puck into the Canadiens' zone. Several players chase the puck into the corner. The Bruins are desperately trying to dig the puck out from the Canadiens defence-man's skates, but it is the Canadiens who come up with the puck. The Canadiens move the puck out into the neutral zone, and their star player aims for the open net and...scores! The Canadiens put the game away on an empty-net goal and win the game 5–3.

See Pull the Goalie

End-to-end: When a player starts with the puck in his own defensive end and skates all the way to the other end of the ice, never once passing the puck.

See Coast-to-coast

Enforcer: The player on a team whose job it is to protect the stars on the team—an essential member of any team with a superstar player. The enforcer is expected to rough up or fight any opponent who dares intimidate his team-mates. NHL players regarded as enforcers include Dave Semenko, Dave Schultz, Tie Domi, Derek Boogaard, George Laraque, Bob Probert and Tiger Williams (the most penalized man in hockey).

E

E

Entry Draft: The annual meeting of NHL teams in which every franchise selects the rights to available amateur players between the ages of 18–20. The draft is held within two to three months of the end of the regular season. The city that hosts the All-Star game is the city that usually plays host to the draft. The first draft in 1963 was held at the Queen Elizabeth Hotel in Montréal, Québec. The draft was subsequently held in Montréal until 1984.

The Entry Draft was known as the Amateur Draft until 1979. The order is determined by the standings at the end of the regular season, with the last-place team usually selecting first overall. The 14 NHL teams that did not make it into the playoffs are entered into a weighted lottery, meaning that the last place team is given more of chance to win than the 14th place team. The remaining teams are then placed according to how they finished in the playoff race.

See Amateur Draft; Draft Lottery

Entry Level Contract (ELC): The first contract signed by a player that still has not played a game in the NHL. They must sign these contracts for their first three years in the NHL if they are between the ages of 18 and 21. Those aged 22 to 23 are deemed entry-level players for two years, and those aged 24 are only at entry level for one year. An entry-level player's signing bonus is currently capped at 10 percent of the player's salary. Performance bonuses can be added to the contract, but they are capped to a maximum of $850,000 per year. If the individual player wins a major award or is top amongst scoring leaders, then the cap rises to $2 million a year. The base salary for an entry-level player is $525,000.

Equalizer: When one team comes from behind to score the tying goal, that goal is said to be the "equalizer."

European Ice Rink: While NHL regulations stipulate that a rink must be 200 feet (61 metres) long by 85 feet (26 metres) wide, European rinks are much larger, measuring 200 feet (61 metres) long by 100 feet (30 metres) wide. The extra room makes for different strategies in the games. North American hockey tends to be more physical while European hockey tends to rely more on passing and individual skill.

Even Strength: When both teams have five skaters on the ice. Term usually used after a penalty is completed by one team and both teams "return to even strength." Also used in keeping track of statistics when a goal is scored at "even strength" as opposed to "on a power play" or "short-handed."

See Penalty Kill; Power Play (PP)

Exhibition Games: Prior to the start of the NHL's regular season, teams play in a series of games that are used to condition the players, help the coaches make roster decisions and promote the league (they also play exhibition games overseas in non-traditional markets). The games are considered "friendly" games because they mean nothing in terms of the regular season or the playoffs.

Expo Hall: Home of the Tampa Bay Lightning during their first season (1992–93). With a seating capacity of just 10,425, the Lightning quickly moved out of the arena once their new home (now called Tampa Bay Times Forum) was ready.

See Tampa Bay Times Forum

E

Extra Attacker: When the referee calls a penalty and the offending team does not have possession of the puck, the official raises his hand to signal the infraction but cannot whistle the play dead until a player from the offending team touches the puck. When this occurs, the goaltender from the non-penalized team is allowed to leave the ice and be replaced by another player, the extra attacker. This gives the team a type of mini power play until the offending team can stop the play by touching the puck.

See Pull the Goalie

Eyelets: Holes that a player uses to thread his hockey skate laces through to tie them up with.

FAHL (Federal Amateur Hockey League): A Canadian men's senior level hockey league that operated from 1904 to 1909, formed in its first incarnation by teams that were not accepted into the Canadian Amateur Hockey League (CAHL). The teams in the league varied from season to season, but the first franchises were the Montréal Wanderers, Ottawa Capitals, Montréal Le National and Cornwall Hockey Club. The Montréal Le National were the first all-Francophone team to play against Anglophone teams in a league. Other teams that played in the league were the Montréal Montagnards, Ottawa Hockey Club (also called the Ottawa Silver Seven), Ottawa Victorias and Brockville Invincibles. The league dissolved in 1909 when some teams left to join the new start-up league called the National Hockey Association (NHA).

See NHA

Faceoff: Also called the "draw." The faceoff may appear to have a simple definition, but putting it into practise can be a complicated procedure. Simply put, the faceoff is used to start the play at the beginning of each period, after a goal and after any stoppage in play. One player from each team approaches the faceoff area, gets into position and waits for the referee or linesman to drop the puck. The winner of the faceoff is the team that gets possession of the puck. In the early days of hockey, the referee would "face" the puck at centre ice, while the players lined up for the opening "bully." As odd as it sounds, this was how the faceoff was described when hockey was still in its infancy.

Originally, the puck was placed on the ice between two players, and only when the referee yelled "play" could the battle for the puck or "faceoff" take place. It was referee legend Fred Waghorne who first dropped the puck for the faceoff to prevent the fighting between the players as they waited for the referee to yell "play." Waghorne positioned the players about a foot apart and had them keep their sticks on the ice until the puck was dropped. From then on, the rules were changed so that players were prohibited from body contact prior to the dropping of the puck, other players not taking the faceoff had to stay at least 15 feet from the puck and all players had to be onside.

There are nine official faceoff spots on the ice: one at centre ice, two on each side of the neutral zone and two inside each defensive zone. However, not all faceoffs must be taken on the designated faceoff circles. Faceoffs can occur anywhere on the ice where an infraction has taken place. For example, if a player shoots the puck over the boards from the neutral zone, the ensuing faceoff takes place from the spot where the player shot the puck. A player can also be thrown out of a faceoff for trying to gain an advantage on the other player by shifting his position outside the allowed faceoff rules.

It is essential for teams to have a reliable player with a good faceoff-win percentage. For example, when a team is winning by one goal with little time remaining in the game, it is essential to win every possible faceoff and keep the puck off the sticks of the opposing team. Winning a faceoff is not easy, and those that are good at it have made it into an art form.

Face Mask: *See* Goalie Mask

Face Wash: If a player wants to draw a penalty on an opponent or just get him really angry, he will rub his sweat-and-spit-covered glove in the opponent's face as if he is trying to get a mustard stain off. Not the most pleasant experience. This usually occurs when players are involved in a pushing and shoving match, often just after a whistle in front of the net.

Fagging: A strange word to find in the hockey lexicon, but it actually means to back check. Fagging was a term used in the early days of hockey to describe when a forward would skate back into his own zone to stop the other team from getting a chance on goal.

Fake; Fake-out: A manoeuvre in which the puck carrier fools another player or goaltender to get the puck past him.

See Deke; Dipsy Doodle

Fan: When a player winds up to take a shot and misses the puck completely—one of the lighter moments in hockey. The term "fan" is used because the player creates a nice breeze with his stick instead of transferring the energy to the puck.

Fans: The people who sit in the seats, cheer for their team and pay the money to watch hockey games. Without fans, there is no NHL hockey. Legions of viewers who tune in every night and the hard-core fans who turn out to their team's home games are the bread and butter of the NHL. The mix of fans at a hockey game is always eclectic. There are the season-ticket holders, there are the fans who see one game a year and pour out all their emotions at that game (usually helped by copious amount of beer) and there are the legions of young kids accompanied by parents who are taking in their first game. Apart from the everyday hockey fan that follows his or her team, in the history of the game there have been some noteworthy fans that stand out for many reasons, not all good or decent.

Of course, there was the time that an angry Montréal Canadiens fan punched then–NHL president Clarence Campbell in the jaw in protest of his suspending of Maurice Richard at the end of the 1954–55 season. The altercation sparked the "Richard Riot" in the streets of Montréal. Then there was the time one stupid fan tried getting at Toronto Maple Leafs enforcer Tie Domi in the penalty box by leaning dangerously over the glass. He got his wish when the glass gave way, sending him and other fans tumbling into the penalty box with Domi. And several Boston Bruins players tussled with the crowd on December 23, 1979, after defeating the New York Rangers in Madison Square Garden. The New York fans made the mistake of reaching over the protective glass to hit Bruins tough guy Terry O'Reilly, who promptly leapt over the glass and into the stands to lay a beating on the fan who assaulted him. The most memorable moment from that melee was O'Reilly beating the fan with his own shoe.

But famously, there was the fan who decided to show the world a little too much. During a stoppage in play in a game

F

between the Calgary Flames and Boston Bruins on October 17, 2002, a very drunk Flames fan named Tim Hurlbut decided to display both his team pride as well as the rest of his body to the 16,000 thousand fans at the game and the millions watching on TV. Hurlbut stood up from his seat near centre ice, stripped off his clothes save for a pair of red socks, and hopped the glass separating him from the ice. The crowd watch half-amused, half-horrified as the drunken idiot lost his balance coming over the glass and fell to the ice, knocking himself unconscious. There he lay on the ice, knocked out and completely naked for the world to see while paramedics came to his aid. He was removed from the ice on a stretcher and later fined $2500 and sentenced to community service for his stupid antics. The cruellest punishment, though, is that his shame will forever be on tape.

Ahh, to be a fan!

Fantasy Hockey: One of the more popular pastimes of the modern hockey fan in which players build a fantasy team from the current roster of NHL players and collect points by the number of goals and assists, penalty minutes, shutouts and wins their "team" accumulates over the regular season. The leagues begin at the start of the NHL season, where participants hold a draft of available players and ends with someone winning a pot of money.

Far Side: The opposite side of the ice to a shooter as he comes into the attacking zone along the boards to the right or the left of the goaltender.

Farm Team: The farm team is an essential part of a professional hockey league. A farm team is always affiliated with an NHL team and is the training ground for its young talent.

162

When a player is sent back to the farm, he is being sent down to the minor leagues to train up to the standards of the NHL. Having a good farm team is essential to the survival of the big brother NHL franchise if it wants a constant supply of talent once older players retire or the team suffers a wave of injuries.

Fibreglass: Material used in the manufacture of sticks and other pieces of equipment. Fibreglass is basically a plastic reinforced with fine fibres of glass, making any product it is applied to extremely light, strong and able to withstand plenty of abuse. Goaltender masks in the '60s and '70s were made primarily out of fibreglass.

Field Hockey: A team sport similar to ice hockey but played on a grass field in which a team attempts to score goals by hitting a ball into the opposing goal using sticks.

Firewagon Hockey: No, this is not a bunch of burning wagons on the ice. This term is used to describe an all-out offensive approach to the game. In firewagon hockey, teams are less concerned with defending their own nets and focus primarily on putting more pucks into the net than the opposing team. The 1980s were exemplary of this brand of hockey.

With the arrival of Wayne Gretzky and his highly skilled Edmonton Oilers teammates, goal production significantly increased in the NHL from the 1970s through the 1980s. During the 1977–78 regular season, Ken Dryden led all goaltenders with the lowest goals-against average at 2.05. Fast forward to the 1986–87 season, and the goaltender with the lowest goals-against average was Montréal Canadien Brian Hayward, with an average of 2.81, followed by

F

teammate Patrick Roy, with a 2.93 average. With a team such as Edmonton scoring a record 446 goals, an average of 5.6 goals per game in the 1983–84 season, firewagon hockey was the best way to describe the style of play that had games ending with scores of 8–1, 10–5 and 12–7.

While the 1980s exemplified firewagon hockey, the term came into being in the late 1940s and was popular through to the Montréal Canadiens five straight Stanley Cups of the late 1950s. Beginning with the arrival of players such as Maurice Richard and Gordie Howe in the 1940s, offence on the ice opened up scoring and ushered in the glory days of the NHL. While many teams still held on to strict defensive principles, the Montréal Canadiens were proponents of a style of hockey that earned their players the nickname "Flying Frenchmen" because of their attack style of hockey.

With a number-one lineup that consisted of Maurice Richard, Elmer Lach and Toe Blake, dubbed the "Punch Line," it was just a matter of time before the rest of the league adopted the Canadiens' style just to be able to keep up on the scoreboard. Although the Canadiens did not win the Cup in the 1944–45 season, Maurice Richard scored an incredible 50 goals in 50 games, finishing with his linemates in the top three in overall scoring. The Toronto Maple Leafs defensive style of hockey dominated to the end of the 1940s, but players such as Gordie Howe, Dickie Moore, Jean Beliveau, Ted Lindsay and Henri Richard could not be kept at bay forever, and fans got to watch some of the most exciting hockey in the game's history.

First All-Star Team: Nothing to do with the annual mid-season All-Star Game, the first All-Star team is selected by the Professional Hockey Writers' Association (PHWA) at the end of the regular season. It is an honour to the players who have played the best hockey during the season. A second All-Star team is also voted upon. Gordie Howe leads in the number of times honoured with 21 (12 first, 9 second) followed by Ray Bourque with 19 total (13 first and 6 second). This practise of selecting a first and second All-Star team began after the 1930–31 season. The honours then went to forwards Aurel Joliat, Howie Morenz and Bill Cook; defencemen Eddie Shore and King Clancy; and goaltender Charlie Gardiner.

First Niagara Center: Home arena of the Buffalo Sabres. Built in 1996, the building was originally named the Marine Midland Arena, then the HSBC Arena, before the First Niagara Financial Group bought the naming rights in 2011. The arena was constructed to replace the now-demolished Memorial Auditorium. The building seats 18,690 for hockey games. On November 16, 1996, just a few months after the building opened, the JumboTron fell to the ice while it was being moved. The incident occurred just a few minutes after several players had finished practise and hours before a scheduled game between the Sabres and Boston Bruins. The game had to be postponed, but nobody was injured. Since construction, the building has under gone several renovations from improving ice quality to increasing seating capacity.

See Buffalo Sabres

First Union Center: Former name of the Philadelphia Flyers home arena from 1998 to 2003. Opened in 1996 as the CoreStates Center.

See Wells Fargo Center

F

Fish-out-of-water: When a goaltender is caught completely out of position and throws his body in any direction to make a save, flopping around like a fish. This manoeuvre does not get much respect from fans or broadcasters, but it can sometimes be effective as a desperation move (just ask Dominic Hasek, who is well known for his fish-out-of-water saves).

See Flopper

Five-hole: The area between the goaltender's legs. One of the seven positions, or "holes," that a goalie must protect.

See Holes

Flash the Leather: A flashy glove save by a goaltender. The term is still used, though goaltenders' gloves or trappers are no longer made out of leather. A goaltender flashes the leather when a shooter blasts a shot to an open part of the net, and the goaltender quickly whips his glove around to make the save. Patrick Roy was well known for overemphasizing his glove saves. When the puck was simply shot into his glove, he would still "flash the leather" as if he had just made a fantastic save.

Fleet Center: Former name of the Boston Bruins home arena from 1995–2005.

See TD Garden

Flip Pass: A pass in which the puck is lifted over an obstacle to reach the intended recipient. For example, if two players break-in on goal on a two-on-one play, and one player wants to pass the puck to the other, but the defenceman is blocking his passing lane, then he can attempt a flip pass. It is used frequently in fast-break situations.

Floater: A weak shot that arches in towards the goal.

Flopper: An unconventional style of goaltending where instead of making a save standing up or in butterfly position, the goaltender basically does whatever they can to stop the puck. Famous flopper goaltenders include Dominik Hasek and Tim Thomas.

See Fish-out-of-water

Florida Panthers: When it was first announced in December 1992 that Blockbuster Video magnate H. Wayne Huizenga was awarded a franchise that was going to be based out of Miami, Florida, many critics were sceptical that the franchise could survive in such a warm climate with a population who had largely (except for the snowbirds) never even seen a hockey game. The team was called the Florida Panthers after the endangered species of panther that is native to the area. The first official move of the Panthers organization was to hire Bryan Murray as its first general manager and Roger Neilson as its first head coach.

F

During the NHL Expansion Draft, Murray was able to cobble together a decent team of veterans and young unknowns, taking New York Rangers goaltender John Vanbiesbrouck, rookie Rob Niedermayer and Scott Mellanby, who would go on to score 30 goals in that first season. The Panthers had one of the most successful expansion seasons in league history, finishing one point below .500 and just missing out on the playoffs for the 1993–94 season. They managed to win a few games, but they were boring, and the Panthers often won by only one goal most of the time thanks to the trap system of hockey. Many sports writers and even other general managers heavily criticized the team for their style. (*See* Trap)

After the 1994–95 season spent looking in on the playoffs from the outside, management fired head coach Roger Neilson and hired Doug MacLean for the start of the 1995–96 season. During the Panthers home opener before the start of the game, a rat found its way into the Panthers locker room. Scott Mellanby reacted by slapping the vermin across the room where it hit the wall and was instantly killed. That night, Mellanby scored two goals in the home opener and later goaltender John Vanbiesbrouck told reporters that he had scored a "rat trick." The story made its way into the news, and at the next home game, a few enthusiastic fans threw rubber rats onto the ice after the Panthers scored.

F

The tradition continued during the season with a reasonable number of rubber rats, but when the Panthers made the playoffs for the first time, that number went into the thousands.

During those 1996 playoffs, the Panthers continued to use their trap system effectively and made it past the Boston Bruins in the first round. They followed up with victories over the Philadelphia Flyers and Pittsburgh Penguins to make it into the Stanley Cup final after just three seasons in the league. Up against the high-flying and high-scoring Colorado Avalanche, the Panthers stood no chance, and although the games remained relatively low scoring, the Avalanche had the goaltending of Patrick Roy to back them

F

up. The Avs swept the Panthers in four straight games to win the Stanley Cup.

The Stanley Cup run of 1996 is probably the only bright spot in the history of the franchise that, despite having several number-one selections in the draft and acquiring players such as Pavel Bure, Olli Jokinen, Jay Bouwmeester, Nathan Horton and Stephen Weiss, they have been unable to win hockey games on a consistent basis. Only three times in their history have they made it to the playoffs, and they have consistently finished at the bottom of the league in points overall. At the beginning of the 2011–12 season, the Panthers started out on a positive note, but their future in Miami will remain uncertain so long as the fans stay away from the arena, and they can't put together a string of winning seasons with some playoff success. After their first playoff appearance in 10 years in 2012, things appear to finally be moving forward for the club.

Florida Panthers Records

Most goals in a season: Pavel Bure, 59 (2000–01)

Most assists in a season: Viktor Kozlov, 53 (1999–2000)

Most points in a season: Pavel Bure, 94 (1999–2000)

Most points in a season, defenceman: Robert Svehla, 57 (1995–96)

Most penalty minutes in a season: Peter Worrell, 354 (2001–02)

Most wins in a season: Roberto Luongo, 35 (2005–06)

Most shutouts in a season: Roberto Luongo, 7 (2003–04)

See Bank Atlantic Center

Flying Frenchmen: Nickname for the Montréal Canadiens during the 1930s, as the team was predominantly composed of French Canadian players.

Forechecking: When one team is in possession of the puck and is trying to get out of their defensive zone to start a rush up the ice, and the opposing team sends in one or two players to stop them in what is referred to as the "forecheck." One player often pesters the puck carrier, trying to pressure him into making a mistake and hopefully turning the puck over to give the opponent a scoring chance.

Forward Pass: Before 1929, scoring in games was not all that high, and goaltenders ruled the league. In one season, Canadiens goalie Georges Hainsworth recorded 22 shutouts in 44 games. Hockey was primarily based around a defensive system, and since forward passing in the offensive zone was not allowed, setting up an offensive rush was difficult. Add to that the fact that teams were allowed to keep as many players as they wanted in the defensive zone, sending just one or two men ahead if they happened to have the lead in the game. All this changed in 1929, when the NHL instituted a set of groundbreaking rules that changed the game forever.

To open up the game and increase the players' point stats, the NHL decided to allow forward passing and penalize a team that kept more than three players (including the goaltender) in the defensive zone while the play moved up the ice. The change in the pace of the game was immediate. Players' scoring percentages skyrocketed and goaltenders' save percentages plummeted. During the previous season, Montréal Canadiens forward Howie Morenz broke the top

F

five among scoring leaders with 17 goals in 42 games. In the next year under the new rules, Morenz increased his output to 40 goals in 44 games.

Foster Hewitt Memorial Award: Named after famed hockey broadcaster Foster Hewitt, the memorial award is presented by the Hockey Hall of Fame. The recipient is selected by the NHL Broadcasters Association annually from the members of the radio and television industry who make a significant contribution to their profession and to the game of hockey during their career. It was first awarded in 1984.

FoxTrax Puck: Many hockey circles are opposed to any changes to the game, but even with all the developments over the years, the game has remained the same: five players with sticks chasing a rubber puck. Players' salaries may have skyrocketed, the number of teams tripled and most people are now watching hockey games from the comfort of their own homes, but the game remains close to its roots. For Canadian hockey fans, the emphasis on tradition has kept them linked to the past even as they looked forward in their pursuit to perfect the game. Each and every change is looked at in minute detail and is not implemented without much debate.

One of the strangest changes was the glow puck, better known as the FoxTrax puck. In the early 1990s, when the NHL expanded into non-traditional markets like San Jose and Tampa Bay, they were faced with educating a fan base that was unfamiliar with the many aspects of the game. While a significant number of fans were willing to embrace the game, the NHL thought that new fans could use some help in following the action on the ice.

To help the NHL reach a wider audience, Fox network was contracted in 1994 to broadcast games in the United States. However, after one full season, the network was getting constant complaints from its audience. The fans liked the fights and the fast-paced action, but a large majority found it difficult to follow the tiny black puck on their TV screens. The Fox network responded to these complaints and, with the approval of the NHL, created the FoxTrax puck to remedy the problem.

F

The FoxTrax puck was simply a regular NHL puck that was cut in half and had a tiny circuit board inside, attached to a shock sensor and infrared sensors. The two halves were then sealed and the puck, with the same weight, balance and rebound as a regular puck, was ready for action. The batteries that powered the puck were designed to last for around 30 minutes, but often it ended up being just 10 minutes. All this technology inside the puck was placed there for a simple reason: so that people sitting at home on their couches could follow the puck more easily.

The infrared sensors relayed information back to the cameras, which would then translate the puck's movements on screen into a bluish glow. When a player hit the puck, a bluish comet tail would light up onscreen indicating the puck's direction,

F

and as an added feature, when the puck moved faster that 70 miles per hour, a red comet tail appeared to obviously indicate that the puck was going really fast.

Reactions to the glow puck were mixed. American audiences welcomed the addition with open arms. However, hockey purists (mostly Canadians) were not happy with the comet tails and bluish glow on their TV screens, and they complained that the glowing puck made their beloved sport look like a video game. The most common response was that it should not be that hard to follow a black puck on a sheet of white ice.

Despite its detractors, the Fox Network kept the glow puck until the end of the 1998 Stanley Cup finals. The following season, the U.S. NHL broadcast rights were handed over to ABC, and the glow puck died along with Fox. Hockey purists everywhere breathed a collective sigh of relief.

Frank J. Selke Trophy: Awarded annually to the NHL's best defensive forward. Named in honour of Frank J. Selke, former general manager of the Toronto Maple Leafs and Montréal Canadiens. The first recipient was Bob Gainey of the Montréal Canadiens at the end of the 1977–78 NHL season. Gainey won the trophy four straight times, which to date is still the most Selke wins by one player. Guy Carbonneau, Jere Lehtinen and Pavel Datsyuk have all won the trophy three times.

Fraternization Rule: During the era of the NHL original six teams, president Clarence Campbell actually enforced a rule that players from one team were not allowed to fraternize with players on another team. This was not just some arbitrary rule for players to follow; it was actually enforced by the league to the point where if one player said "Hello" to an opposing player off the ice, they would be fined. This helped to foster a hatred for opposing players whether in uniform or out. In the days of the original six, players often remained on the same team for most of their careers, making the dislike of the other teams even more evident. But when the league expanded in 1967 from six teams to 12 and players began to move between teams more freely, the non-fraternizing rule was harder to enforce and it eventually died.

Freeze: The ice.

Freeze the Puck: When players hold the puck against the boards with either their sticks or their skates in order to get the referee to whistle the play dead. Goaltenders can also

freeze the puck when a loose disk enters the goal crease. Freezing the puck outside the goal crease can earn a goaltender a two-minute minor penalty.

Frozen Pond: When hockey was first being played in the early 1800s, there were no state-of-the-art arenas or man-made outdoor rinks. Hockey was played on out on the frozen ponds, rivers and lakes in the cold Canadian winters. When frozen ponds are mentioned, they bring to mind an idyllic time when hockey was played purely for the fun of it in a much simpler time.

G: Abbreviation for Goaltender used in marking statistics, and also the abbreviation for Goals when used in scoring stats.

GA: Abbreviation for Goals Against used in stats.

GAA: Abbreviation for Goals-Against Average used in stats.

GF: Abbreviation for Goals For, as written in team stats.

GP: Abbreviation for Games Played, as written in the league standings.

GWG: Abbreviation for Game-Winning Goals used in players' stats.

Gallery Gods: Fans in the nosebleeds or upper decks. The term originated to describe fans in the old Boston Garden, but it is now used throughout the hockey world. Gallery gods are also known as "real fans" in the modern-day parlance because lower bowl seats are almost entirely bought up by corporations.

Game Ho!: No one alive would remember celebrating a goal by screaming "Game ho!" but that's exactly what early hockey players shouted in the first few decades of hockey when they scored a goal.

177

Game On!: Heard frequently during street hockey games. After moving the nets out of the way, players will yell "Game on!" after a car has passed and the game can resume.

Game Misconduct: A penalty that is usually imposed when a player intentionally attempts to injure another player. The offending player is suspended for the remainder of a game, and a substitute player is allowed to replace the penalized player. A game misconduct carries an automatic fine of $200, and the case is reported to the NHL Commissioner, who can impose further fines or suspend the player from upcoming games.

List of Game Misconduct Penalties

Certain major penalties, generally stick infractions

Continues or attempts to continue a fight

Fighting off the playing surface or with an opponent who is off the playing surface

First or second player to leave the players' bench during or to start an altercation

First to intervene in an altercation (third man in)

Interferes with a game official in the performance of their duties

Leaving the penalty bench during an altercation

Obscene gestures

Persists to challenge or dispute an official's ruling

Physically abuses an official

Player who has been ordered to the dressing room but returns to the bench or the ice

Player who deliberately attempts to injure a manager, coach or other non-playing club personnel in any manner

Garbage Goal: A goal that does not take much effort or talent to score. This type of goal is often scored when a goaltender lets out a juicy rebound or is out of position.

Gauntlets: Alternate name for hockey gloves. For many years, hockey players did not wear gloves of any kind, and if they did, they often wore just a regular pair of leather winter gloves. But as the game developed, and the play became faster and more violent, players needed something to protect their hands from errant sticks. Some of the first gloves used in hockey were cricket gloves. The gloves protected the hands from slashing but were not made to accommodate the range of movement needed by hockey players. The first version of hockey-specific gauntlets did not appear until 1904, when Eaton's department store began selling them in their catalogue for $1.75 for the pair.

The basic construction of the hockey glove has changed little over the years. The biggest difference has been in the materials used to protect the players' hands from injuries. In the past, gloves were made mostly of foam padding and leather, but

modern hockey players wear gloves made from hard plastic and dense foam covered in nylon, which offers better protection against slashes and the occasional flying skate blade.

Gaylord Entertainment Center: Former name of the home arena of the Nashville Predators from 1999 to 2007. Currently known as the Bridgestone Arena.

See Bridgestone Arena

General Manager: Official team person responsible for the acquisition of new players, the negotiating of contracts and other functions within the team. Must answer to the president of the team and to the owners of the franchise.

General Motors Place (GM Place): Former name of the home arena of the Vancouver Canucks. GM Place opened on September 21, 1995, and was built to replace the Canucks old home arena, the Pacific Coliseum.

See Rogers Arena

Give-and-go: A passing exchange between two players on the attack. The players pass the puck to each other quickly so as not to give the defenders or the goaltender any indication which player is going to shoot the puck.

Glendale Arena: Former name of the home arena of the Phoenix Coyotes.

See Jobing.com Arena

Gnash: Mascot of the Nashville Predators. The name of the blue sabre-tooth tiger is a form of word play on the city's name. Gnash was introduced in 1998 when the team was founded. He has become known for his stunts on the ice to entertain fans during the intermissions. He has occasionally been known to play pranks on fans of the visiting teams, sometimes going as far as hitting them with a pie in the face.

Goal Crease: The painted area directly in front of the net. NHL regulations state that the goal crease must measure eight feet (2.4 metres) wide and six feet (1.8 metres) deep. Players are generally allowed to enter the goal crease, but if they come into contact with the goaltender, they can be charged with a two-minute goaltender interference penalty.

See Goaltender Interference

Goal Judge: With the abundance of cameras that are now focused on the ice and the advent of the instant replay, it seems rather pointless to continue the tradition of the goal judge, but at one time, goal judges were the most important officials on the ice. Called goal umpires in the early days of hockey, they were an essential part of the game when hockey goals had no nets and there were no cameras for instant replays.

The net used to be marked by two simple poles stuck in the ice, which made it rather difficult at times to decipher if the puck had actually crossed the line on the front side of the goal. Add to that the fact that players would often crash through the goal, sending bodies flying over the goal line at the same time as the puck, making the goal judges' decisions the source of much scrutiny and controversy. When nets were finally introduced, the goal judge moved from his spot directly behind the net to a little perch behind the boards. In the days before instant replay, given the

181

importance of the goal judges' decisions, they were often the target of aggression from both players and fans.

One famous incident involved a goal judge, Montréal Canadiens legend Aurel Joliat and a mob of angry fans. Joliat crashed the front of the goal and, to the best of his knowledge, put the puck past the goaltender and into the net. The goal judge didn't see it that way and refused to call the goal. Joliat immediately flew into a rage, jumped over the boards and began to rain down blows on the poor judge. But even when Joliat was pulled off the judge, the official's ordeal was far from over. Fans broke open the gate of his booth and tried to finish the job the Canadiens player had started. The battered and bruised judge had to be removed from the arena under police escort.

Today, the goal judge's job is a lot less controversial and definitely less dangerous. The modern-day goal judge simply signals whether the puck has passed completely over the goal line with the push of a button that turns on a red light. It is not the job of the goal judge to decide whether or not the goal was legally scored. This is left to the discretion of the referee or the video goal judge who can overturn the goal judge's decision at any time.

Goalie Mask: Now an essential part of a goaltenders equipment, it is hard to imagine a time in the NHL when goaltenders went bare-faced up against guys like Maurice Richard, Boom Boom Geoffrion and Bobby Hull, but it wasn't until 1959 that a goaltender first donned a mask on a permanent basis. From the dawn of hockey until November 1, 1959, no goaltender, except Clint Benedict, who briefly wore a leather mask because of a broken nose, ever wore a protective facemask to prevent injuries. And injuries were common

for NHL goaltenders. Terry Sawchuk had over 600 stitches to his face in his career, and it was hard to find a goaltender without a crooked nose or missing teeth.

Despite the dangers, it was considered a sign of toughness to go without protection, and any goaltender who dared put on a mask was seen as weak. It took Montréal Canadiens goaltender Jacques Plante's bold decision to finally break the stigma. During a game against the New York Rangers on November 1, 1959, Andy Bathgate of the Rangers whistled a shot that broke Plante's nose, sending a gush of blood all over his jersey and the ice. Plante was rushed into the dressing room to get bandaged up and put back out onto the ice. Plante refused to return to the ice unless he was allowed to wear the protective mask he had been using in practise. Head coach Toe Blake did not like ultimatums or the fact that his goaltender would be seen in something that was deemed cowardly, but he had no choice but to relent.

From that historic game on, Plante wore a mask until the day he retired. Soon, other goaltenders followed suit, and by the 1970s, no goaltender went without that essential piece of hockey equipment. The final goaltender in the NHL to go without a mask was Pittsburgh Penguins Andy Brown, who last went mask-less on April 7, 1974, in a 6–3 loss to the Atlanta Flames. Over the years, goalies have worn many iconic masks: Gerry Cheevers' "scar" mask, Ken Dryden's "bleu, blanc, rouge" mask, Gilles Gratton's "tiger" mask, Canucks goaltender Gary Bromley's "skull" mask and Jason Voorhees "killer" mask.

Goaltender: Glenn Hall once described being a goaltender as "60 minutes of hell." The goaltender is the last line of defence for a team and is often the most important position on the team. It has been said that a team cannot win in the playoffs without superb goaltending, and more often than not, history has proven this maxim to be true. The goaltender's office is his goal crease, the blue-painted area just in front of the net. When hockey first began, goaltenders wore the same protective equipment as players. But as the game evolved and shots became harder, goaltenders began wearing specially designed equipment to protect them from the direct impact of the puck.

The goaltender can use all parts of his body to stop the puck from entering the net. Unlike the players, the goaltender is allowed to legally freeze the puck to cause a stoppage in play. If the goaltender's stick breaks, he is allowed to continue to use it whereas a player must immediately drop theirs or incur a penalty. Also if a goaltender is penalized for an infraction, a player from his team must serve the penalty for him. However, if the goaltender receives a misconduct penalty, he is removed from the ice and replaced by the back-up goalie.

When hockey was still in its infancy, goaltenders followed a different set of rules. At one time, goaltenders were strictly stand-up goaltenders because the rules stated that if they fell to the ice to make a save, they would receive a two-minute penalty. And this penalty was, by the way, one the goalie had to serve himself, leaving a defenceman to cover the net for the duration of the penalty. It wasn't until the arrival of goaltender Clint Benedict into the NHL that the position changed.

Never one to conform to regulations, Benedict set out on a lengthy campaign to get the rules changed in his favour. Starting from his days in the National Hockey Association (NHA) to his first year in the NHL with the Ottawa Senators, Benedict developed a unique technique on the ice so whenever he was called upon to make a save, he would fake losing his balance and fall to the ice. He fell to his knees so much that he was given the nickname "Praying Benny." Referees became so frustrated with Benedict's antics that the matter was brought before league president Frank Calder, and on January 9, 1918, Calder changed the rule to allow goaltenders to fall to the ice to make a save.

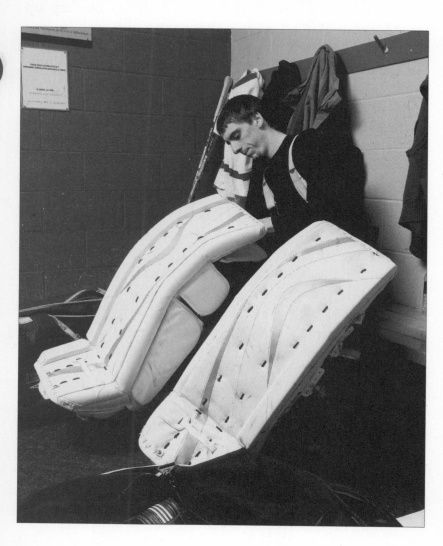

Other goaltenders would come along and alter the game, like Jacques Plante, Terry Sawchuk and Glenn Hall, whose dedication and unique styles influenced an entire generation. Plante changed the game by donning a goalie mask on a regular basis, but his acrobatic style also became a trademark, and many young Québec goaltenders coming up behind him copied his style.

Terry Sawchuk was a warrior in the net. No other goaltender before him attacked the puck with such fearless abandon. Playing the majority of his career without a mask, Sawchuk crouched low to the ice to track the movements of the puck, something others were not keen on doing because of the possibility of getting sticks, pucks and skates in the face.

Glenn Hall loved to hate his job; he actually threw up before most games. However, there was no other goaltender more dedicated to his position, and he still holds the record to this day of playing in 502 consecutive games.

Every goaltender has a specific style. For the most of the history of the NHL, goaltenders could have been classified as playing the stand-up style, which means staying on their feet to make a save rather than dropping to the ground. There were a few different styles around the league, but things did not really change that much until the mid 1980s, when a young goaltender named Patrick Roy broke onto the scene.

Roy had received his training in a new style of goaltending called the butterfly style. His goaltending coach Francois Allaire noticed the young goaltender was having trouble stopping pucks in the lower half of the net, so Allaire taught

187

Roy to drop to his knees and splay his legs outward. As the majority of NHL shots on goal happen in the lower half of the net, the butterfly style took away a huge option for shooters. Roy subsequently perfected the style and changed the game as a result. All up-and-coming goaltenders copied his new style.

Another unique style, or lack there of, came from Dominik Hasek. Probably best defined as a flopping style, Hasek would basically do anything he could to stop the puck. Where another goaltender would make a sliding pad save, Hasek threw his entire body, arms and legs flailing in the air, just to stop the puck. Most of the time it worked.

Stripped of all the extras, styles and strengths, goaltending comes down to a mental game. Naturally, goaltenders must have strong bodies, good skating and fundamentals, but the best weapon of any goaltender is his mind. It is the common strength that is found in all the great goaltenders. They are only human, and on many nights, even the best, including Patrick Roy and Jacques Plante, had bad games. But it was their ability to bounce back from those games, to learn and to adapt that made them great. It is this quality that makes the goaltender one of the most important keys to success for an NHL team.

See Butterfly Goaltending; Stand-up Style

Goaltender Glove: What the goaltender uses to catch the puck.

See Trapper

Goaltender Interference: When an attacking player either impedes a goaltender's ability to make a save or comes into more than incidental contact with the netminder. For as long as there have been goaltenders in the net, players have been getting in their way. Throughout the history of the league, goalies have long complained that the NHL does not use the goaltender interference penalty for their protection. During the 1998–99 NHL season, the league attempted to protect goaltenders by disallowing any player to enter the goaltender's crease in the front of the net. If so much as a toe was in the goal crease when a goal was scored, it was automatically disallowed regardless of whether or not the

G

189

goaltender was interfered with. Luckily that rule was abolished before the start of the next season.

Goal Mouth: The area just in front of the goal line and behind the goal line inside the net.

Goal Suck: A term heard more often on streets and in local arenas than in the professional ice palaces of the NHL. A goal suck is a player that always stays within striking distance of the opponent's goal and plays zero defence. Though this type of player is generally not well respected, he always seems to manage a breakaway on goal from time to time.

See Loafer

Gobble Up the Puck: When both teams have a chance at the puck and someone comes away with it. Normally used in reference to when a goaltender grabs the puck in the middle of a scramble in front of the net.

Goon: A player on the ice who cannot skate very well, does not have much of a shot, is much bigger than the average player and whose sole purpose is to start and finish fights. Few goons remain in hockey these days, but those who grew up watching hockey in the 1970s are well aware of the term "goon." Among the more notable goons in hockey history are Sprague Cleghorn, Dave "Tiger" Williams, Dave Schultz and Tie Domi. A goon should not be confused with an enforcer. A goon will set out to injure, while the enforcer's role is to protect his teammates.

Goose Egg: A colourful term for a goaltender getting a shutout, that is, allowing zero goals in a game.

See Shutout

Gordie Howe Hat Trick: Gordie Howe was well known for his ability to put the puck into the net, but he would fight as readily as he would score. A Gordie Howe hat trick is when a player scores a goal, gets an assist and gets into a fight in the same game. Though not an official statistic, it is seen as a badge of honour for some players to have on their resumes. The first known incident of a player having a goal, an assist and a fight happened on, appropriately enough, December 26 (Boxing Day), 1917, and was accomplished by Toronto Arena's forward Harry Cameron. Gordie Howe's first Gordie Howe hat trick came on October 11, 1953, against the Toronto Maple Leafs.

G

Although Howe had the feat named after him, he only accomplished the triple play twice in his career. Many other players have since passed Mr. Hockey's standard; even Sidney Crosby is one fight away from tying Howe's mark. Brendan Shanahan is the current record holder with 17 Gordie Howe hat tricks, while Jarome Iginla is still currently active with seven to his name.

Grandfather Clause: An exemption from a new rule instated by the league. Some examples of this would be when the league made it mandatory for all new players to wear helmets in 1979. Those players who were already in the league and wished to do so did not have to wear a helmet. Craig MacTavish was the last NHL player to go without a helmet when he retired as a member of the St. Louis Blues in 1997.

Grapes: Nickname of the one and only Don Cherry. He received the nickname from a series of restaurants that he used to own called Don Cherry's Grapevine and a TV show out of Hamilton of the same name. He also had a radio show titled *Don Cherry's Grapeline*.

Great One: With 61 NHL records held or shared and a career filled with amazing play, it's not difficult to see why Wayne Gretzky was given the nickname "Great One."

Gretzky had been breaking records since he started playing hockey. Even before he was a teenager, he scored 378 goals in 82 games. Everyone watching the skinny kid from Brantford, Ontario, knew that he was destined for hockey greatness. The time he spent on his backyard rink practicing his shooting and skating and visualizing how the game is played paid off for the young star.

When Gretzky outgrew the backyard rink, he made his way to the professional ranks at 17 years of age. The sports world was waiting to see what the young prodigy could do, as many suspected that this skinny kid would not be able to stand up against the men of the NHL. But Gretzky proved them all wrong, scoring 51 goals and 86 assists in his first year in the NHL with the Edmonton Oilers.

The 1981–82 season was Gretzky's breakout year, where he established his "Great One" status. At the tender age of 20, Gretzky was on track not only to break but shatter Maurice Richard's 50 goals in 50 games record set in 1944–45, which had only been equalled during the 1980–81 season by Mike Bossy of the Islanders. Although averaging one goal per game is hard, Gretzky destroyed the record, reaching 45 goals in 38 games. He then finished the record off in Great One–style, scoring five goals against the Philadelphia Flyers on December 30, 1981. Gretzky finished that year with 92 goals and 120 assists for a record-breaking 212 points.

After being traded to the Los Angeles Kings in 1988, Gretzky continued his greatness when he broke the all-time points record in regular season play in 1989, a record he still holds with 2857 points. Just a few years later, Gretzky zeroed in on Gordie Howe's total goal record of 801. Gretzky broke that record on March 23, 1994, when the Kings played the Vancouver Canucks before a crowd of 16,000-plus fans packed into the Great Western Forum. The awaited moment came in the second period on a rush started by Luc Robitaille and Marty McSorley, with Gretzky following close behind. Robitaille carried the puck into the Vancouver zone and passed it to Gretzky, who had McSorley with him for a two-on-one. Gretzky hit McSorley with a pass. McSorley could have shot but instead passed it back to Gretzky, who had the wide-open net and shovelled it in for goal number 802.

Some of Gretzky's records might be broken some day, but others are certainly untouchable, never to be outdone. He truly was the Great One!

Great Western Forum: Former home of the Los Angeles Kings from 1967 to 1999. Seated 16,005 for hockey games and was also the home of Los Angeles Lakers. The Kings now play in the Staples Center.

See Staples Center

Greensboro Coliseum: Home of the Carolina Hurricanes from 1997 to 1999. Built in 1959, the Greensboro Generals of the Eastern Hockey League called the Coliseum home until the league folded in 1973. Several other teams played under the Coliseum's roof during its history, but it wasn't until the Hartford Whalers became the Carolina Hurricanes in 1997 that the NHL came calling. The Coliseum was the best temporary home for the new NHL franchise as construction of their more modern facility was underway in Raleigh.

It was not a match made in heaven, however, as the people of Greensboro did not flock to the arena to watch the hockey games. So in an effort to build up a scarcity of tickets and artificially inflate the price, the owners blocked off a large section of the seats with a green curtain. National media mocked the move and dubbed the blocked off area the "green acres." Once the Raleigh Entertainment and Sports Arena was complete, the Hurricanes were more than happy to move into their new home. The Coliseum remains open to concerts, basketball games and other large events, and even underwent a major renovation in 2011.

See PNC Arena

Gretzky's: Famous sports-themed restaurant in downtown Toronto owned by the "Great One" Wayne Gretzky.

Gretzky Trade: Wayne Gretzky was and still is the greatest player in the history of the game. With the Edmonton Oilers, he established countless records and many milestones since joining the NHL in 1982. It was thought impossible that any general manager or owner in their right mind would want to get rid of a dynamic player of Gretzky's calibre. After all, he was responsible for bringing the Stanley Cup to Edmonton four times and had made the Oilers the most powerful club in the league.

By 1988, Gretzky was the king of hockey and could do no wrong in the eyes of all Edmonton Oilers fans. Any idea of Gretzky leaving the club never even entered people's minds. He was an Oiler for life, and that was final. Gretzky was Canada's proud little treasure that no one wanted to share.

After the 1988 Stanley Cup victory celebrations died down and the players were relaxing over the summer, strange rumours began swirling around the NHL that the Oilers were on the verge of making a major, multi-player deal that could possibly involve Gretzky. Most fans in Edmonton simply dismissed the rumours as simple lies. Rumours always tend to creep into the hockey world during the off-season, more the product of bored sportswriters rather than having any grains of truth. But this time was different— this story had legs. But despite the rumblings, when Oilers management called an emergency press conference on August 9, 1988, most of the hockey world was still caught off-guard.

At the press conference, the room fell eerily silent as Oiler management walked in and took their seats. With a rather sedate look on his face, Oilers owner Peter Pocklington took his seat, shuffled a few papers, took a deep breath and uttered the words that broke millions of hearts.

"Gretzky has been traded to the Los Angeles Kings," he said as flash bulbs illuminated the room.

What everyone in the room that day was unaware of was that Pocklington and charismatic Kings owner Bruce McNall had signed the deal two weeks earlier. The reason they had not told the world of their little secret was that the Oilers season ticket drive was on and any news of Gretzky leaving the city surely would have affected sales.

The trade was monumental not just for the fact Gretzky was leaving for the warmer climes of southern California but that a slew of other players were also involved in the deal. Along with Gretzky, the Oilers sent enforcer Marty McSorley and Mike Krushelnyski to L.A. in return for Jimmy Carson and Martin Gelinas. The Oilers also received several of the Kings first-round draft picks in 1989, 1991 and 1993, as well as a chunk of change reported to be in the area of $15 million.

After Pocklington finished his announcement, it was time for Gretzky to address the media. No signs of happiness were visible on his face as he sat down and shuffled closer to the microphone. Taking a couple of breaths, Gretzky proceeded to confirm the news that nobody wanted to hear.

"For the benefit of Wayne Gretzky, my new wife and our expected child in the new year, it would be for the benefit of everyone involved to let me play for the Los Angeles Kings," said Gretzky, choking back tears. "I promised Mess [Mark Messier] I wouldn't do this."

Although it might not have been apparent then, the Gretzky trade was more than just a transfer of players from one team to another. When a player of his calibre and stature was brought into a market where football and basketball reigned supreme, his arrival changed the game. Gretzky brought a renewed interest in the game of hockey and hope for a team struggling to put fans in the seats. Overnight, the Los Angeles Kings became the hottest ticket in town. Gretzky was a star in a town that worshipped stars.

See Edmonton Oilers; Los Angeles Kings

Grinders: A player who works best in the corners, digging out pucks and getting physical with the other team. Used by the coach mainly in a defensive role on the third and fourth line. Grinders do not tend to score much but are valuable to the success of a team.

Gross Misconduct: A serious infraction that occurs when a player, coach, manager or trainer purposely violates the rules of the game. The offending individual is suspended for the remainder of the game and is assessed an automatic $200 fine. If a player incurs three game misconduct penalties during the regular season, then that player receives an automatic $1000 fine and is suspended for the next league game. In the event of any subsequent game misconduct penalties, the suspension is increased by one game.

G

List of Gross Misconduct Penalties

Banging boards with stick in protest of an official's ruling

Continuing or attempting to continue a fight

Deliberately breaking stick or refusing to surrender stick for measurement

Deliberately throwing any equipment (including stick) out of playing area

Entering or remaining in the referee's crease

Fighting off the playing surface (or with another player who is off the playing surface)

Inciting an opponent

Instigating a fight

Interfering or distracting opponent taking a penalty shot

Knocking or shooting puck out of reach of an official

Leaving bench to speak to official

Gross Misconduct Penalties (continued)

Refusing to change non-regulation piece of protective equipment (second violation)

Use of profane or abusive language

Verbal abuse of an official

Guardian: Another name for a goaltender, as in the one who guards the net from being scored on.

HP Pavilion: Formerly known as the Compaq Center and the San Jose Arena, the now-dubbed HP Pavilion was built in 1993 as the home for the San Jose Sharks. It is commonly known as the Shark Tank or the Tank. It seats 17,562 for a hockey game and has also been the home for the NBA's Golden State Warriors and the San Jose Sabercats of the Arena Football League. The building originally opened under the name San Jose Arena. In 2001, the naming rights were sold to Compaq, then in 2002, when HP bought Compaq, the arena was renamed the HP Pavilion.

See San Jose Sharks

HSBC Arena: Former name of the home of the Buffalo Sabres from 1999 to 2011. Now called First Niagara Center.

See First Niagara Center

Habitants: Alternative nickname for the Montréal Canadiens, also shortened to "Habs." The French word refers to the early settlers who farmed along the St. Lawrence Gulf and the river. The term was used by the settlers themselves and other classes from the 17th century up until the early 20th century, when the usage of the word declined in favour of the more modern *agriculteur* (farmer). As the

Montréal Canadiens were one of the first professional, pre-dominantly French hockey teams, they were given the nickname *"Les Habitants."* A common misconception about the Montréal Canadiens' "CH" logo is that the "H" stands for Habitants, but "CH" actually stands for *"Club de Hockey."* The first man to refer to the team as the "Habs" was American Tex Rickard, former owner of Madison Square Garden, who in 1924 told a reporter that the "H" stood for *Habitant*, or Habs as he called them, because he was either unable or unwilling to say the word in French.

Hacking: Slashing. An infraction in which a player swings his stick at an opponent and earns a minor penalty.

See Slashing

Halifax Rules: These are some of the earliest known rules for the game of hockey as published by a Nova Scotia newspaper reporter named James Power. Power recorded the rules as related to him by the head of the Dartmouth Amateur Athletic Association, Byron Weston, who had played hockey in the Halifax–Dartmouth area as early as the 1850s. The rules were carried to Montréal when the first official game was played in 1875.

The Rules

A small block of wood was used as the puck.

The puck was not allowed to leave the ice.

The stones marking the place to score goals were placed on the ice at opposite angles to those used today.

Slashing was not allowed.

The stick could not be lifted above the shoulder.

Halifax Rules (continued)

When a goal was scored, ends were switched.

Players had to keep "on side" of their sticks.

The forward pass was permitted.

The same players played the entire game.

A penalized player could not be replaced with another player.

The game had two 30-minute periods with a 10-minute break in between.

The goalkeeper had to stand for the entire game.

Goals were decided by the goal umpires, who stood at the goalmouth and rang a handbell.

Halifax Style of Hockey: An early style of hockey used mostly during informal games where two goal posts without netting were turned to face the sideboards rather than toward the action. The players were allowed to score from either side of the posts, making the job of the goaltender a rather dizzying one.

Hamilton Tigers: NHL team from 1920 to 1925. When the Abso-Pure Ice Company had finished building a 4000-seat artificial ice rink in Hamilton in 1919, the company thought a good way to fund their project was to have an NHL franchise in the city. It just so happened that the Québec Bulldogs were looking to get out of the NHL at the time, so a deal was struck to bring the Bulldogs to Hamilton. The Abso-Pure Ice Company paid $5000 for the franchise and started operations for the start of the 1920–21 season, but they inherited a club that had won only four games in the previous season despite having goal-scoring legends Billy Burch and Joe Malone on their team. For the first four seasons, the Tigers never won more than 10 games out of the 24 played each season and inevitably missed the playoffs every year.

The fortunes of the franchise only turned around when brothers Shorty and Red Green were added to the team for the start of the 1924–25 season. With everything on the ice finally going smoothly, the Tigers started to win hockey games, propelling the team from last place to the best team in the league, ahead of powerhouse clubs like the Montréal Canadiens and the Toronto St. Patricks. For the first time in franchise history, the Tigers were going into the playoffs with a good shot at going all the way and winning the Stanley Cup, but on March 9, 1925, everything changed.

On that day, the Tigers players got together and confronted team owner Percy Thompson and demanded that they be paid an extra $200 for playing in the postseason. The players had a genuine reason to feel like they were not being compensated properly as the league had expanded for the first time that year, adding the Montréal Maroons and Boston Bruins. With six teams instead of four, the season was extended from 24 to 30 games, and the players believed they should be paid accordingly for the extra games, just like players on the other teams in the league were. Despite the rationality behind the players' demands, league president Frank Calder was not sympathetic to the their complaints and threatened to suspend or fine them if they did not meet their contractual obligations.

The players decided they would rather quit hockey than be taken advantage of by management. With either side standing pat, Calder, along with the owner of the Tigers, disqualified the team from participating in the playoffs.

The Tigers first-round opponents, the Montréal Canadiens, went into the Stanley Cup finals against the Victoria Cougars and ended up losing the best-of-five series three games to one. At the end of the season, with no players remaining on their roster, the Tigers' owners were more than happy to sell the franchise rather than deal with player issues again. The Hamilton Tigers moved south of the border and became the New York Americans. Efforts to get an NHL team to return to Hamilton continue but without much success.

H

See New York Americans

Hand Pass: In game action, when a player passes the puck with his hand to a teammate outside of their defensive zone, the referee will whistle the play dead, calling a hand pass, and then set up for a faceoff.

Handcuffed: When the goaltender has a difficult time stopping an easy-looking shot, he is said to be handcuffed. For example, a shot handcuffs a goaltender when he can't seem to control the puck after it hits his glove.

Handle the Puck: To touch or hold onto the puck. If any player other than the goaltender closes his hand on the puck, the referee calls an automatic two-minute minor penalty. A player may grab the puck out of the air; however, he must immediately knock it down or place the puck on the ice. If a player knocks the puck in the air toward a teammate, the referee or linesman will call a "hand pass" and a faceoff is taken in the area of the infraction. However, a hand pass to a teammate while in the defensive zone is permitted.

The goaltender cannot hold onto the puck for longer than three seconds if there is no pressure from the opposing team. If the goaltender does not release the puck after three seconds, a two-minute minor penalty to the goaltender is assessed.

Hanging from the Rafters: At a hockey game, whenever there is a sell-out crowd including standing-room only, the broadcaster calling the game will inevitably describe the full arena for the viewers or listeners at home saying that the fans are "hanging from the rafters."

It is an old hockey saying based on a real-life situation where fans have indeed "hung from the rafters" just to get a better view of the ice. The term was first used to describe the fans at the old Detroit Olympia Stadium. The standing-room-only area near the top of the steep arena was known for having one of the worst views in the arena, so spectators intent on getting a better view of the action would reach up and grab the overhead rafters, pulling themselves above the rest of the crowd. Broadcasters naturally saw this and simply described what they saw, people literally "hanging from the rafters." Today, the term is more descriptive than anything else, used by broadcasters with a penchant for the dramatic. The rafter-hanging tradition at the Olympia Stadium continued until the building was replaced by Joe Louis Arena in 1977.

Hanson Brothers: Three crazy fictional brothers from the 1977 movie *Slap Shot*. The characters were based on three actual brothers—the Carlson brothers—two of whom starred in the film, but the third brother could not appear in the film as he had been called up by the Edmonton Oilers for the World Hockey Association (WHA) playoffs. In the film, the three brothers were Jack Hanson (portrayed by David Hanson), Steve Hanson (portrayed by Steve Carlson) and Jeff Hanson (portrayed by Jeff Carlson). The three brothers were famous for starting violent fights, interrupting the coach's pre-game speech and wearing extremely thick eyeglasses.

See Slap Shot (movie)

Hard Around: A hard shot into the offensive zone that follows the boards into the corner, behind the net and into the opposite corner. The hard around is used to set up offensive plays, particularly power plays.

Hart Memorial Trophy: Named in honour of Dr. David Hart, who donated the original trophy to the NHL in 1923. It is the oldest and most prestigious of the individual awards

205

H

in hockey as it celebrates the player who is judged most valuable to his team during the regular season. Members of the Professional Hockey Writers' Association (PHWA) vote to determine the winning player.

The Hart Trophy was first awarded in 1924 to Frank Nighbor of the Ottawa Senators. The original trophy was retired in 1960 to the Hockey Hall of Fame, and a new trophy was commissioned and named the Hart Memorial Trophy after Dr. David Hart passed away.

Wayne Gretzky won the trophy a record nine times during his career, eight of which were consecutively. The Montréal Canadiens, as a team, has the most players in history to have won the trophy, a record 16 times; the Boston Bruins are second with 12 and the Detroit Red Wings and Edmonton Oilers won it nine times. Notable players who have won the trophy are Detroit Red Wings Gordie Howe (six times), Boston Bruins Eddie Shore (four times) and Bobby Orr (three times) and Montréal Canadiens Maurice Richard (once).

Hartford Civic Center: Former home arena of the New England Whalers of the WHA and the Hartford Whalers of the NHL (1975–97). Now known as the XL Center, the original Hartford Civic Center opened in 1974 as a multipurpose arena. It served as the home of the New England Whalers until January 18, 1978, when the roof collapsed after a heavy snowstorm. Luckily, there were no injuries, but the building was forced to close while extensive renovations were done. The renovated arena reopened two years later and sat 15,635 people for hockey games. The arena played host to the 1986 NHL All-Star Game, the 1994 NHL Entry Draft and was home to the Hartford Whalers until their last game on April 13, 1997, when they defeated the Tampa Bay Lightning by a score of 2–1.

Hartford Whalers: When it was announced that a new professional league would be starting up in 1972, a group of New England businessman led by Howard Baldwin put in a bid for a franchise. The World Hockey Association (WHA)

207

granted their proposal, and in 1972, the New England Whalers played their first season out of Boston, playing their home games at Boston Gardens. The club signed a host of former NHLers and managed to steal a few players from others clubs and formed a competitive team when the season began. By the end of the 1972–73 season, the Whalers had the best record in the league and went on to win the inaugural Avco Cup, the WHA championship. After scheduling conflicts with the owners of Boston Gardens, the NHL's Boston Bruins, the Whalers owners decided to relocate the team to Hartford, Connecticut, for the beginning of the 1974–75 WHA season.

By January 1975, the Hartford Civic Center was completed, and the team moved into their new home. Although the Whalers never again won the Avco Cup, they did have a loyal following of fans and managed to ice a competitive team for most of their seasons in the WHA, with players such as an aging-yet-still-competitive Gordie Howe, Dave Keon, Mike Antonovich, Gordie Roberts and Mike Rogers.

When the WHA folded in 1979, the NHL readily accepted the Whalers into the new league as they were one of the more financially stable clubs at the time. The only condition of acceptance into the league was issued by the Boston Bruins: the club had to drop "New England" from their name. It was agreed upon, and the Hartford Whalers were born.

The Hartford Whalers did not start off their life in the NHL as well as they had in the WHA. The 1979–80 season was a series of ups and downs that saw the return of Gordie Howe (age 51) to the league and saw the city of Hartford fully embrace their team, but the team on the ice could not compete against the stronger NHL clubs and ended the season with a winning percentage below .500. Despite their win-loss record, they still made the playoffs, but they faced off against the defending Stanley Cup champion Montréal Canadiens and were promptly swept out of the hunt for the Cup.

That was the lone bright spot for the Whalers as the team posted consecutive losing seasons until 1985, when they finally began to turn their fortunes around. The main reason for their success was leading scorers Ron Francis and Kevin Dineen and the goaltending of Mike Liut, who powered the club into the playoffs for the first time since 1980. With all three players at the top of their game, the Hartford Whalers were a tough team to beat, playing a hard-hitting, defensive-oriented game. In the 1986 playoffs, the Whalers managed to contain the high-scoring Québec Nordiques, defeating them in three straight games in the best-of-five series before moving on to face the Montréal Canadiens.

The series against the Canadiens is without a doubt one of the most exciting in Whalers history. Every game played felt like a game seven, both teams playing with intensity and mutual hatred, making for entertaining hockey. Unfortunately for the Whalers, the Canadiens won the series in overtime of game seven and eventually went on to win the Stanley Cup.

In the 1986–87 season, the Whalers put in their best season since joining the league, finishing atop their division, but again found disappointment in the playoffs when the Québec Nordiques got their revenge in the first round, eliminating the Whalers from Stanley Cup contention. Following 1986–87, the Whalers once again fell into the middle of the league standings and spent the next several years in and out of the playoffs, and whenever they did make into the post-season, they never made it past the first round.

There were still more dark days ahead for the Whalers. The second darkest day in their history occurred on March 4, 1991, when Whalers management traded franchise star Ron Francis, along with Ulf Samuelsson and Grant Jennings, to the Pittsburgh Penguins for John Cullen, Zarley Zalapski and Jeff Parker. Ron Francis had been the face of the organization and was one of the most popular players on and off the ice. What made everything worse was that newly acquired Jeff Parker suffered a career-ending injury just two weeks after the trade, and then Francis became an integral part of the Penguins' success in winning back-to-back Stanley Cup championships in 1991 and 1992.

The Whalers did everything they could in the '90s to salvage their club, including hiring Brian Burke as their general manager, but their losing ways continued. While things deteriorated on the ice, the owners in the boardroom were looking for a way out of a financial mess. The team could barely sell the required amount of season tickets, and the lack of any playoff success really hurt the team's financial outlook. If the club was going to succeed, they needed to build a fancy new arena with luxury boxes and corporate seats just to stay competitive as the league expanded and upgraded. Owner Peter Karmanos tried to come to a financial agreement with the Connecticut governor to help save the club, but talks fell apart. It was announced in 1996 that the Whalers would be leaving Hartford at the end of the 1996–97 season and move to Raleigh, North Carolina, to become the Carolina Hurricanes. The last home game was played on April 13, 1997, and Kevin Dineen scored the team's final goal.

Despite the ups and downs of professional hockey in Hartford, several attempts over the years to bring a franchise back to the city have left many hockey fans hopeful that they will see the Whalers return.

See Carolina Hurricanes

Harvey the Hound: Beloved mascot of the Calgary Flames, Harvey the Hound comes in at an imposing six-foot-six and weighs approximately 200 pounds. The 25-year NHL veteran made his debut with the team in 1983 and has been a fixture behind the bench, in the stands and out in the community ever since. Harvey is famous for his hat and his hanging red tongue that was once famously ripped out by Edmonton Oilers head coach Craig MacTavish, when the mascot got a little too close to the coach during a game.

Hash Marks: Often referred to by announcers but seldom explained, the hash marks are a wonderfully colourful way of describing the setup lines within the four faceoff circles. When two players line up within the faceoff circles to the left or right of the goal, they must stand behind the series of lines painted on the ice before the linesman will drop the puck. If one of the players cross the hash marks, he can be thrown out of the faceoff and a teammate will have to replace him.

Hat Trick: Three goals scored by a player in one game. When the third goal is scored, it is traditional for the fans to throw their hats on the ice in celebration. This strange ritual

H

goes back many years to one enthusiastic hockey fan and an opportunistic hockey player.

Prior to 1946, when a player scored three goals, it was called a "three-goal game" and fans did not throw anything on the ice. All that changed one fateful day, when fashionable Chicago Blackhawks forward Alex Kaleta walked into a Toronto haberdashery owned by Sammy Taft. Kaleta had a game that night against the Leafs and made a bet with the hat maker and ardent Leafs fan. Kaleta bet the hatter that if he scored three goals in the game that night at Maple Leaf Gardens, Taft would have to give him a hat of his choice for free. Knowing that Kaleta was not the greatest goal scorer and that a three-goal game was difficult to come by, Taft gladly took the bet from the young forward.

That night, Kaleta scored his three goals against the Leafs and walked into the hat store the next day to collect his winnings. Newspapers eventually got wind of the story, and

Taft was quoted in all the major dailies in the city as saying, "Yeah, that was some trick he pulled to get that hat." From that day forward, whenever a player scored three goals in one game, it was known as a "hat trick." Never one to pass up a good marketing opportunity when it arose, Taft offered a free hat to every Toronto Maple Leafs player who scored a hat trick in a home game. Eventually, Taft retired from haberdashery, and since then, hockey fans have picked up where he left off and throw their hats on the ice every time a player pots three goals.

See Natural Hat Trick

"He Shoots! He Scores!": Famous line coined by broadcaster Foster Hewitt that he used to call when a goal was scored.

Head Butt: When one player hits another with his head. Any player caught head butting receives an automatic match penalty.

Headman the Puck: A term used more often these days with the new rule that has removed the red line at centre ice, allowing players to make a two-line pass. When a player "headmans the puck," he quickly passes it up to a player who has snuck in the back door behind the defencemen. Headmanning the puck is part of the more open, offensive style of hockey that the league has been trying to promote when they tweaked the rules at the start of the 2005–06 season.

Heel of the Stick: The bottom portion of the stick that connects the straight part of the shaft to the flat edge of the blade.

Helmet: A hockey player's head protection. You would think that in a sport as fast and as rough as hockey, the helmet would have been one of the first pieces of equipment to become standard for every player, but it wasn't until 1979 that the NHL passed a rule requiring all players entering the league to wear helmets.

Helmets in early 20th-century sports weren't used a lot, a practise that seems unimaginable today. The hockey

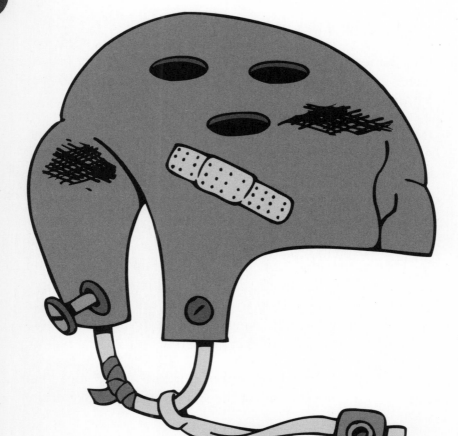

helmet got its start when player/inventor Barney Stanley presented a prototype to the NHL's board of governors at their annual meeting in 1927. At that time, no NHL or professional player had ever worn a helmet during a regular-season game unless he was recovering from an injury, and players were not about to start. The NHL board rejected Stanley's idea flat out.

The ole "brain bucket" would have served many players well in the early days as several high-profile players were forced to retire from the game prematurely because of head injuries. Among them was Irvin "Ace" Bailey of the Toronto Maple Leafs, whose career ended when he smacked his head on the ice after receiving a vicious body check from Eddie Shore. Boston head coach Art Ross began experimenting with helmet designs after the Bailey incident, and when he settled on one he liked, he made several of his players wear them during a game against the Ottawa Senators. The experiment only lasted one game as the players opted out, preferring to risk injury rather than don the bulky headgear again.

The first-ever recorded instance of a player wearing a helmet was in 1913, when Moose Johnson of the New Westminster Royals in the Pacific Coast Hockey Association donned a crudely made helmet to protect the broken jaw he had suffered in a game. The last helmet-less player in the NHL was Craig MacTavish, who retired from the game in 1997.

High Stick: An infraction in which a player hits an opponent in the neck or face with his stick. The result is usually a two-minute minor penalty, but if blood is drawn, the offending player must sit in the penalty box for four minutes.

Hip Check: When a player uses his hip to check an opponent. Because the impact is to the lower part of the body, the person being checked often gets thrown into the air.

Hobey Baker Award: Annual award given to the top U.S. National Collegiate Athletic Association (NCAA) men's hockey player. It is named after former hockey star and World War I veteran Hobey Baker, who played hockey for Princeton University. Baker was the most popular athletic star in the United States in his day, playing for the university's hockey team as well as starting as the captain of the football team. He was an accomplished scholar and was well known in the social circles of Manhattan's nightlife and party circuit. Baker even caught the eye of famed writer F. Scott Fitzgerald, who immortalized the young athlete in his novel *This Side of Paradise*, depicting him as he lived—a handsome young man with the world in the palm of his hand.

On the ice, Baker was one of the most talented players around. His physical size meant he could hit as hard as the toughest players, but his athleticism meant he was always a constant threat to score. His fans filled arenas everywhere he went, but when World War I broke out, Baker put aside his studies and athletic aspirations to do his duty as a citizen. He survived his time in the war as a pilot in the U.S. Air Force, but just before returning home from his base in Paris, Baker wanted to take one last flight. He was a few hundred feet in the air when the plane's engine cut out. He could not recover the plane and died in the ensuing crash.

Baker left behind a legacy with various symbols of success that bear his name. The Hobey Baker Memorial Award and the arena where his old Princeton Tigers still play is named after him as well. In 1945, when the Hockey Hall of Fame opened in Toronto, Baker was one of the first players to receive his spot in the pantheon of hockey's greatest players.

Hockey: The etymology of the name is difficult to trace back to a single source, and there are a number of possible origins for the name of the sport.

Hoquet is an old French word used to describe a shepherd's crook or bent stick. There was also a field game played in ancient France called *hoque*, but there is little evidence that the game was ever played in Canada or on ice. *Hoquet* was brought to England with the invasion of William the Conqueror in 1066, and the word gradually evolved into the form and spelling we recognize today.

As far back as the early 1400s in England, there is reference to a game variously called *hawkey, hawkie, horkey, hooky, hoky* and *hockey*. It was played during harvest festivals, when young boys got covered in mud playing in the fields with curved sticks and a ball.

In 1527, in Ireland, a book of statutes refers to a sport that used "the horlinge of the litill balle with hockie stickes or staves."

The Middle Dutch word *hokkie*, meaning "shack" or "doghouse," was commonly used to refer to a goal. Several Dutch paintings from the 16th century depict people playing a hockey-like game on ice.

The game had many names in the beginning, but it was around the mid-1800s that it became more widely known as hockey. There are several written reports of military men playing the game of hockey in their free time, including one from a British army officer stationed in Kingston, Ontario, in 1843, who wrote in his journal: "Began to skate this year, improved quickly and had great fun at hockey on the ice."

But historians generally agree that other communities claim primordial ties to early forms of hockey, citing the amount of anecdotal and physical evidence found in Nova Scotia, more specifically in the Halifax–Dartmouth area, that firmly place it as ground zero for the birthplace of hockey in "Canada's Ocean Playground."

The landscape of Nova Scotia provides the perfect outdoor arena for winter sports. Dotted with thousands of lakes, ponds and rivers, the province was the ideal testing ground to develop a new winter sport. The fertile land of Nova Scotia and the natural harbour in Halifax attracted an influx of early European settlers in the late 17th century. With the expansion of Nova Scotia's settlement in the 1700s came a wave of immigrants from all over Europe who had to adapt to their new environment. In addition to adjusting economically and socially, the new arrivals also had to change their sporting traditions to fit the landscape and the long, cold winters. As the area was predominantly settled by the Scottish and the Irish, they brought over their games of shinty and hurling.

Going back a few centuries before the arrival of the Europeans, the aboriginals of the area, the Mi'kmaq, had been playing their own stick-and-ball games, similar to the early form of hockey.

With the convergence of the new immigrants and the Mi'kmaq in the Windsor–Halifax–Dartmouth area, the games mixed, and a new sport began to emerge, something many began to refer to as hockey on ice. It was out of this melting pot of sports that a more recognizable form of hockey began to take shape in around the 1840s, and only a few decades later, the first official game was played on March 3, 1875, in Montréal, and a couple of decades after that, the Stanley Cup was born in 1893. Up until the birth of the Stanley Cup, the nexus of the game centred on a handful of cities, mainly Montréal, Ottawa and Toronto, but that quickly changed.

When the Cup was first awarded in 1893, teams weren't overly eager to win the actual trophy because it stood just a few centimetres off the ground and came with a stipulation that teams could not keep it—what was the point? But as each year passed and the battle to be crowned Cup champion intensified, a legend and mythology started to surround the Cup, and teams went to great lengths to get the chance to win it. Hockey has been a Canadian game, played by Canadians and watched by Canadian fans since its inception. But professional hockey couldn't remain locked up in Canada forever, and by the early 1900s, several American teams had established a presence in the rink and had even won a Stanley Cup.

One of the biggest early hockey players in the United States was Hobey Baker. The suave, handsome scholar from New York City played in only 45 games in his brief hockey career, but in those games, had no trouble bringing out the sophisticated crowds of the big city. Unfortunately, Baker was killed in a plane crash just after World War I ended, but in no way did hockey end with him. Hockey fever spread throughout the U.S., and teams from California to Boston began to pop up throughout all levels of hockey. Eventually,

H

the NHL was formed in 1917, and among many teams in the U.S., pro squads were also organized in Vancouver, Edmonton, Winnipeg and Québec City.

From its humble beginnings on a pond in Nova Scotia to the modern global game that it is today, hockey is here to stay. The game of hockey would have never survived if it had not been so fully embraced by the nation that created it.

Hockey By Any Other Name:

Baddin: A folk variety of field hockey played in Cheshire, England, in the 19th century.

Bandy: Similar to ice hockey but played on a larger surface the size of a soccer pitch. This sport is popular in Russia and Scandinavian countries. The National Bandy Association was established in 1891.

Cheuca: A game similar to field hockey played by the Aracuano natives of Argentina.

Hurley / Hurling: The most closely related game to modern hockey. Founded in ancient Ireland, the game resembles field hockey but allows more physical contact.

Keretizein: An ancient Greek game not unlike field hockey, played with bent sticks and a ball.

Khong kangjei: Also known as "Manipuri hockey" or "wrestling hockey." The game is played mainly along the border between India and Burma. Player use sticks similar to hockey sticks to move a ball about a field. A player is allowed to carry the ball, but a goal can only be scored when the ball is hit with a stick. If an opponent tackles a player, the tackled player must submit to a trial of strength, basically a wrestling match. The winner of the match receives possession of the ball.

Knattleikr: An ancient Scandinavian game in which a wooden ball was hit with curved sticks. It may have been played on iced-over fields.

Koora (Arab ball): A type of field hockey played in Algeria near Menea.

Melat: A violent medieval ball game in French Brittany played with hard, curved sticks. The church frequently banned the game because of the numerous brawls that started during the games.

Oochamkunutk (*See* Mi'kmaq): A cross between lacrosse and field hockey, played by the natives of Nova Scotia generations before the arrival of the Europeans.

Ringette: A sport similar to hockey in which players use a stick without a blade and a large ring instead of a puck. Sam Jacks of North Bay, Ontario, invented the game in 1963.

Roller hockey: The rules are similar to those of modern ice hockey, but this sport is played on in-line roller skates on a cement surface.

Underwater hockey: Not all variations of hockey are played on hard surfaces. Underwater hockey is played on the bottom of a swimming pool. The players move a weighted puck with short sticks across the bottom of the pool to the opposing team's goal. The game was invented in 1954 in England and was originally called "octopush."

H

Hockey Hall of Fame: A museum located in Toronto, Ontario, dedicated to the history and preservation of hockey. It houses exhibits about the players, teams, builders and others surrounding the game that have been an integral part of the history of the sport. Originally established in Kingston, Ontario, by James T. Sutherland, the first class of members were inducted in 1945. The museum was moved to Toronto in 1958 after the NHL removed its support of the Kingston location. It was located at Exhibition Place from 1961 to 1993 before moving into its current building, the former Bank of Montréal building in downtown Toronto. Every year, a committee of former players and Hall members selects new inductees. The Hall of Fame also has many interactive exhibits, including the NHLPA Be a Player Zone and the Sports Shootout Zone. As of 2011, there are 251 players in the Hall of Fame (including two women), 100 builders and 15 on-ice officials.

Hockey Mom/Dad: More than just the parents who wake up at 4:30 AM to drive their children to the hockey arena, hockey moms and dads are the driving force behind the millions of kids who dream of one day making it into the professional ranks. Hockey moms and dads are the people who pick up their kids' spirits when they lose the championship and cheer them on in every game from the frigid stands of arenas across North America. Occasionally, the hockey moms' and dads' love for the game and their children leads to the odd scuffle with other hockey parents, but they can be forgiven, after having woken up at 4:00 AM every weekend during hockey season.

Hockey Night in Canada: Most Canadians know it as a television program, but Hockey Night in Canada began

as a radio broadcast in November 1931. Back then, it was called the "General Motors Hockey Broadcast" on the Canadian National Railway radio network, and it only transmitted the Saturday night hockey games of the Toronto Maple Leafs. In 1934, Imperial Oil of Canada took over the

H

sponsorship of the program, expanding its coverage to the Montréal Canadiens and Montréal Maroons. Then in 1936, the broadcast was handed over to the Canadian Broadcasting Corporation (CBC). The show got the name Hockey Night in Canada from its host Foster Hewitt who welcomed listeners every night to "Hockey Night in Canada." From Ontario to British Columbia, the weekly show featured only Toronto Maple Leafs games hosted by Foster Hewitt and colour commentator Percy Lesueur, while from Québec eastward the French population tuned into Canadiens games and the voice of Rene Lecavalier, and the English population would listen to Doug Smith and Elmer Ferguson broadcast the Montréal Maroons games.

When television arrived on the scene, *Hockey Night in Canada* began airing in 1952, just a few weeks after television broadcasting opened up in Canada. In French Canada, the broadcasts were called *La Soiree du Hockey*.

The television show's first theme music was titled "Saturday's Game," composed by Howard Cable, but that song was replaced by the now-iconic 1968 composition by Dolores Claman's, "The Hockey Theme." The song has now been played for so many years, week and after week, that it almost became a second national anthem to most Canadians. Just hearing the first few notes of the song, any Canadian would be able to name the tune. But in 2008, the CBC lost its licence to the song, and it was quickly bought up by the CTV network and is now used for their hockey broadcasts on TSN.

In the history of *Hockey Night in Canada* that has seen such broadcasting legends as Danny Gallivan, Dick Irvin Jr.,

Bob Cole, Foster Hewitt, Ted Darling, Dave Hodge and Ron MacLean, none have been more famous (or infamous) than Don Cherry. Hired in 1981 by the CBC as a full-time colour commentator, Cherry did not last long in that position given his habit of openly cheering for one team (mostly the Bruins and the Leafs and was extra critical of the Canadiens). The CBC then created a show for Cherry that aired in the first intermission called "Coach's Corner" with co-host Dave Hodge. In 1987, Hodge was replaced by current co-host Ron MacLean. The show was an instant hit and has made Don Cherry (for better or worse) a Canadian institution. His weekly tirades on the virtues of Canadian hockey, toughness and smart play are what keep people tuned in. Whether they agree or not is a different story.

What started out as a simple radio broadcast has expanded into one of the most popular shows in Canada, now including "Coach's Corner," the "Hot Stove," a weekly double header and both pre- and post-game coverage on game night. The French broadcast *La Soirée du Hockey* ended in 2006 when French broadcasting rights to all Montréal Canadiens games went to RDS (Réseau des Sports).

Hockey Sweater, The (Le Chandail de Hockey): A short story written in 1979 by Canadian author Roch Carrier. Although a simple tale of a young Montréal boy who receives a Toronto Maple Leafs jersey from his mother when all he wanted was a Montréal Canadiens number 9 jersey (Maurice Richard's), it is widely considered to tell a deeper story of the linguistic and cultural differences of Anglophone and Francophone Canadians at the time. The story represents just how important hockey is to many Canadians and how a simple sweater can make a big difference in

225

someone's life. The story was made into a National Film Board animated short film called *The Sweater*, and Roch Carrier's words even appear on the back of the $5 bill: *"Nous vivions en trois lieux: l'ecole, l'eglise, et la patinoire; mais la vrair vie etait sur la patinoire."* ("We lived in three places: the school, the church, and the skating rink; but our real life was on the skating rink.")

Holding: Any action in which a player holds or grabs onto another player and impedes his movement on the ice. The infraction receives a two-minute minor penalty.

Holes: The seven distinct "holes" a goaltender needs to cover:

1. At the corner of the net along the ice on the goaltender's stick side

2. At the corner of the net along the ice on the goaltender's glove side

3. On the goaltender's glove side, near the upper crossbar

4. On the goaltender's stick side, near the upper crossbar

5. Between the goaltender's legs; called the "five-hole," it is the only hole named by its number at the present time

6. Between the goaltender's torso and the stick side

7. Between the goaltender's torso and the glove side.

Holy Grail: A diehard hockey fan's term of endearment for the Stanley Cup.

See Stanley Cup

Home Team: Used to designate the team playing in their home city. "Home team advantage" is another term often used, which simply means that the home team has the added boost of having its fans' support, and during any stoppage in play, the home team is allowed the final line change. This gives the home team coach the ability to match players and skills better than the visiting team.

See Visiting Team

Honda Center: Current name of the home of the Anaheim Ducks. Formerly known as the Anaheim Arena, Pond of Anaheim and Arrowhead Pond of Anaheim. The arena complex opened in 1993 and was the home of the Los Angeles Clippers from 1994 to 1999. Although now exclusively the home of the Anaheim Ducks, the building also housed the Anaheim Bullfrogs of the Roller Hockey International league, Anaheim Splash of the Continental Indoor Soccer League, Anaheim Piranhas of the Arena Football League and Anaheim Storm of the National Lacrosse League. Seating capacity for hockey games is 17,174 seats.

See Anaheim Ducks

Hooking: An infraction is which a player uses the blade of his stick to hook another player to slow him down. Under the new, stricter NHL guidelines, even though contact may be minimal, as long as the offending player puts his stick around the waist of his opponent, the referee will call a hooking penalty. It is by far the most common penalty in hockey.

Hot Dog: A player who loves to show off his skills and take all the glory for himself.

Hot Moment: An old-time hockey term for a fight.

Howitzer: Not the classic field artillery cannon used in warfare, but a player with a hard slapshot. The puck travels so fast that it seems as if it has just come out of a cannon. "Sheldon Souray blasted a howitzer past a surprised goaltender."

See Slapshot

Hurley: Traditionally, the word "hurley" is used to refer to the stick used in the game of hurling, but it can also be used to describe the game itself in a colloquial manner.

Hurley-on-ice: The name for an early version of hockey. The same rules applied as for regular hurling, but the game was played on ice. As the game began to evolve further away from its roots, the name changed.

See Hurling

Hurling: Field game that originated in ancient Gaelic times, around 3000 years ago. The object of the game is for players to use their sticks (or hurleys) to knock a small ball between their opponent's goalposts. The game is a cousin of hockey. Hurling was brought to Eastern Canada in the early 17th and 18th centuries, and because of the long winters, the sport eventually evolved to where it was played on ice. Hurling employs a similar strategy as in hockey with forwards, defencemen and goaltenders. Hurling is still played today, mainly in the United Kingdom, Europe, Australia, New Zealand and South Africa.

Hybrid-style Goaltending: A cross between butterfly and stand-up goaltending, hybrid style is not used by many goaltenders today, but the ones who do use it have found some of the greatest success in the NHL. A hybrid goaltender is equally adept at dropping to his knees to make a butterfly save as well as making a classic Terry Sawchuk–style kick save. The hybrid style is one of the most effective ways of keeping the opposing shooters guessing whether to shoot the puck high or low. The two most effective practitioners of this style are Martin Brodeur and Dominik Hasek, whose

unpredictability and flair for making big saves have kept them at the top of the goaltending world since they broke into the NHL.

See Butterfly Goaltending; Stand-up Goaltending

I

Ice Palace: A hockey arena. Hockey is so uniquely connected to Canadian culture that we give regal names to the places where the sport is played. It seems fitting to call the sheet of ice where so many hopes and dreams are played out on a weekly basis, where battles are won and lost and where legends are made, an ice palace.

The "Ice Palace" was also the name of the first hockey rink opened in the U.S., in New York in 1894.

Iceburgh: Official mascot of the Pittsburgh Penguins. The large, plushy penguin first appeared in the 1991–92 season and has been a part of the team ever since. He even made an appearance in the 1995 action film *Sudden Death* starring Jean-Claude Van Damme. In the movie, filmed in Pittsburgh's Civic Arena, the hero Darren McCord (Van Damme) has to chase down the villain who was dressed in the mascot costume.

Icing the Puck: This occurs when a player in his own defensive end shoots the puck the length of the ice and a player from the other team touches the puck first. The red line is used as the marker for icing. If, for example, a player shoots the puck but has not yet crossed the red line, then the linesman will call icing. Icing is waved off when a player

231

on the offending team touches the puck before the defence-men, when the puck does not make it past the goal line or when the goaltender comes out and plays the puck.

Igloo: Nickname of the former home of the Pittsburgh Penguins, Mellon Arena, in reference to its dome-shaped roof.

See Civic Arena

Illegal Curve: The NHL defines an illegal curve on a stick as follows:

> *The curvature of the blade of the stick shall be restricted in such a way that the distance of a perpendicular line measured from a straight line drawn from any point at the heel to the end of the blade to the point of maximum curvature shall not exceed one-half inch.*

Many people believe that the curved stick makes the puck fly faster when shot, but this is false. There are three benefits to a curved stick:

- The player has more control over the puck, making it easier to stick handle around the ice and to take a pass.

- In a curved stick, the puck tends to fall into the same pocket on the blade so that every time the puck leaves the blade, the player's shots and passes are more consistently delivered.

- The puck will spin a little more, making some shots a little less predictable for the goaltender.

The NHL has guidelines for players to follow, and should a player be suspected of having an illegal curve and is caught by the referees in a game, that player is given a two-minute minor penalty. One of the most famous illegal curved stick calls happened in the 1993 Stanley Cup finals.

In the playoffs, every advantage counts. Sometimes luck helps you out and sometimes a little inside information about the other team helps. In game one of the Stanley Cup finals between the Montréal Canadiens and Los Angeles Kings, in which the Canadiens lost 5–1, a few Montréal players noticed that Kings defenceman Marty McSorley's stick blade looked a little odd. The players informed their head coach, Jacques Demers, who decided to hold onto this information in case he needed it later.

That time came in the second game of the series when the Canadiens were down 2–1 with less than two minutes remaining in the period. Demers asked the referee to check McSorley's stick for an illegal curve, hoping that the hunch would pay off. Demers' instincts were good, and McSorley was assessed a two-minute penalty that the Canadiens used to tie the game and eventually win it in overtime. Using the momentum, the Canadiens went on to win the series and the franchise's 24th Stanley Cup.

Illegal Equipment: The NHL has strict regulations as to the size and fit of players' equipment, and any player who alters his gear to gain advantage is penalized if caught. For example, goaltender Tony Esposito was famous for making alterations to his equipment, including stuffing extra padding into his leg pads and stitching netting under his arms. In the NHL, players have also tried to get away with illegal curved sticks and goaltenders have tried illegal padding.

See Illegal Curve

In the Slot: The real estate in front of the goaltender and between the faceoff circles. The slot is the place on the ice where every true goal scorer is born—Monopoly's Boardwalk for hockey. Because it is such a sought-after piece of territory, it is often the scene of most hockey scrums and fights. If a player can get open in the slot, he has a direct shot at the goaltender, but if a defenceman is doing his job properly, the slot's availability is quickly shut off. With a quick shot and deadly accuracy, Brett Hull was one of the most effective players at finding an opening in the slot and putting the puck in the net.

See Doorstep; Kitchen

Infirmary: Area in an arena where players go to get medical attention during and after games.

See Sick Bay

Influenza Epidemic (a.k.a. Spanish influenza): Throughout World War I, soldiers fought in trenches across Europe. Confined to these cold trenches, fighting and sleeping in dirty water beside dead or dying soldiers and an army of rats, many soldiers developed what appeared to be cold symptoms. As soldiers began returning home from the war, a virus known as influenza started to spread among the populations of the world. Over 21 million people worldwide died from the flu also known as the Spanish influenza. In Canada and the United States, entire communities were wiped out. In an attempt to minimize the effect of the disease, government officials closed schools, large celebrations and family gatherings were discouraged and sporting events were cancelled.

In only its second year, the NHL faced a major roadblock to establishing itself in North America. The Spanish influenza had begun to affect not only the players but also the fans who came to watch the games. Attendance at the games was significantly reduced by the government warnings to avoid public gatherings. Banners were plastered all over the cities warning people how to avoid contracting the virus. An air of panic spread across North America as families and communities began to splinter because of the number of cases that developed. The players and teams in the NHL were not immune to the disease either.

At the start of the 1918–19 season, the NHL had managed to sign up only three teams to play for the season and a chance for the winner to play against the rival league of the Pacific Coast Hockey Association (PCHA). The teams were the Ottawa Senators, the Montréal Canadiens and the Toronto Arenas. But halfway through the season, the Toronto Arenas withdrew from the league because of financial problems, and the league was forced to play a best-of-seven series between the remaining Senators and Canadiens, with the winner scheduled to battle the Seattle Metropolitans, winner of the PCHA title.

Led by Newsy Lalonde, the Canadiens emerged victorious as they easily beat the Senators four games to one. While preparing for their battle against Seattle, several Canadiens players began to fall ill. At first, most thought it was the common cold, but the symptoms progressed, and by the time of the final game—which was scheduled for April 1, 1919—several of the players had fallen seriously ill.

With more players becoming violently ill from influenza, the decision came down from NHL management just before the start of the final game of the Stanley Cup playoffs that the game would be cancelled, and because the series was tied, no winner would be declared. Four days after the decision to cancel the playoffs, Canadiens star "Bad Joe" Hall lost his life to the influenza virus in a Seattle hospital, proving that the league had done the right thing in cancelling the playoffs and potentially saving other lives.

Injured Reserve (IR) List: Every team makes a list of the players who are unable to play for an extended period of time because of injury. A player placed on injured reserve can be replaced by another player without exceeding the roster limits of 23 players per team.

Instigator Rule: A player who is deemed the instigator of a fight is given an additional two-minute penalty. Any instigator of a fight in the final five minutes of the game is treated more harshly with not only the instigator minor penalty of two minutes, but also a major penalty for fighting (five minutes), a 10-minute misconduct (which is significant if the game goes into overtime) and an automatic one-game suspension. Additionally, the coach is fined $10,000.

See Major Penalty; Misconduct Penalty

Insurance Goal: When a team is already leading the game by one tally and scores another to take a comfortable lead.

Inter-conference Play: Games played between teams in different conferences. There are only a few games between conferences per year for each team, and in some seasons, two teams might not meet at all.

Inter-divisional Play: Games played between teams in different divisions. Less games are played per year between inter-divisional teams than against teams in the same division.

Interference: An infraction in which one player deliberately obstructs or impedes another player who does not have possession of the puck. An interference penalty can also be given if a player accidently drops his stick, glove or helmet and another player knocks it out of his reach.

International Ice Hockey Federation (IIHF): Founded in May 1908 in Paris, France, as the *Ligue International de Hockey sur Glace*. The founding nations of the federation were France, Great Britain, Switzerland and Bohemia (Czech Republic). Today, the federation has 51 member countries, including Canada, Mongolia, India and even North Korea. While Canada and the United States are part of the federation, it has little power in North America over hockey decisions as the NHL is considered the highest hockey organization. Hockey Canada and USA Hockey are other independent organizations. The main function of the IIHF is to govern, develop and organize hockey throughout the world, helping to promote the sport to new generations. It is also responsible for the business side of the game, such as arranging sponsorships, licensing and merchandising in connection with IIHF events. The IIHF presides over hockey in the Olympic Games and the World Championships.

International Ice Hockey Rink: Every rink outside North America follows IIHF guidelines when it comes to the size of the playing surface. To increase the speed and the number of goals scored, international rinks are considerably wider—98 feet (30 metres)—than the NHL rinks, which are 200 feet (61 metres) by 85 feet (26 metres). At the larger size, players have more space to manoeuvre and hopefully, for the fans, score more goals.

See European Ice Rink; Rink

Izod Center: Current name of the former home of the New Jersey Devils. The team moved into the modern Prudential Center in 2007 and their former arena was renamed the Izod Center. The building was built in 1977 and sat over 19,000 fans for a hockey game. Was also called Continental Airlines Arena from 1996 to 2007 and the Brendan Byrne Arena from 1981 to 1996.

See Prudential Center

J

Jack Adams Award: NHL trophy handed out annually to the head coach deemed to have contributed the most to his team's success during the regular season and playoffs. The trophy is named after hockey legend Jack Adams, who played professional hockey from 1917 to 1927 (Toronto Arenas, Vancouver Millionaires, Toronto St. Pats and Ottawa Senators) but also coached for the Detroit Red Wings organization from 1927 to 1947. The Jack Adams Award was first awarded in 1974 to Philadelphia Flyers head coach Fred Shero. Of note, Don Cherry also won in 1976. Pat Burns has won the Adams award the most, winning three times and for three different clubs (Montréal '89, Toronto '93, Boston '98).

James Norris Memorial Trophy: Award handed out annually to the NHL's best defenceman during the regular season. Winners are selected by votes from the Professional Hockey Writers Association (PHWA). It is named in honour of James E. Norris, former owner of the Detroit Red Wings from 1932 to 1952. The trophy was first given out at the conclusion of the 1953–54 season to the Red Wings Red Kelly. Then Doug Harvey of the Montréal Canadiens won the award seven times in eight years. Only Bobby Orr beat that record, winning it eight times in a row from 1968 to 1975.

The Red Wings Nicklas Lidstrom has won the trophy seven times.

Jarring Hit: A really hard check delivered by one player to another. Usually makes the crowd cheer.

See Bodycheck

Jaw Fest: A heated discussion between two players or occasionally two coaches on the bench.

Jennings Trophy: *See* William M. Jennings Trophy

Jersey: A term for a hockey sweater.

Jobing.com Arena: Current home of the Phoenix Coyotes. Opened in December 2003 to replace the older America West Arena, the Jobing.com Arena (formerly known as the Glendale Arena) seats 17,799 fans for hockey games and also serves as a concert hall. The Coyotes played their first game on December 27, 2003, against the Nashville Predators in a 3–1 losing effort.

See Phoenix Coyotes

Jock Strap and Cup: The essential piece of equipment for any male hockey player to protect his family jewels.

Joe Louis Arena: Current home of the Detroit Red Wings. Named after boxer and former heavyweight champion Joe

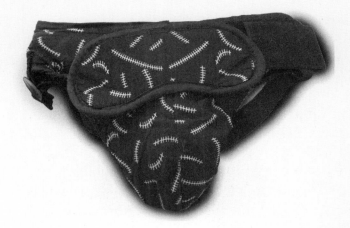

Louis, who grew up in Detroit. The arena replaced the iconic Detroit Olympia stadium in 1979. The building, along with Madison Square Garden and Nassau Veterans Memorial Coliseum (both in New York), are the only three arenas in the NHL without corporate names. The Red Wings played their first game in Joe Louis Arena on December 27, 1979, in a 3–2 losing effort to the St. Louis Blues. The building seats 20,066 spectators for a hockey game. It is one of the older buildings in the NHL, and the Red Wings have looked for a new site to build an arena, but they have recently renewed the agreement to lease the building for another 30 years.

See Detroit Red Wings

Johnny-on-the-spot: A term for a player who is always in the right place at the right time to slip the puck into an open net.

Journeyman: A player who bounces around from team to team, never staying with one club for more than one or two seasons at a time.

Jubilee Rink: Was the home arena of the Montréal Canadiens from 1909 to 1910 and briefly in 1919. Originally built in 1908, it held just 3200 spectators. It was destroyed by fire in 1919.

Juiced: In the world of modern sports, juiced has come to mean two different things. When a player puts all his power into a shot, he is said to have "juiced the puck." And, no longer just the title of Jose Canseco's autobiography, "juiced" has also come to mean any player who is using drugs (usually steroids) to enhance his performance.

Junior A: The second highest level of junior hockey in Canada (highest being Major Junior). In Québec, it is called Junior AAA. This is one level below the Canadian Hockey League (CHL).

Junior B: Third highest level of junior hockey in Canada. Called Junior AA in Québec. Generally a locally based system of hockey.

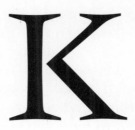

Kansas City Scouts: The original incarnation of the New Jersey Devils franchise, the Kansas City Scouts entered the NHL in 1974 along with the Washington Capitals. Before the start of their first season, the Kansas City franchise searched for a name for the team, finally settling on the "Jayhawkers," but after the Chicago Blackhawks complained that the name was too similar to their name, the team dropped that name and adopted the name "Scouts" in honour of a famous statue located in a city park.

The Scouts put their team's hopes into the hands of head coach Bep Guidolin, a former NHL player who is most famous for being the youngest player to play in an NHL game at the age of 16 years and 11 months in November 1942. The team struggled to fill their lineup as the World Hockey Association (WHA) continued to steal much of the talent available, and as a result the Kansas City Scouts were not a very good team. General manager and former NHL great Sid Abel did the best he could to fill his roster, but the club faltered. The Scouts finished their first season in the NHL with a record of 15–54–11 and landed well out of a playoff spot.

Kansas City seemed willing at first to support the Scouts through one bad season, but in the 1975–76 season, the

Scouts only won 12 games, and with each passing game, fewer and fewer fans showed up to fill the stands. With an average of 8000 fans showing up per game to a 17,000-seat arena, the Scouts could not survive and were forced to relocate to Colorado, where they became the Rockies, then eventually moved again and became the New Jersey Devils.

See Colorado Rockies

Keepaway: A game usually played outside on frozen ponds with friends in which one player attempts to keep the puck away from all others for as long as possible.

Kenora Thistles: An amateur hockey team based in Kenora, Ontario, that was founded in 1896. Although the town had a population of just 4000, several of the players on the team had grown up playing on the same teams and worked well together on the ice. The Thistles challenged the Ottawa Silver Seven for the Stanley Cup in 1903 and lost, but in 1907 they tried again, this time against the Montréal Wanderers and they won. However, just two months after winning the Cup from the Wanderers, the Montréal team reclaimed their trophy from the Thistles in another Stanley Cup challenge.

> *Kenora Thistles Stanley Cup Roster:* Roxy Beaudro, Eddie Geroux, Silas Griffis, Joe Hall, Tom Hooper, Billy McGimsie, Russell Phillips, Tom Phillips and Art Ross.

Kid Line: The Toronto Maple Leafs "Kid Line" of Charlie Conacher, Harvey "Busher" Jackson and Joe Primeau was so named because none of them was older than 23 when they first started playing together, and they were the dominant line of the Leafs in the early 1930s. The line was one of the major reasons the Leafs won the Stanley Cup in 1932 and helped the team to four Stanley Cup final appearances in six years. All three players are in the Hockey Hall of Fame.

King Clancy Memorial Trophy: The NHL award given out annually to the player who best exemplifies qualities of leadership on and off the ice and who has given back to his community. Named in honour of Francis "King" Clancy, former legend on the Ottawa Senators and Toronto Maple Leafs in the 1920s and 1930s. The trophy was donated in 1988 by Toronto Maple Leafs owner Harold Ballard, who greatly admired Clancy. The first recipient of the award was the Calgary Flames' Lanny MacDonald.

Kitchen: The area inside the goaltender's crease or directly in front of the goalie. "The game plan is to get into Dominik Hasek's kitchen."

See Doorstep; In the Slot

Kneeing: Considered one of the dirtier infractions in hockey. Hitting an opponent with a knee on knee often leads to one of the players either being taken out of the game or injured so severely that he is out for the season. A major or misconduct penalty is usually given for kneeing because it is an intentional attempt to injure. Kneeing is considered a cheap shot.

Knuckle Puck: One of the most deceptive ways to shoot a puck. The shooter lays the puck on its edge and takes a wrist shot or slapshot on net. The puck is supposed to flip through the air at a deceptive speed, hopefully confusing the goaltender so that he is unable to stop it. The term is borrowed from baseball's knuckleball.

Kraut Line: Milt Schmidt, Woody Dumart and Bobby Bauer were nicknamed the Kraut Line because all three players came from Kitchener (formerly named Berlin), Ontario, a town known for its German heritage. First put together on the same line for the 1938–39 season, the Kraut Line helped the Boston Bruins to their second Stanley Cup. In the second year as linemates, the trio led the league in scoring. Schmidt was in first with 52 points, Dumart was second with 43, and third place was Bauer with 43 points as well (Dumart scored more goals). The Kraut Line shone again in 1940–41, leading Boston to their third first-place regular-season finish and their second Stanley Cup victory, beating the Detroit Red Wings in four straight games. The line was broken up when all three were called into military service for World War II, but the trio continued their on-ice antics on the military hockey team, dominating all hopeless challengers.

L

LNH (*Ligue Nationale de Hockey*): French abbreviation for the National Hockey League.

Lady Byng Memorial Trophy: NHL trophy presented each year to the player who has best exhibited the qualities of sportsmanship and gentlemanly conduct. The award is named in honour of the wife of Governor General Viscount Byng of Vimy (1921–26), Marie Evelyn Moreton or, as she was also known, Lady Byng.

A fan of the Ottawa Senators, Lady Byng wanted to promote gentlemanly conduct among the players, so she donated the trophy to the NHL at the end of the 1924–25 season. The first trophy was given to the Ottawa Senators forward Frank Nighbor. From 1928 to 1935, New York Rangers forward Frank Boucher won the most Byng trophies, at seven, while Wayne Gretzky comes in second with five wins. After Boucher's final win in 1935, Lady Byng was so impressed with his dedication to playing a clean style of hockey that she gave him the original trophy and had another made for the NHL. Bill Quackenbush and Red Kelly are the only two defencemen to win the Lady Byng Trophy. No goaltender has ever won.

Lamplighter: A player who lights up the goal lamp by scoring a lot of goals.

See Light the Lamp

Lane: An opening in the flow of the game where a player might skate into to get clear, take a pass or take a shot.

Larceny: When a goaltender makes an impossible save on a shooter, robbing him of an otherwise sure goal. The term can also be used when a player jumps into the path of a shooter with an open net and takes away a golden opportunity for a goal.

See Rob (of a Goal)

Laser Beam: A very hard and accurate shot.

Lateral Movement: Used to describe the side-to-side movement of goaltenders.

Laying on the Lumber: A slang term for slashing. When a player swings his stick at an opponent, chopping him down or connecting stick to stick, he is said to be laying on the lumber.

See Slashing

Lead Pass: When a defender passes the puck up the ice to a streaking forward. It is hoped that a lead pass will lead to a fast break or a breakaway.

LeafsTV: Television station owned by the Toronto Maple Leafs on which they primarily show Leafs games and other programming related to the franchise, the players and the fans.

Left Wing Lock: A defensive strategy in which the left wing drops back to play parallel to the defence when the other team tries to exit their zone.

Les Glorieux: Another one of the many nicknames for the Montréal Canadiens.

See Habitants

Lester B. Pearson Award: Now called the Ted Lindsay Award.

See Ted Lindsay Award

Lester Patrick Trophy: Presented by the NHL and USA Hockey to the person who contributes the most to the game of hockey in the United States. Players, coaches, referees and executives are eligible for the trophy. It is considered a non-NHL trophy because it can be given out to anyone, even those not associated with the NHL.

The New York Rangers presented the trophy in 1966 to honour the great Lester Patrick, who was once the general manager and coach of the team. The trophy was first given out to Detroit Red Wings coach Jack Adams. The trophy is a little different from other hockey awards as it can be given out posthumously to those who have at one time made a contribution to U.S. hockey. For example, in 1987, it was given to Hobey Baker, famed American hockey player who tragically died just after the conclusion of World War I.

Lid: A colloquial term for a helmet.

See Helmet

Lie: The angle made by the shaft of the stick and the blade.

Lift the Stick: When one player uses his stick to lift another player's stick off the ice in order to either separate his opponent from the puck or prevent him from getting control of it.

Light the Lamp: Score a goal. When a goal is scored, the goal judge switches on a red light situated just behind the top of the net to signal that a point has been scored. Hector "Toe" Blake of the old Montréal Canadiens scored so many times in his career that he earned the nickname "Ole Lamplighter."

See Lamplighter

Line Matching: A system in which a coach will pair up his most effective lines against the other teams' lines depending on the progress of the game. This is an essential strategy for any coach.

Lines: A three-player forward unit. Forward lines are usually broken down into first, second, third and fourth lines, with the first line being the scoring line while the fourth tends to be the defensive or checking line.

Linesman: An assistant to the referee. Two linesmen are on the ice during a game, and it is their job to call infractions such as offsides, icing, high sticks, hand passes and the freezing of the puck. In rare cases, a linesman can advise the referee of an infraction on the ice if the ref fails to see it, but it is ultimately the referee who makes the final call. However, a linesman is allowed to assess a bench minor if a player or a member of the coaching staff is verbally abusive. Linesmen are also responsible for most of the faceoffs and usually get to break up scrums and fights.

See Referee

Lineup: The team's complete roster submitted to the on-ice officials before the start of a game.

Lip: Saying nasty things to the referees, as in "He's really giving the referee some lip." It can also be a term for top of the goal crease.

See Badgering

Loafer: An opportunistic player who loafs or lingers around the neutral zone awaiting a long pass from one of his teammates for a fast break on goal.

See Goal Suck

Lob: A type of shot used when a player in the defensive zone wants to clear the puck down the ice and avoid icing the puck all the way to the other end. To relieve the pressure in the defensive zone, a player will lift or lob the puck over the heads of his opponents, clearing it into the neutral zone and slowly into the opposing team's end.

See Soft Dump

Lockout: In the history of the NHL (so far), there have been two lockouts, in which, because of the business relations between the NHLPA, the NHL and the owners, the NHL regular season and the playoffs have either been cut short or have not occurred at all.

Lockout 1994–95

After the 1993–94 season was played without a collective bargaining agreement between the players and the owners, the 1994–95 season never began as the players were "locked out" of the league, and games were put on hold until the issues could be resolved. The main issue at hand was the implementation of a salary cap that the owners wanted and the players protested. Both the players and the owners agreed that many of the smaller market teams could not survive against the big clubs, and so to even the playing field, the league and the owners wanted to tie salaries of the players to revenue in order to subsidize the smaller teams, while the NHLPA sought revenue-sharing options to help the smaller market teams. But after a 104-day lockout, the only thing both sides could agree on was the implementation of a salary cap for rookies. After the lockout ended on January 13, 1995, the NHL season was cut short to 48 games. The New Jersey Devils won the Stanley Cup that year.

Lockout 2004–05

Since 1917, on only two occasions has the Stanley Cup has not been awarded: in 1919, when the Spanish influenza epidemic forced the cancellation of the Stanley Cup finals between the Montréal Canadiens and the Seattle Metropolitans, and in 2005, when a lockout resulted in the cancellation of the entire season and playoffs. The cancellation of the season was a direct result of the failure of the 1994–95 collective bargaining agreement (CBA), and the lockout began at 12:01 AM on September 16, 2004, the day that the old CBA expired. Small-market teams were spending nearly 80 percent of their revenues on players' salaries and could not keep up with the larger markets of Toronto and New York. The league and the NHLPA needed to come to some agreement in order to save the game from financial collapse, but this was easier said than done. The league presented the NHLPA with six concepts to achieve financial harmony and franchise sustainability, but the NHLPA rejected all six concepts, and as a result, a CBA was not signed and so began the waiting game. After 44 weeks without hockey, the NHLPA finally voted in favour of a salary cap and revenue sharing on July 21, 2005. It was a tough year for Canadian hockey fans, one they hope to never see again, but it might happen again if both sides cannot agree to new terms as the current CBA expires on September 15, 2012.

See Influenza Epidemic

Long Bomb: A puck that is slapped on net from far out, sometimes out past the blue line or even centre ice. It should be an easy save, but sometimes a long bomb can handcuff a goaltender. Every goaltender dreads letting this type of shot into the net.

Longshot: A player deemed not likely to make it on the team, given his talent level in comparison with the rest of the league.

Loose Change: A puck that lies on the ice and that nobody can seem to find.

Loose Play: A team that plays a game with absolutely no effort or "jump" in their skates—a coach's worst nightmare. When players don't cover their positions and turn over the puck easily, they are said to be playing "loose" hockey.

Lord Stanley of Preston: When Frederick Arthur Stanley, Earl of Derby, Lord Stanley of Preston, was first appointed Governor General of Canada by Queen Victoria in 1888, he had never seen, let alone heard of, the game of hockey. But that year, during the Englishman's first winter on Canadian soil, he was invited to the annual Montréal Winter Carnival and witnessed an exhibition game between the Montréal Victorias and the Montréal Amateur Athletic Club. The two teams put on an exciting match for the new Governor General, with the Victorias winning by a score of 2–1. The next day, the *Montréal Gazette* reported that Lord Stanley "expressed his great delight with the game of hockey and the expertise of the players."

Even Lord Stanley's children got involved in the hockey phenomenon, with three of his sons playing for the Ottawa

257

Rideau Rebels. After three years of cheering on his sons and his local clubs, Lord Stanley noticed the game lacked what other sports in his native England had—a trophy, something that teams from across Canada could compete for and aspire to attain. So Lord Stanley sent out a letter to be read at the league championship victory celebration of the Ottawa Hockey Club on March 18, 1892. He could not attend because he was called back to England.

The letter read:

> I have for some time been thinking that it would be a good thing if there were a challenge cup which should be held from year to year by the champion hockey team in the Dominion (of Canada). There does not appear to be any such outward sign of a championship at present, and considering the general interest which matches now elicit, and the importance of having the game played fairly and under rules generally recognized, I am willing to give a cup which shall be held from year to year by the winning team. I am not quite certain that the present regulations governing the arrangement of matches give entire satisfaction, and it would be worth considering whether they could not be arranged so that each team would play once at home and once at the place where their opponents hail from.

Back in London, England, Lord Stanley commissioned silversmith G.R. Collis and Company to create a trophy for 10 guineas (about $1300 CDN today). Engraved on the side of the cup were the words, "Dominion Hockey Challenge Cup," and on the opposite side, "From Stanley of Preston." The Cup was then shipped across the Atlantic to Canada, where teams might begin to fight to hold it above their heads.

Lord Stanley never witnessed a Stanley Cup match himself, having been recalled to England by the Queen. Lord Stanley

later became Lord Mayor of Liverpool and the Chancellor of the University of Liverpool. He died at the age of 67 on June 14, 1908.

Lord Stanley's Mug: Another nickname for the Stanley Cup.

See Stanley Cup

Los Angeles Kings: Hockey in California does not sound right, but there have been teams in the Golden State since the days of the Pacific Coast Hockey Association (PCHA) and the Western Hockey League (WHL), including the Los Angeles Monarchs and Los Angeles Blades. The NHL decided to venture into the City of Angels in 1967 after awarding Canadian businessman Jack Kent Cooke the rights to a franchise in the city. Cooke named his team the Kings and chose purple and gold as their colours because the colours are associated with royalty.

The new club did not have a home for the start of the 1967–68 season as the Forum was still under construction, so the team moved into the Long Beach Arena for their first year. The Kings opened their first season at home with a 4–2 victory over the Philadelphia Flyers. Several months later, the Forum officially opened, and the Kings played those same Flyers in their new building, this time losing 2–0. General manager Larry Regan tried his best to fill his team with quality players, but in a league that was dominated by Toronto, Montréal, Boston and New York, it was difficult for any of the new expansion clubs to compete. The Kings finished their first season with a respectable record of 31–33–10. The Kings lost their first attempt in the playoffs in the first round to the Minnesota North Stars. Things only got worse over the next few seasons for the Kings, who won just 14 games in the 1969–70 season.

The turnaround for the franchise came when goaltender Rogie Vachon joined the team during the 1971–72 season. With solid goaltending, the Kings still needed frontline scoring. From 1972 to 1975, the Kings were a good team, but any successes in the playoffs eluded them without scoring help. They finally got some scoring punch in 1975 by acquiring Marcel Dionne in a trade with the Detroit Red Wings and getting some supplemental scoring from Butch Goring. Even with frontline scoring and solid goaltending, the Kings could not find traction in the playoffs past the second round.

The beginning of the 1980s were less kind to the Kings as they fell to the bottom of their division, and even the rise of young star Bernie Nicholls could not help the team in their pursuit of Lord Stanley's Mug. In 1987, the Los Angeles Kings looked like a franchise with a limited air supply. Fan support was dwindling with each bad season, and the team did not seem to have much of a future. Then along came Bruce McNall, who purchased the Kings in 1987 and completely changed the fortunes of the club with one simple announcement in the summer of 1988: Wayne Gretzky was about to become a Los Angeles King. (*See* Gretzky Trade)

At the start of the season before Gretzky's arrival, the Kings only managed to sell 4500 season tickets, but by the opening day of the new Gretzky era, the Kings had sold 13,000 season tickets. The Kings not only attracted regular sports fans, but at nearly every home game, you would also find celebrities like Jack Nicholson, Kurt Russell and Goldie Hawn now cheering for the Kings.

Gretzky was good for the bottom line, and the team on the ice saw an upswing in their standings. The year before Gretzky arrived, the Kings had finished the season with just 68 points and had only scored 318 goals, but with Gretzky, the Kings improved their season and finished with 91 points and scored 376 goals and finally made it out of the first round of the playoffs for the first time since 1982. The players flanking Gretzky on the left and right wings had banner years under the Great One's tutelage. Linemate Bernie Nicholls had previously been a respectable goal scorer with a career high 46 goals in one season, but in his first year playing with Gretzky, Nicholls saw his scoring output increase to 70 goals.

L

The Gretzky effect was not just confined to Los Angeles. Selling hockey in the southern United States was something the NHL had always set its mind on, but they never seemed to be able to create a lasting foothold. Of the teams that have tried to take hold in the southern U.S., most have either failed or barely managed to keep solvent. Hockey is a winter sport of ice and snow. In the south, most people have never seen snow, let alone heard of this crazy game Canadians call hockey. Gretzky got a whole new generation of kids interested in hockey. Where before there had been no hockey programs for kids, suddenly communities began to build the infrastructure needed to support the development of the game.

At the NHL level, Gretzky's impact on the game could be seen as well. With the sudden interest in hockey in the south, the NHL finally felt comfortable bringing in new franchises. By 1994, the list of southern-based U.S. franchises had expanded to include the San Jose Sharks, Anaheim Mighty Ducks, Dallas Stars, Tampa Bay Lightning

and Florida Panthers. Within another five years, the NHL added the Phoenix Coyotes, Carolina Hurricanes and Colorado Avalanche to the list of NHL teams, and while Gretzky cannot be credited completely with the expansion of hockey into the southern states, his immediate success in Los Angeles had showed the league that it was possible to thrive in non-traditional markets.

In the Gretzky era, the Kings had a new look, a new fan base and a new reason to hope. But while Edmonton went on to win another Cup in 1990, the Kings never made it back to the finals until 1993, when they faced the Montréal Canadiens and ultimately lost the Stanley Cup final in five games. By the 1995–96 season, the Kings were no longer at their peak and decided to retool their club by trading Gretzky to the St. Louis Blues. Bruce McNall placed the Kings into bankruptcy, forcing the club to sell off their higher-priced players.

After Phillip Anschutz and Edward P. Roski saved the Kings from bankruptcy court, the Kings set about rebuilding their franchise. Through the late 1990s and into the early 2000s, the Kings had a few good seasons and a few bad ones, but they never made it far into the playoffs. Players came and went as the seasons passed, but the franchise still had not found the right combination of players for success. All of that changed in 2012 when the Kings entered the playoffs as the eighth-seeded team and knocked off the top-three teams in the Western Conference: the Vancouver Canucks, St. Louis Blues and Phoenix Coyotes. Buoyed by the brilliant play of goaltender Jonathan Quick and hard-nosed captain Dustin Brown, the Kings defeated the New Jersey Devils in the Stanley Cup finals and finally captured the franchise's first championship.

263

Los Angeles Kings Records

Most goals in a season: Bernie Nicholls, 70 (1988–89)

Most assists in a season: Wayne Gretzky, 122 (1990–91)

Most points in a season: Wayne Gretzky, 168 (1988–89)

Most points in a game: Bernie Nicholls, 8 (1988–89)

Most points in a season, defenceman: Larry Murphy, 76 (1980–81)

Most points in a season, rookie: Luc Robitaille, 84 (1986–87)

Most penalty minutes in a season: Marty McSorley, 399 (1992–93)

Most wins in a season: Jonathan Quick, 39 (2009–10)

Most shutouts in a season: Rogie Vachon, 8 (1976–77)

See Staples Center

Love Tap: Tongue-in-cheek term used when a player slashes another player or hits him hard.

See Slashing

Lumber: A hockey stick. Long, long ago, hockey sticks were made of wood or "lumber." Actually, the first hockey sticks were carved out of a single piece of hardwood.

See Stick

LW: Statistical abbreviation for Left Wing.

MCI Center: Former name of the Washington Capitals home arena.

See Verizon Center

MCL: Abbreviation for medial collateral ligament, a ligament along the knee that connects the femur to the fibula. Injuring one's MCL is a common injury in hockey, especially when players collide knee to knee.

See Kneeing

MVP: Abbreviation of most valuable player. The Conn Smythe Trophy goes to the MVP of the playoffs.

See Conn Smythe Trophy

Madison Square Garden (MSG): Colloquially known as The Garden, it is the home arena of the New York Rangers. The current version of Madison Square Garden was constructed in 1968. Former locations were built in 1879, 1890 and 1925 before moving to its present location. MSG houses the arena, the Pennsylvania Train Station as well as numerous shops and restaurants. The building also serves as a concert hall, the third busiest in the world behind the Manchester Evening News (MEN) Arena in Manchester and the O2 Arena in London, England. The arena is also the home of the NBA's New York Knicks. Over the years, MSG has undergone numerous renovations to improve the seating and modernize its facilities. It is widely known as one of the ugliest arenas in the NHL, given its round, prison-like appearance. It seats 18,200 spectators for a hockey game.

See New York Rangers

Major Penalty: A five-minute penalty that is assessed for a serious infraction of the rules. The referee automatically gives a major penalty to the offending player or players when there is a fight or when a minor penalty such as slashing is committed with the intent to injure another player.

List of Major Penalties

Boarding

Butt-ending

Charging

Checking from behind

Clipping

Cross-checking

Elbowing

Fighting

Head-butting

Hooking

Illegal check to the head

Interference

Kneeing

Major Penalties (continued)

Slashing

Spearing

Man On: When a player is chasing the puck and has his back to the play, his teammates will yell "Man on!" to let the player know that an opposing player is right on his heels.

Manhandle: When one player heavily checks and pushes another player, as in "Probert just manhandled Jones in the corner."

Maple Leaf Gardens: With two Stanley Cups under their belt, the Toronto St. Patricks were one of biggest draws in town in 1926 since joining the NHL nine years earlier. There was just one problem with the huge demand for tickets— the Mutual Street Arena, or Arena Gardens as it was more commonly called, that had been the home of Toronto's NHL team since 1917 had seen better days and couldn't house the growing number of fans. Conn Smythe knew another arena had to be built in order for the franchise to survive, and he envisioned a grand hockey palace that was to be the envy of all the other teams in the league. A few obstacles stood in Smythe's way, however.

As early as 1927, when Smythe purchased the Toronto franchise, he had planned for a new arena. And with the team's general success on the ice, his confidence in moving ahead with his decision soared. Smythe started to secure the necessary financial support he needed and, by 1930, began the difficult task of finding the perfect location. Several sites were considered, including one at the corner of

Yonge and Fleet streets, but the final spot chosen was a lot bounded by Carlton, Wood and Church streets. The same architectural firm that designed Toronto's Union Station was selected to build the new arena, and on June 1, 1931, construction began on Maple Leaf Gardens. Smythe wanted the building ready for the opening game of the 1931–32 season and pushed the construction crew to finish the arena as quickly as possible. The paint had barely dried when, just 166 days later, on November 12, 1931, Maple Leaf Gardens was open to host its first NHL game.

Maple Leaf Gardens has seen some of the most incredible moments in hockey history. For example, it was on Maple Leaf ice that the NHL had its first All-Star game on February 14, 1934, as a benefit for injured Toronto star Ace Bailey to help him pay his bills and take care of his family. The Maple Leafs defeated the NHL All-Stars by a score of 7–3, and at the end of the game, Bailey's famous number 6 jersey was the first jersey in NHL history to be retired. The good times continued through to the 1970s, when the team's glory days finally appeared to be over. Toronto's fortunes didn't change in the 1980s, and it wasn't until the early 1990s that things started to turn around again. It was thus decided a new home was needed to welcome in the newest era of the Toronto Maple Leafs.

Construction began, and on February 13, 1999, the Maple Leafs played their final game under the Gardens lights in a 6–2 loss to the Chicago Blackhawks, and Doug Gilmour scored the final goal in the Gardens history. The Toronto Maple Leafs now play their games at the Air Canada Centre, where the hope still lives on that a Stanley Cup banner will one day be raised again in the rafters.

See Air Canada Centre (ACC)

Mask: Metal cage or fibreglass face protection worn by forwards, defencemen and especially goaltenders.

See Goalie Mask

Masterton Trophy: *See* Bill Masterton Memorial Trophy

Match Penalty: The most serious of game penalties. An automatic ejection from the game is given to any player who deliberately tries to injure another player, with the added punishment of a five-minute penalty to be served by another member of the team.

List of Match Penalties

Attempt to injure (in any manner)

Biting

Boarding

Butt-ending*

Charging

Checking from behind

Clipping

Cross-checking

Deliberate injury (in any manner)

Elbowing

Goalkeeper who uses his blocking glove to the head or face of an opponent*

Grabbing of the face mask

Hair pulling

Head-butting*

High-sticking

Illegal Check to the Head

Kicking a player

Kneeing

Punching and injuring an unsuspecting opponent*

Slashing

Slew-footing

Spearing*

Match Penalties (continued)

Throwing stick or any object

Wearing tape on hands in altercation*

Infraction must have match penalty assessed if injury results

Maurice "Rocket" Richard Trophy: Established in 1999, the Maurice Richard Trophy is awarded annually to the leading goal scorer in the NHL. It was donated by the Montréal Canadiens in honour of the legendary Maurice "Rocket" Richard, who was well known for his goal-scoring abilities. The Anaheim Ducks Teemu Selanne was the first winner of the award in 1999, scoring 47 goals. Alexander Ovechkin has scored the most goals in one season with 65 to win the trophy in 2007–08. Steven Stamkos won in 2010 with 51 goals and again in 2012 with 60 goals.

McNichols Sports Arena: Home arena to the Colorado Rockies from 1976 to 1982 and the Colorado Avalanche from 1995 to 1999. McNichols Sports Arena, named after a long-standing mayor of Denver, was originally constructed in 1975 and also served as the home to the Denver Nuggets of the NBA. One of the smaller arenas in the NHL when it was first constructed, it originally sat just 15,900 spectators, which was boosted up to 16,061 after renovations in 1986. The McNichols Sports Arena was demolished in 1999, and the Nuggets and the Avalanche moved into the new Pepsi Center.

See Pepsi Center

Mellon Arena: Former name of the home of the Pittsburgh Penguins.

See Civic Arena; Consul Energy Center

271

Memorial Cup: The championship trophy of the Canadian Hockey League (CHL). It is awarded every year after a four-team, round-robin tournament between a host team and the CHL's member leagues, the Ontario Hockey League (OHL), Québec Major Junior Hockey League (QMJHL) and Western Hockey League (WHL). The trophy was originally created for the Ontario Hockey Association (OHA) championship. It was first proposed by Captain James T. Sutherland during World War I as a way to remember the OHA players who died during the war. It was created in 1919 and was originally known as the OHA Memorial Cup, and the league donated the Cup to be the championship trophy for all the junior champions of Canada. The trophy is one of the most sought-after hockey trophies apart from the Stanley Cup.

Metropolitan Sports Center: Former home arena of the Minnesota North Stars. It was constructed in 1967 when the North Stars joined the NHL. It seated 15,000 spectators and at its time was considered one of the nicest arenas in the NHL for its modern style and sight lines for the fans. One year after the North Stars moved to Dallas in 1993, the arena was demolished.

Miami Arena: Former home of the Florida Panthers, from 1993 to 1999. Also served as the home of the Miami Heat of the NBA. Seating just 14,703 for a hockey game, the arena was far too small for the Panthers to continue, forcing them to move to the new Bank Atlantic Center in 1999. The Miami Arena was demolished in 2008.

See Bank Atlantic Center

Mighty Ducks of Anaheim: Former name of the Anaheim Ducks.

See Anaheim Ducks

Mi'kmaq: The Aboriginal tribe that lived in Nova Scotia before the arrival of the first Europeans. The abundance of water bodies in the area provided the Mi'kmaq with a constant supply of fish, and the expansive, dense land was ideal for hunting animals. But when the bitter cold of winter swept across the land and froze the lakes, ponds and rivers, fishing became much harder. The Mi'kmaq, however, developed a creative way of taking advantage of the frozen water for recreational purposes—they played a game for amusement that was strikingly similar to hockey. This game was called *oochamkunutk*.

Even though the exact details of the game have been lost to history, it's believed that two teams of no more than 10 men each took to the ice with sticks fashioned out of a single piece of wood, and then attempted to shoot a wooden or stone disk past the opponent's goalposts. The Mi'kmaq did not use skates, but because their game was similar to hockey and existed in the same geographical region where, it's argued, hockey came into being—*oochamkunutk* deserves to be included as a member of hockey's earliest influences.

See Hockey

Minnesota North Stars: When it was announced in 1965 that the NHL was expanding from 6 to 12 teams, a partnership of nine businessmen, led by Walter Bush Jr., formed to seek a franchise for the Twin Cities. On February 9, 1966, NHL president Clarence Campbell announced that

Minnesota, Oakland, Los Angeles, Philadelphia, Pittsburgh and St. Louis would be awarded franchises.

Walter Bush Jr. appealed to the public for their help in naming the team, and of the 1536 entries received, it came down to five names: the Norsemen, the Voyageurs, the Blades, the Mustangs and the North Stars. On May 25, 1966, the new Minnesota North Stars were unveiled to the public. The name is derived from Minnesota's state motto, "*L'Etoile du Nord*," which means "The Star of the North" in French.

A few months after naming the team, a mad rush to complete the team's new arena began. It was a blessing the North Stars started on the road, as the construction crews had yet to finish the arena when the season began. Even by the home opener on October 21, 1967, crews were installing seats as fans arrived.

Despite a few bumps along the way, the North Stars got off to a good start for an expansion club. They finished the season in fourth place in the Western Division and made it into the playoffs, where they reached the semifinals before being eliminated by the St. Louis Blues.

Although the North Stars didn't have much in the way of postseason success, fans kept coming in the hopes that the team would eventually develop into a contender. But as the decade wore on, the North Stars' fate grew dim. From 1974 to 1979, the North Stars made the playoffs only once and didn't even make it out of the preliminary round. As a result of the team's poor performance, fans stopped going to the games, and by 1979, the team was on the verge of folding operations completely.

However, just as things seemed doomed to fail, the North Stars saw the coming out of a young Bobby Smith, who won the Calder Trophy as the top rookie of the 1978–79 season. The team also saw the emergence of Steve Payne who, along with Al MacAdam, led the North Stars in scoring during the 1979–80 campaign with 42 goals.

The addition of some young talent energized the club and finally brought about some success on the ice. The 1979–80 season saw the return of the North Stars to the playoffs, and they made it all the way to the semifinals before being eliminated by the Philadelphia Flyers. The Stars had reasserted their position as one of the top teams in the league, but it was the arrival of a young rookie named Dino Ciccarelli that would propel the team deeper into the playoffs than they had ever been before.

Finishing the 1980–81 season in third place in the Adams Division put the North Stars in the playoffs for the second year in a row, but with a young lineup, the team was not expected to make it into the later rounds. However, through sheer scoring power, forwards Dino Ciccarelli and Steve Payne helped the team move all the way to the Stanley Cup final against the defending champion New York Islanders. Their opponents, however, were no pushovers, and the Islanders easily defeated the North Stars in five games.

It was a tough break for the Stars, but an excellent sign for the future of the franchise. With the team's postseason success, fans began to return to the stadium to fill the seats and cheer on their team. But the euphoria only lasted a handful of seasons before the team began to miss the playoffs again in the late '80s, and talk once again turned to moving the franchise to another city.

The 1990–91 NHL season was by no means a success for the North Stars. They had to battle hard for every win, and by the end of the regular season, they had only scraped together 27 victories and 39 losses. But by some miracle of hockey statistics, the Stars made the final playoff spot in their division and had a second chance to prove to their fans that they could be a factor in the NHL.

It wasn't going to be easy as the first team they faced was the league-leading Chicago Blackhawks and the Vezina-winning goaltender Ed Belfour. But with some timely saves from goaltender Jon Casey and the veteran presence of Bobby Smith and Brian Propp, the Stars defeated the Blackhawks in six games and went on to make their second trip to the Stanley Cup finals in a decade.

The run to the finals brought much-needed life and revenue back into the North Stars franchise, but their Cinderella run ended there. They faced the Pittsburgh Penguins, who proved too deep in scoring talent, and the Stars simply could not put enough goals in the net to match.

In the final game, the Penguins handed the Stars the most lopsided loss in the Stanley Cup finals since 1905 by beating them 8–0. It was an embarrassing way for the Stars to finish off their magical run, and it was ultimately their last appearance in the Stanley Cup finals. The early 1990s were hard times for some markets in the NHL, as the realities of big city business began to hurt the NHL franchises located in the smaller cities like Québec, Winnipeg and Minneapolis. The NHL was about to go through a major update in the next decade, with teams across the league in the planning stages of modernizing their stadiums to accommodate more fans and more revenue-winning luxury boxes and corporate seats. The teams that could not provide the housing and fans to put into the seats started to fall to the wayside. Add to that a struggling team on the ice, and it was a certain recipe for a franchise to fold. By the 1992–93 season, North Stars team owner Norman Green announced that he could no longer operate the team in a market that had been losing money since 1985. Minneapolis lost their beloved North Stars to the city of Dallas, Texas.

See Dallas Stars

Minnesota Wild: The effort to return NHL hockey to Minneapolis began the moment the final buzzer sounded at the end of the North Stars 1993 game-seven playoff defeat, their last game as a Minnesota team. Only four years later, on June 25, 1997, the NHL announced that Minnesota Sports & Entertainment, a limited partnership formed by Bob Naegele Jr., had won the rights to open a franchise back in the great state of Minnesota, with 2000–01 as their opening season.

The appeal was put out to the public to send in their best ideas for a name for the Minnesota team. After going through thousands of submissions, it came down to just six: Blue Ox, Freeze, Northern Lights, White Bears, Voyageurs and Wild. The name "Minnesota Wild" was unveiled to the public along with the logo of a wild animal that appears to look like a wild cat or, to some, a bear, with the silhouette of a forest, a setting sun and a red sky. The Wild never specified what animal was on the logo, as the design was more about symbols of the state and the hockey team: the mouth of the wild animal resembles one of Minnesota's many rivers and its eye doubles as a star in the sky, in homage to the North Stars. "We think it best represents what Minnesota hockey fans hold most dear," said the newly named chief executive officer of the new team, Jac Sperling.

Former player Doug Risebrough was named general manager, and the process of constructing a new team began. A new stadium called the Xcel Energy Center was to be built on the site of the former Saint Paul Civic Center in St. Paul. Jacques Lemaire was named the team's first coach, and the team's future superstar, Marian Gaborik, was selected third overall by the Wild at the 2000 NHL Entry Draft. Gaborik scored the first goal in Wild history at their debut game on October 6, 2000, against the Anaheim Ducks. The Wild did not have much success in the beginning, but the young team quickly adapted to the pace of the NHL's top teams and, by 2002–03, were classed among them. Led by Gaborik, Wes Walz and Andrew Brunette, the Wild finished the season with 42 wins and enough points to get them into the playoffs for the first time.

In the first round of the playoffs, the Wild went up against a tough Colorado Avalanche, and by the end of the fourth game, the Avs seemed to have put the Wild away, but the young team surged back, winning the next three games to advance into the second round. Up against a determined Vancouver Canucks squad, the Wild once again needed seven games to win before moving on to the Conference Finals, one step away from the Stanley Cup finals. However, it was not to be as the Anaheim Ducks sent Minnesota off in four straight games.

Since that playoffs run, the Wild have missed out on the playoffs some seasons and made it in others, but they have never managed to make it out of the first round. The Wild have tried changing the players, the coaches and the general managers, but the team continues to search for that elusive chemistry that wins Stanley Cups. Minnesota, though, has a solid fan base that has stuck with the club through the good and the bad.

Minnesota Wild Records

Most goals in a season: Marian Gaborik, 42 (2007–08)

Most goals in a game: Marian Gaborik, 5 (December 20, 2007 vs. New York Rangers)

Most assists in a season: Pierre-Marc Bouchard, 50 (2007–08)

Most points in a season: Marian Gaborik, 83 (2007–08)

Most points in a season, defenceman: Brent Burns, 46 (2010–11)

Most points in a season, rookie: Marian Gaborik, 36 (2000–01)

Most penalty minutes in a season: Matt Johnson, 201 (2002–03)

Best plus-minus in a season: Keith Carney, +22 (2006–07)

Most wins: Niklas Backstrom 160
(as of end of 2011–12 season)

Most wins in a season: Niklas Backstrom, 37 (2008–09)

Most shutouts in a season: Niklas Backstrom, 8 (2008–09)

See Xcel Energy Center

Minor Hockey: From as early as five years of age, kids can enter into the North American hockey system. As they get older and their skills improve, they move through the various levels in the system. Not all the levels are age restricted. If a child is bigger than others or is far better, then his or her

age doesn't matter and the player is moved up to the higher levels. Sidney Crosby entered the professional NHL at 18 years of age, as did Wayne Gretzky.

Tykes or Squirts: Ages 5–6; kids learn the basics of the game
Novice: Ages 7–8; emphasis is on moving away from pack-style hockey
Atom: Ages 9–10
PeeWee: Ages 11–12
Bantam: Ages 13–14
Midget: Ages 15–17
Juvenile/Junior: Ages 18–20

Minor Penalty: A penalty of two minutes is assessed for the listed offences. During the two-minute penalty, the offending player sits out his sentence in the penalty box and can only return when the two minutes are over or the opposing team scores a goal.

List of Minor Penalties

Boarding

Charging

Clipping

Closing hand on puck

Cross-checking

Delay of game

Diving

Elbowing

Goalkeeper interference

High-sticking

Holding

Holding the stick

Hooking

Illegal equipment

Illegal stick

Instigator

Interference

Kneeing

Leaving penalty bench too early

Leaving the crease (goalkeeper)

Minor Penalties (continued)

Participating in the play beyond the center red line
(goalkeeper)

Roughing

Slashing

Throwing puck towards opponent's goal (goalkeeper)

Throwing stick

Tripping

Unsportsmanlike conduct

Miracle on Ice: Refers to the U.S. national hockey team's win in 1980 at the Olympics. At the start of the Olympics in Lake Placid, New York, nobody gave the young team from the United States any hope of beating powerful teams from countries like Sweden, Finland, Czechoslovakia and especially the Soviet Union. But when the upstart team from the U.S., led by university hockey coach Herb Brooks, beat the Czechs, Norwegians, Romanians and West Germans, people began to take a second look at the young squad. When it was announced that the U.S. would play the Soviet Union for a place in the gold-medal game, many people thought it a death knell for the U.S. team.

The Soviets had destroyed the Americans 11–3 in an exhibition game just a few days earlier. The Soviets were the picture of robotic discipline, playing an emotionless yet highly effective style of hockey that had made them international hockey champions in the 1970s. The Americans were the exact opposite of the Soviets. They were young, overemotional and had not played together until a few weeks before the start of the Olympics. Few people gave the U.S. much hope of winning against the Soviets.

The atmosphere at the Lake Placid arena was decidedly one-sided as the teams took to the ice, the Americans in their red, white and blue uniforms, and the Soviets in red, the communist colour. Right from the start, however, the Americans surprised the Soviets, playing a physical game and not letting up on their forechecking. The Americans also needed a stellar performance from their goaltender Jim Craig, who was, fortunately, having the best game of his life. Soviet goaltender Vladislav Tretiak was not having the greatest game and let in two goals before being replaced by back-up goalie Vladimir Myshkin. This move seemed to spark the Soviets, who pulled ahead 3–2 by the end of the second period.

In the third, the U.S. tied the game with a goal by Mark Johnston, sending the American fans wild. The winning goal came off the stick of U.S. team captain Mike Eruzione, who blasted a hard shot from 10 metres away. The puck went through the pads of the surprised Soviet goaltender. The world was in shock that the mighty Soviets had lost to the young American amateurs, but these amateurs were just as shocked as the rest of the world. The United States then went on to beat Finland and won their first Olympic gold medal in hockey in 40 years. Broadcaster Al Michaels famously cried, "Do you believe in miracles?"

Misconduct Penalty: A penalty assessed for a serious infraction, such as when a player uses abusive language toward the officials or does not obey the referee's requests. The referee indicates a misconduct penalty by placing both hands on his hips. In the event of a misconduct penalty, the player is removed from the ice for 10 minutes, and a substitute player is permitted to replace the penalized player. The offending player must also pay an automatic fine of $100 if the offence causes injury to the face or head of the opponent by means of his stick.

Moncton Victorias: A professional hockey team based in Moncton, New Brunswick. They played in the Maritime Professional Hockey League from 1910 to 1913. In 1912, they challenged and lost to the Québec Bulldogs in a best-of-three series by a score of 9–3 and 8–0.

Montréal Canadiens: Founded in 1909 by J. Ambrose O'Brien, the Montréal Canadiens were born out of the division between the owners of the Eastern Canadian Hockey Association (ECHA) and a group of businessmen seeking their own franchise. Jimmy Gardner and O'Brien joined forces and formed the National Hockey Association (NHA). Montréal had an already-established group of teams, like the Montréal Hockey Club, Montréal Shamrocks and the Montréal Victorias, but all were run and populated by English communities. French Montréal had no professional team to call their own. So when it was announced that the NHA season would start in 1909, O'Brien put a team together, and since it was made up of mostly French players, naming the team was relatively easy. On December 4, 1909, at a meeting in room 129 of Montréal's Windsor Hotel, the Montréal Canadiens were born.

The task of building the team was given to Jack Laviolette, who had many connections in the French hockey world. He had to act fast because the team's debut game against the Cobalt Silver Kings was set for January 5, 1910, at the Canadiens home arena, the Jubilee Rink. In less than one month, Laviolette had managed to assemble a competitive team. He snagged star players like Didier Pitre and Newsy

Lalonde, along with Joe Cattarinich, Ed Decary, Arthur Bernier, Georges Poulin, Ed Chapeleau, Ed Millaire, Noss Chartrand and Richard Duckett. Around 3000 fans turned out on that cold January day to watch the Canadiens beat the Kings 7–6 in overtime.

In 1911, the owners of the Montréal Canadiens ran into some legal trouble from Georges Kennedy, who owned a French Canadian team called Le Club Athletique Canadien that operated in Montréal east end. Kennedy wanted to get his hands on an NHA franchise, and so he threatened to take the Canadiens to court for stealing his team name. O'Brien did not want the legal hassle and was willing to hand over the rights of the team while he focused on his other teams (O'Brien also owned other teams in Ontario). The change in ownership did nothing to stop the rise of the Canadiens. With Georges Vezina minding the net, the Canadiens quickly established themselves as one of the dominant teams in the NHA, finally winning their first Stanley Cup in 1916 in a series against the Pacific Coast Hockey Association (PCHA) Portland Rosebuds. The Canadiens won the best-of-five series in the fifth game by a score of 2–1. Montréal had their first Cup of many.

When the NHA disbanded and the NHL formed in 1917, the Montréal Canadiens joined Ottawa, Toronto and the Montréal Wanderers in the new league. After the Wanderers were forced out of the league when their arena burnt down, it was just Ottawa, Toronto and the Canadiens left in the NHL. Montréal missed out on a chance at the Cup in 1918, but made it all the way to the Stanley Cup finals in 1919 before the series was cancelled because of the Spanish influenza epidemic that ended up killing two members of the Canadiens organization. (*See* Influenza Epidemic)

From 1919 to 1923, the Canadiens were a decent team, but the Senators were the dominant force in the league at the time. It wasn't until the arrival of a young man named Howarth "Howie" William Morenz from a small Ontario town that things began to turn around for the club. With the new additions of Aurel Joliat and Billy Boucher as well, the Canadiens finally had a team that could challenge the mighty Senators. With Morenz leading the way, the Canadiens beat the Senators in the NHL finals before moving on to the Stanley Cup finals against the West Coast Hockey League's (WCHL) Calgary Tigers, who they easily beat to win the franchise's second Stanley Cup.

The Canadiens made it back into the Stanley Cup finals in 1925 but ultimately lost to the last non-NHL team to win the Cup, the Victoria Cougars. The Canadiens faltered in the following season, but they regained composure and were one of the dominant teams through much of the late 1920s with Howie Morenz leading the way, but playoffs success eluded them. That is, until 1930 and 1931, when Morenz and the Canadiens won back-to-back Stanley Cups. But the remainder of the decade was a dark time for the Canadiens.

Morenz began to show signs of slowing down, not putting up the same numbers or giving his all in the playoffs. While the Canadiens still had the chance to get something good in return, they traded Morenz to the Chicago Blackhawks along with Lorne Chabot and Marty Burke in exchange for Lionel Conacher, Roger Jenkins and LeRoy Goldsworthy. But the trade did nothing for Morenz or for the Canadiens' fortunes on the ice. Hoping to relive some of that early magic, the Canadiens reacquired Morenz for the start of the 1936–37 season, and although he wasn't the Morenz of old, the fans were happy to have him back. The season was going well for the Canadiens until January 28, 1937, when in a game against the Blackhawks, Morenz went into the corner to retrieve the puck and got his skate stuck between the ice and the boards at the same moment Hawks defenceman Earl Seibert delivered a crushing check. Morenz twisted. Only able to bear so much strain, his leg snapped. It was said that the break could be heard throughout the arena.

Morenz lay in hospital for two months while his team battled the rest of the season, ending up in second place overall

M

in the league. Doctors were hopeful he could soon return to his feet, but told him he would never play hockey again. On March 8, 1937, tired of lying in bed, Morenz got out of bed, took one step in his room and fell to the floor. He died suddenly from what doctors deemed to be a pulmonary embolism in the brain. However, faced with the possibility of never playing hockey again, many said Morenz died of a broken heart. The Canadiens ended up faltering in the playoffs that year and fell to the bottom of the league until the arrival of the Canadiens next superstar Maurice Richard in 1943.

Alongside Elmer Lach and Toe Blake, Richard became the goal-scoring star of the decade and beyond. His exploits on the ice made him a hockey legend and, to the people of Québec, an icon. Richard's legend grew with nearly every game and every season. In the 1944 playoffs, Richard led the team with 12 playoff goals as the Canadiens won another Cup. Then, during the 1944–45 season, he accomplished what many in the hockey world deemed impossible at the time—he scored 50 goals in 50 games. Backstopped by goaltender Bill Durnan, the Canadiens won another Cup in 1946, but fell short for the rest of the decade while Toronto and Detroit rose to prominence.

Montréal won another Cup in 1953, and all the while, Maurice Richard remained the centre of attention for the Canadiens, even though the lineup boasted players like Bert Olmstead, Bernie Geoffrion, Doug Harvey, Jean Beliveau and Jacques Plante. Richard became even more of a celebrated figure in Québec and a hated figure outside it when, in March 1955, he was suspended for the remainder of the season and the playoffs after punching out a referee during a game against the Bruins. The suspension by league president

Clarence Campbell was made all the worse because the Canadiens were in a battle for first overall against the Red Wings, and without their star player, fans became upset.

Everything came to a boiling point when the Detroit Red Wings rolled into town for the final game of the season on March 17, 1955, and Clarence Campbell made the decision to attend the game that evening. An angry crowd gathered outside, carrying signs denouncing the NHL president as a tyrant and a hater of French people, and inside the Forum, things got even worse when the Red Wings started winning the game. Throughout the game, fans threw food, newspapers and insults at Campbell, and then all hell broke loose when one fan tossed a smoke bomb, setting off what became known as the Richard Riots. Overnight, enraged Canadiens fans caused over $100,000 in damage. In the playoffs, the Canadiens lost in the Stanley Cup finals to those very same Detroit Red Wings in the seventh game. Many feel that had Richard been allowed to play, the Canadiens might have won the Cup.

Over the next five seasons, though, the Canadiens were the premiere team in the NHL, winning five Stanley Cups in a row. After the fifth Cup, Montréal bid a fond farewell to Maurice Richard, who retired from the game on top.

The 1960s and 1970s brought more Stanley Cups and more legendary players to Montréal. Players like Guy Lafleur, Henri Richard, Yvan Cournoyer, Bobby Rousseau, Jacques Lemaire, Ken Dryden, Steve Shutt, Bob Gainey, Serge Savard, Larry Robinson, Guy Lapointe, and many more, made the Canadiens one of the dominant teams for those two decades. But the 1980s saw the rise of the New York Islanders and the Edmonton Oilers, who both stole the spotlight from the Canadiens. Montréal did manage to win another Cup in 1986 thanks to a young rookie goaltender named Patrick Roy, but the league was expanding with new franchises and the dynasties of old would never again return.

With Roy in nets, the Canadiens won the Cup again in 1993, but since that Cup, the Canadiens moved out of the historic Montréal Forum in 1996 and into the Bell Centre. The team has had a few good seasons in its new home, but it has failed to return to the Stanley Cup finals in the new millennium. From 1995 to 2005, the Canadiens were a team without identity. They went through several coaches and general managers, trying to find the right combination for success, but nothing ever worked. Despite their valiant efforts, the Canadiens never made any serious progress in the playoffs.

There was a brief glimmer of hope at the end of the 2009–10 season when the eighth place–overall Canadiens defeated the first-place Washington Capitals in the first round, and then defeated the Pittsburgh Penguins, thanks to some excellent work on defence by Josh Gorges and Hal Gill, and show-stopping goaltending by Jaroslav Halak. But it was all for naught when the Canadiens met the Philadelphia Flyers in the Eastern final and were eliminated from Stanley Cup contention in five games. Montréal fans are made of hardy stuff, however, and they continue to stick with their team in the blind hope that the Canadiens will one day bring back the years of *Les Glorieux*. Now led by star goaltender Carey Price, the Canadiens hope to build on a young team and take their fans where they last left them in 1993.

Montréal Canadiens Records

Most goals in a season: Steve Shutt (1976–77) and Guy Lafleur (1977–78), 60

Most goals in a season, defenceman: Guy Lapointe, 28 (1974–75)

Most power play goals in a season: Yvan Cournoyer, 20 (1966–67)

Most power play goals in a season, defenceman: Sheldon Souray, 19 (2006–07)

Most assists in a season: Pete Mahovlich, 82 (1974–75)

Most points in a season: Guy Lafleur, 136 (1976–77)

Most points in a season, defenceman: Larry Robinson, 85 (1976–77)

Most points in a season, rookie: Mats Naslund (1982–83) and Kjell Dahlin (1985–86), 71

Most penalty minutes in a season: Chris Nilan, 358 (1984–85)

See Bell Centre; Centre Bell

Montréal Forum: Today on the site of the old Montréal Forum there sits the hollowed-out carcass of what was once the greatest building in the NHL. Instead of Stanley Cup banners and the echoes of the greats of the Canadiens are the latest movie posters and the din of shoppers looking for a sale at the electronics store.

The Forum played host to some of the greatest players in the history of the game and was the home of many Stanley Cup championship teams. It was the historic home for the Montréal Canadiens from 1926 to 1996, but the building had originally been constructed for another team. In 1924, a group of wealthy Montréal businessmen got together and decided to form a new Montréal team called the Maroons. But in order for them to be admitted into the league, they were required to build a new arena to house the team. A site was chosen on the corner of Ste-Catherine and Atwater, and in 159 days, the Montréal Forum was open for business. Although the building was constructed for the Maroons, the Montréal Canadiens ended up playing many "home" games in the Forum as their official residence at the Mount Royal Arena was becoming too small. It was actually the Canadiens who played the first game in the Forum on November 29, 1924, scoring a 7–1 win over the Toronto St. Pats.

In the building's 70 years of existence, the Forum underwent major renovations in 1949 and again in 1968 to accommodate the ever-increasing crowds. The Montréal Maroons eventually moved out of the building in 1938 after folding the franchise, leaving it to the Canadiens. But with a seating capacity of just under 18,000, the Canadiens needed a new arena for a new era. The Canadiens played their last game in the Forum on March 11, 1996, when they beat the Dallas Stars 4–1. Today, the building houses a movie theatre, restaurants and a host of shops.

Montréal Hockey Club: Founded in 1886, the Montréal Hockey Club was the first powerhouse team in hockey. They were the first to win the Stanley Cup in 1893, followed by wins in 1894, 1902 and 1903. When the Stanley Cup became a professionals-only trophy in 1907, the Montréal Hockey Club continued to play on the amateur circuit until 1932, when the team was sold and they became the Montréal Royals.

> *1893 Montréal Hockey Club Stanley Cup–winning Roster:* Billy Barlow, Allan Cameron, Archie A. Hodgson, Alex Irving, Alex Kingan, George Lowe, Tom Paton, Harviland "Harvie" Routh and James A. Stewart.

Montréal Maroons: From 1924 to 1938, Montréal was the home to two NHL teams. Created to appeal to the anglophone community of Montréal, the Maroons were named after the colour of their jerseys. In their first season, the Maroons filled their lineup with a bunch of aging veterans, and their age showed when they finished with a record of 9–19–2, well out of a playoff spot. In the off-season, they added speedy forward Nels Stewart and goaltender Clint Benedict, helping round out the veterans with some scoring talent. The team finished the season second overall and landed their first berth in the playoffs. The Maroons made it all the way into the Stanley Cup finals, where they beat the Victoria Cougars for their first championship win. The Maroons went on to win another Stanley Cup in 1935, led this time by the goaltending of Alex Connell. But the team was on shaky ground.

After bowing out of the playoffs early for the next two seasons and completely missing it in 1938, the Maroons owners asked the league if operations could be suspended for a year while they got their financial house in order. The NHL granted the request, but the team never returned. The money, the competition for fans in Montréal with the Canadiens and the outbreak of World War II kept the club from ever returning. The franchise was dismantled, leaving the Canadiens as the only team in Montréal, and Maroons players were dispersed throughout the league. The owners tried to sell off the franchise in the coming years, but no buyers could be found. The franchise was finally and officially put to bed in 1947.

Montréal Shamrocks: Founded in 1886, the Shamrocks were an amateur hockey club that got their name because the team was made up of residents from the Irish Catholic neighbourhood of Griffintown, in Montréal. Several players from the Shamrocks went on to greatness and induction in the Hockey Hall of Fame, including Jimmy Gardner, Jack Laviolette (first captain coach and general manager of the Montréal Canadiens) and Didier Pitre. They won the Stanley Cup in 1899 and 1900 after finishing first in the Canadian Amateur Hockey League and successfully defended their championship in three challenges in between their Cup wins. The Shamrocks never became a professional team, playing in amateur leagues until around 1914.

Montréal Victorias: One of the first organized hockey clubs ever, the Montréal Victorias played out of the Victoria Skating Rink, the same arena that hosted the first organized hockey game in 1875. While there is no clear date of when the Victorias were founded, it was some time between 1875 and 1881. The team only played games for fun until 1886, when the Amateur Hockey Association of Canada was founded. The team played in this league until 1898 and was one of the most dominant clubs, winning the Stanley Cup in 1895, 1897, 1898 and 1899 before losing the title to the Shamrocks. When the Stanley Cup became a professionals-only trophy, the Victorias remained an amateur club, competing for the Allan Cup, winning the trophy in the first year it was awarded in 1908. The club played in various amateur leagues up until 1939, when it ceased its activities at the outbreak of World War II.

See Allan Cup

Montréal Wanderers: The Montréal Wanderers were founded on December 3, 1903, but had no league to call their own. They had tried to join the Canadian Amateur Hockey League but were rejected, so in response, the Wanderers, along with several other teams, helped create the Federal Amateur Hockey League (FAHL) on December 5, 1903. Right from the start, the Wanderers were one of amateur hockey's top teams as many of the players had previously been part of the successful Montréal Hockey Club. Just a few months after creating the team, the Wanderers challenged the Ottawa Hockey Club for the Stanley Cup on March 2, 1904, resulting in a 5–5 tie. The Wanderers then wanted to move the tie-breaking game to Montréal, but when the Ottawa Hockey Club refused, Montréal forfeited the series in protest.

From 1903 to 1911, the Wanderers and the Ottawa Hockey Club (also known as the Silver Seven) shared the Stanley Cup and developed one of the fiercest rivalries in the sport.

M

Among the Wanderers lineup were future Hall of Fame members Moose Johnson, Lester Patrick, Hod Stuart and Ernie Russell. During that time, the Wanderers won the Cup four times (1906, 1907, 1908, 1910).

The Wanderers later joined the National Hockey Association (NHA), winning the O'Brien Cup in its first year of existence and the team's final Stanley Cup in 1910. However, the team began to falter in the NHA standings as many of its players from the glory days began to retire or changed teams. By the time the NHA folded and the NHL was formed, the Wanderers were not the same club that they once were. Along with the Montréal Canadiens, the Toronto Arenas and the Ottawa Senators, the Wanderers opened the 1917–18 inaugural NHL season, but just four games into it, the Wanderers' home rink, the Montréal Arena, burned down. After the fire, the team tried to survive but ended up folding the club after having played just six games.

See O'Brien Cup

Mount Royal Arena: Home arena of the Montréal Canadiens from 1920 to 1926. The arena held approximately 10,000 fans (including standing room). It was where the Canadiens played their first game on January 10, 1910. The Canadiens moved into the new Montréal Forum in 1926. The arena was converted into an auditorium, where legendary opera singer Enrico Caruso once sang. It was then converted into a commercial building. On February 29, 2000, the structure was destroyed in a fire and now a supermarket fills the space.

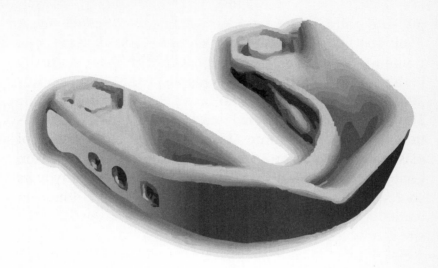

Mouthguard: A protective plastic covering for players' teeth. Some studies have claimed that it also helps in the prevention of concussions.

MTS Center: First opened in 2004, it now the home of the newly returned Winnipeg Jets. The building's naming rights is owned by Manitoba Telecom Services. It is one of the smaller arenas in the NHL, seating just 15,004 fans, but its close quarters makes it a tremendously loud building. Before the arrival of the Jets in 2011, it served as a concert hall and home of the American Hockey League's Manitoba Moose.

Mutual Street Arena: From 1912 to 1931, the arena was the premiere venue in Toronto to see a hockey game. It was the home of the Toronto Tecumsehs, Toronto Blueshirts, Toronto Ontarios and Toronto Shamrocks, all members of the National Hockey Association (NHA) at different periods from 1912 to 1917. The arena had an artificial ice surface, just the third of its kind in Canada, and seated about 7500 spectators. When the NHL was formed, it became home to the Toronto Arenas, the franchise that eventually became known as the Toronto Maple Leafs. The arena was also the site of the first radio broadcast of a hockey game and an NHL game and was where Foster Hewitt made his radio debut. The Toronto Maple Leafs left the building in 1931 to move into Maple Leaf Gardens. After the Leafs were gone, the building remained open as a venue for other sports and entertainment events. It closed its doors on April 30, 1989, and was demolished a few months later. The site is now a city park.

NHA (National Hockey Association): The predecessor league to the NHL, the NHA was founded in 1909 by J. Ambrose O'Brien after the rival Canadian Hockey Association refused to allow his Renfrew Creamery Kings into the league. So O'Brien got together with the owner of the Montréal Wanderers, Cobalt Silver Kings, Ottawa Senators and Montréal Shamrocks and created the National Hockey Association. To bring in the interest of Montréal's French community, O'Brien also created the Montréal Canadiens. O'Brien donated a trophy under his name to be the championship trophy of the NHA. The champions of the NHA would then move onto a Stanley Cup final against other league champions.

The league began in January 1910, and the Montréal Wanderers were the first champions of the NHA and winners of the Stanley Cup. After the first season, the Silver Kings and Shamrocks dropped out of the league and were replaced by the Québec Bulldogs.

The Ottawa Senators won the 1910–11 season. In the off-season, O'Brien made critical changes to the way the game was played by eliminating the rover position and switching from seven- to six-player hockey. It was in that same off-season that the Pacific Coast Hockey Association (PCHA) was created. The PCHA made life difficult for the NHA as it stole many players by offering them more money, but the NHA persisted.

Eventually, in 1917, the league got into a legal battle with one of its owners. Eddie Livingstone had been a pain in the NHA's side since the Toronto Shamrocks joined the league. After several years of illegal trades, not to mention purchasing the Toronto Blueshirts without league permission, the NHA owners and managers got together and decided to suspend the league and create a new one without the involvement of Livingstone. After the 1916–17 NHA season, the league was dissolved, and the remaining teams— the Canadiens, Wanderers and Senators—left to create the National Hockey League (NHL).

NHL (National Hockey League): When the league was founded in 1917, it had just three teams—the Montréal Canadians, Montréal Wanderers and Ottawa Senators. Today, there are 30 teams across North America, with seven in Canada and 23 in the United States. From 1917 to 1926, the NHL shared the rights to the Stanley Cup with the Pacific Coast Hockey Association and the Western Canadian Hockey League. In 1926, after both leagues folded, the NHL became the only league able to win the Cup. The first American team in the NHL was the Boston Bruins, who joined the league in 1924. The Montréal Canadiens have won the most Cups in the NHL with 22 (two while part of the NHA). From its beginnings, the league was run by a president until 1993, when the office of the commissioner was formed and Gary Bettman was installed.

NHL Entry Draft: *See* Entry Draft

NHLPA (National Hockey League Players Association):
The organization in charge of overseeing that the rights
of the players are respected and that the owners do not take
advantage of them. The first NHLPA was formed by Detroit
Red Wing Ted Lindsay and Montréal Canadien Doug Harvey
when the league refused to release pension financial
information to the players who requested it. The owners
broke this first attempt at a union by trading the players
involved or sending them to the minor leagues. The NHLPA
that exists today started in 1967 when players from the
original six teams met and elected Bob Pulford as their
representative and Alan Eagleson as their director. The
NHLPA then took their case to the board of directors of
the NHL and had the owners recognize the union as legiti-
mate. Bob Goodenow sat as director of the NHLPA through
the 1994 and 2005 lockouts. Ted Saskin took over after
Goodenow, only lasting until 2007 after he was removed
for acts of misconduct. Paul Kelly followed, then Donald
Fehr, who currently sits as executive director of the NHLPA.

NJ Devil: Official mascot of the New Jersey Devils that first
appeared in 1993. He is a cartoonish version of the red devil
man wearing a New Jersey Devils uniform.

Nail: To check another player extremely hard. "Oh, he
nailed him into the boards."

Nashville Predators: Joining the NHL in 1997 alongside
fellow expansion clubs Columbus, Atlanta and Minnesota,
the Nashville Predators were the first team to begin playing
in the league for the 1998–99 season. David Poile, former
general manager of the Washington Capitals, was hired as
the team's man in charge of building a team out of nothing.

N

His first step was to hire head coach Barry Trotz. Then came the addition of free agents Jayson More, Rob Valicevic and Mark Mowers, followed by the expansion draft, where they added Greg Johnson and Andrew Brunette and goaltenders Mike Dunham and Tomas Vokoun.

The Predators played their first game on October 10, 1998, posting a 1–0 loss to the Florida Panthers before a sellout crowd at the new Nashville Arena (now called Bridgestone Arena). Their first victory came three nights later against the Carolina Hurricanes, 3–2 on home ice. Andrew Brunette scored the franchise's first goal and the first win went to goaltender Mike Dunham. The season was not much of a success on the ice as the club finished with a record of 28–47–7, but the people of Nashville completely embraced the team, producing six straight sell-outs to end the season.

Cliff Ronning was the Predators top scorer for a number of years, but the club was unable to back him up and the Predators missed out on the playoffs their first five years in the league. Despite the issues, the management stood behind head coach Barry Trotz, knowing that most expansion teams go through a building process. The 2003–04 season saw the Predators turn things around led by David Legwand and the goaltending of Vokoun, who played in 73 games that season. The Predators finished the season with a record of 38–29–11–4 and just managed to squeak into the playoffs. In their first franchise appearance in the playoffs, the Predators had to face the Detroit Red Wings. The Predators put up a good fight against the Wings, managing to win two games, but the Wings took the series in six games.

After the lockout in 2004, the Predators added some offensive depth by getting Paul Kariya from the Colorado

Avalanche. Kariya and Steve Sullivan were the top point getters on the club with 31 goals each, while goaltender Chris Mason stepped up to take some of the pressure off Vokoun. The Preds finished the season with their best record yet at 49–25–8. But despite all the positives, the team was once again eliminated from the hunt for the Cup in the first round, this time by the San Jose Sharks in five games. In the 2006–07 season, the Predators signed centre Jason Arnott and traded Scottie Upshall and Ryan Parent to the Philadelphia Flyers for Peter Forsberg. The added punch upfront led the team to a franchise record 110 points by the end of the season, but playoff success continued to elude them, losing again to the San Jose Sharks in the first round.

After the loss in the playoffs, it was reported that the Predators might be sold and could be set to leave Nashville. CEO of Research In Motion (RIM), makers of Blackberry, Jim Balsillie was rumoured to be interested in buying the team and moving them to Hamilton, but this deal was struck down, and instead the team was sold to a group of local executives and remained in Nashville.

During the off-season, the Predators lost most of their big-salaried players like Forsberg and Kariya, but despite the losses, the team still put together another winning season and once again were booted out in the first round of the playoffs. The 2008–09 season saw the team struggle and miss out on the playoffs for the first time in five years. The 2009–10 Preds added Marcel Goc, Francis Bouillon and Patric Hornqvist to the lineup and returned to their winning ways with the help of new franchise goaltender Pekka Rinne. The emergence of Shea Weber as one of the best defencemen in the league did not hurt the club's fortunes

N

either. Despite a good season, the Predators fell short in the playoffs, losing yet again in the first round, this time to the Chicago Blackhawks.

For the 2010–11 season, Shea Weber was made team captain, and the Preds added Matt Halischuk, Sergei Kostitsyn, Anders Lindback and Blake Geoffrion to the club. They were a younger team and had a new life in their skates. They were helped in the offensive department when forward Mike Fisher joined the club from Ottawa in February. The team finished with a 44–27–11 record and finally achieved some success in the playoffs when they beat the Anaheim Ducks in six games, finally making it to the second round. For the first time since the franchise was inaugurated, Nashville had a sense of excitement that they could be a competitor, but they lost that hope in the second round when the Vancouver Canucks sent them packing in six games.

In the 2011–12 playoffs, the Predators were bolstered by the addition of defenceman Hal Gill and forwards Alexander Radulov and Andrei Kostitsyn and made it past a tough Detroit team in the first round, winning the series in five games, but they came up short against the Phoenix Coyotes, losing in five games. Despite the loss, hope remains for the Predators in the future, and with rabid fan support, the team can only move forward.

Nashville Predators Records

Most goals in a season: Jason Arnott, 33 (2008–09)

Most goals in a season, defenceman: Shea Weber, 23 (2008–09)

Most assists in a season: Paul Kariya, 54 (2005–06)

Nashville Predators Records (continued)

Most points in a season: Paul Kariya, 85 (2005–06)

Most points in a season, defenceman: Kimmo Timonen, 55 (2006–07)

Most points in a season, rookie: Alexander Radulov, 37 (2006–07)

Most penalty minutes in a season: Patrick Cote, 242 (1998–99)

Most wins in a season: Tomas Vokoun, 36 (2005–06)

Most shutouts in a season: Pekka Rinne, 7 (2008–09)

See Bridgestone Arena

Nassau Veterans Memorial Coliseum: Home arena of the New York Islanders. Built in 1972, it is currently the second oldest building in use in the NHL (Madison Square Garden is the oldest, built in 1968). It seats 16,250 for hockey games. The arena is considered obsolete by modern NHL standards, but efforts to replace the arena have been unsuccessful, leaving the future of the Islanders in question.

See New York Islanders

National Hockey League Alumni Association: The NHL alumni association was created in 1999. It provides programs and assistance for all retired NHL players. Their mission statement is:

The National Hockey League Alumni brings together former NHL players to: Support and participate in charitable causes, primarily those youth oriented; Assist former players in their transition to life after hockey; Promote the game of hockey.

305

National Hockey League Officials Association: Created in 1969 out of a need to improve working conditions, salaries and other benefits for all officials in the NHL.

Nationwide Arena: Home arena of the Columbus Blue Jackets. Seats 18,500 for hockey games. Nationwide was the arena in which a young fan named Brittanie Cecil died in 2002 as a result of injuries sustained from a hockey puck flying into the stands and striking her in the head. As a result of this tragedy, protective netting was installed in every arena in the NHL. Cecil's death was the first fan fatality in the NHL's history.

See Columbus Blue Jackets

Natural Hat Trick: When a player scores three goals in a row without any other player on either team scoring during his run. It is a rare occurrence in professional hockey.

Neck Brace: A supportive pad wrapped around the neck of a player that has sustained a neck injury.

Negate the Icing: When the linesman is about to call icing, he raises his arm to signal the infraction. The icing is called off if the goaltender touches the puck or the opposing team touches the puck first, and in doing so, they are said to "negate the icing" and play is allowed to continue.

See Icing the Puck; Wash Out

Net: The goal. The first hockey goals did not have nets and were simply two blocks of whatever material was available (usually rocks), spaced evenly apart to demarcate the area of the goal. During the 1800s, cricket terminology once again found its way into the new game as the "goalposts"

became known as "rickets." As the game evolved, two metal poles took the place of the rocks as goal-line markers. Since it was difficult to decide whether or not a goal had been scored, an umpire was stationed directly behind the goal to call the goals. The goal umpire would stand slightly behind the net dressed in heavy winter attire, and whenever a goal was scored, he would ring a loud brass bell. Depending on the affiliations of the goal judges, not all their decisions could be trusted, so another alternative had to be found to appease all parties.

Fishing nets were first attached to the metal posts in the late 1890s to make the job of the goal judge easier, but it wasn't until 1912 that one innovative goaltending legend invented the modern hockey net. Percy LeSueur had long been a student of the game, and he was always looking for ways to improve it. In 1912, he made a few modifications to the nets used at the time, most notably the addition of a crossbar, giving the hockey net the basic shape that is still used today.

Netminder: A goaltender, the one who "minds the net."

See Goaltender

Neutral Zone: The area between the blue lines. It is designated the neutral zone because it is in neither the offensive nor the defensive zone.

New Jersey Devils: The New Jersey Devils began their life as the Kansas City Scouts, followed by the Colorado Rockies. It took two failed attempts before the franchise finally succeeded in finding a home for itself. Starting out in 1982, the Devils were still not a very good club. They had inherited many of the players and many of the problems from their previous incarnations.

The Devils' first season was a complete disaster. The 1982–83 season saw the team limp out with a paltry 17–49–14 record, just three points above last place in the league (occupied by the Penguins and Whalers). The following season was even more embarrassing. One game in particular beautifully illustrated the gulf between the top-tier teams and the lowly Devils.

On November 19, 1983, Wayne Gretzky and the Edmonton Oilers came to town and completely embarrassed the organization. The Devils put former Oiler Ron Low in net that night, but the players' familiarity with Low did little to keep

Gretzky and company from blasting eight goals into the Devils net before Low was mercilessly pulled and Glenn "Chico" Resch came in as relief. Before the massacre was over, the Oilers had amassed a 13–4 rout. It got even worse when Gretzky commented to reporters after the game: "It got to the point where it wasn't even funny. They're ruining the whole league. They had better stop running a Mickey Mouse operation and put somebody on ice." For the remainder of the season, many Devils fans began to wear Mickey Mouse ears.

Things did not begin to improve for the Devils until later in the decade, with the emergence of young stars like Kirk Muller, John MacLean and Pat Verbeek. By the 1987–88 season, the fans had removed their Mickey Mouse ears and began to wear their jerseys with pride. Kirk Muller finished the season with 94 points, goaltender Sean Burke emerged as a possible franchise netminder and the club finished with enough points to just make it into the postseason for the first time. New Jersey surprised everyone in the league by beating the New York Islanders in the first round and the Washington Capitals in the second to make it into the conference finals against the Bruins. The Devils were quickly proving they were no longer pushovers, and though they lost to the Bruins, it took them seven hard-fought games.

The Devils slipped over the next few years, missing the playoffs one season then exiting early in another. Team president and general manager Lou Lamoriello made a decision that changed the future of his team—and changed how the game of hockey was played in general—when he hired Jacques Lemaire as head coach for the start of the 1993–94 season.

The lineup that season included Scott Niedermayer, Stephane Richer, Bobby Holik, Claude Lemieux, Scott Stevens and Calder Trophy–winning goaltender Martin Brodeur. With Brodeur in net and Niedermayer and Stevens on defence, the Devils finished the season with 106 points and the lowest goals-against in the league. The Devils lost in the conference finals to the New York Rangers, but the following season, Lamoriello managed to keep the same nucleus of players together, and into the strike-shortened 1994–95 season, the Devils once again finished atop league standings. In the playoffs that year, they rolled past the Bruins, Penguins, Flyers and embarrassed the Red Wings in the Stanley Cup final with a series sweep, claiming their first Stanley Cup as a franchise. The success of the team was owing to the skills of the players but also their commitment to the team system installed by Lemaire.

Though the Devils did have quality players, Lemaire knew that his team was not offensively oriented like other clubs. Lemaire therefore developed his infamous "trap" defence system. Keeping two defencemen back on the play and plugging up the neutral zone did not make for exciting hockey, but when up against the Mario Lemieux's and Jagr's of the league, the Devils were at least provided with a chance to compete every night. Soon afterward, other teams in the NHL began adopting the neutral zone trap, and offensive production in the league fell off dramatically. In 1984–85, 16 players finished with over 100 points, but by 1996–97, just two players had over 100 points.

Under Lemaire, the Devils were a top-tier team, but as teams began to adjust their style to counter the Devils, the club's postseason success began to fade. After an early exit from the 1998 playoffs at the hands of the Ottawa Senators, the Devils fired Lemaire and replaced him with Robbie Ftorek. But the new coach had the same problem: regular-season success, but postseason failure. Half way through the 1999–2000 season, Ftorek was replaced by assistant coach Larry Robinson. This proved to be the spark the Devils needed as they finished the regular season strong and dominated in the playoffs, winning the franchise's second Stanley Cup. They almost won again in 2001, making it all the way to the Stanley Cup finals, but it was the Avalanche and Ray Bourque who won the Cup that year. The Devils won another Cup in 2003.

Since that last Cup, the Devils have consistently iced a quality team, but any more postseason success has since eluded them. They have changed coaches several times since 2003, employing Brent Sutter, Claude Julien, Lou Lamoriello (interim), John MacLean, Pat Burns, Jacques Lemaire (twice) and have settled on Peter DeBoer for now. While Martin Brodeur remains in the Devils net today, having broken every conceivable goaltending record, the club's future seems, as always, to depend on the goaltender. This leaves many to wonder about New Jersey's success without Brodeur and whether they can bring back the glory.

New Jersey Devils Records

Most goals in a season: Brian Gionta, 48 (2005–06)

Most goals in a playoff season: Claude Lemieux, 13 (1995)

Most assists in a season: Scott Stevens, 60 (1993–94)

Most points in a season: Patrik Elias, 96 (40 G, 56 A) (2000–01)

Most points in a season, rookie: Scott Gomez, 70 (1999–2000)

New Jersey Devils Records (continued)

Most penalty minutes in a season: Krzysztof Oliwa, 295 (1997–98)

Most wins in a season: Martin Brodeur, 48 (2006–07)

See Prudential Center

New York Americans: Before the New York Rangers entered the NHL, Manhattan had the New York Americans. Founded in 1925 by notorious bootlegger William V. Dwyer, the Americans were mostly players from the former Hamilton Tigers franchise, Dwyer having bought the majority of the team before the start of the 1925–26 season. Among the starting lineup for the club's first game on December 15, 1925, were such talents as Billy Burch and brothers Red and Shorty Green. The Americans played the Montréal Canadiens that night, losing the match 3–1, but the new franchise wasn't the flop that many had predicted, finishing with a respectable 12–20–4 record, out of the playoffs but not last in the league.

Despite their losing record, Manhattanites fell for their new hockey team. Seeing the potential for success, the owners of Madison Square Garden started their own franchise, the Rangers, one year after the Americans joined the league. It was a rivalry that quickly built up to the level of Montréal versus Toronto, but while the Rangers got better and eventually won a few Stanley Cups, the Americans struggled each season.

Even though they had legendary players like Roy Worters, Nels Stewart and Sweeney Schriner in their lineup over the years, the Americans missed out on the playoffs most years, only making it out of the opening round of the playoffs twice. When World War II broke out, many of the Americans' most talented players (who were actually Canadian) left to join the military, leaving the club worse off than before. The franchise moved to Brooklyn for the 1941–42 season in an effort to save its hide, but after missing the playoffs yet again, the Americans were forced to close their doors.

New York Islanders: Before the start of the 1972–73 hockey season, the World Hockey Association (WHA) wanted to have a hockey team in the brand-new Nassau Veterans Memorial Coliseum, but officials in the local community did not consider the WHA a real professional league with a chance of lasting for decades and sought to block a WHA franchise. The only way to do so was to get an NHL franchise to take the WHA's potential place. Lawyer and passionate sports fan William Shea, who had already helped bring the New York Mets to Major League Baseball (MLB), petitioned the NHL for a new team on Long Island, and despite the protests from the Rangers, NHL president Clarence Campbell agreed to allow a new franchise into the league.

The team was christened the New York Islanders, and Bill Torrey was given the job of constructing a franchise out of nothing. Torrey's strategy was simple: build a team for the future. At the 1972 NHL Amateur Draft, Torrey selected Billy Harris and signed goaltender Billy Smith. Torrey knew that the first few seasons would not be successful, and when the 1972–73 season mercifully came to a close, the Islanders had won just 12 games and lost 60. But the last-place team gets to pick first at the draft, and the Islanders added Denis Potvin to the club, and in the off-season, Torrey added head coach Al Arbour.

With Arbour on board and a growing roster of young talented players, the Islanders made their first appearance in the playoffs in 1974–75 and made an immediate impression, beating the rival Rangers in the opening round and the Pittsburgh Penguins in the quarterfinals to make it all the way to the semifinals before being eliminated by the eventual champion Philadelphia Flyers. The Islanders again made it to the semifinals in 1975–76, but were stopped short by the eventual Cup champion Montréal Canadiens. The Islanders used these years to gain experience and let their young players develop.

By 1978–79, the Islanders were the top team in the regular season, and Bryan Trottier, Mike Bossy, Denis Potvin and Clark Gilles were among the top scorers in the league. The Islanders finally broke through in the playoffs in 1979–80, making it to the Stanley Cup finals against the Flyers and winning the series in six games.

While Gretzky and the Oilers were tearing up the regular-season stats, the Islanders had the experience and talent to win four straight championship titles. However, like the Islanders did in the 1970s, accumulating young talent and gaining experience, the Edmonton Oilers were busy doing the same. After losing the Stanley Cup to the Islanders in 1983, the Oilers returned to the playoffs the next year, determined to teach the now aging lineup of the Islanders a lesson, and as fate would have it, the Islanders and Oilers met up in the finals for the 1984 championship. The speedy, high-scoring Oilers had their revenge, beating the Islanders in five games.

The Islanders continued to be a top-tier team in the 1980s, replacing aging players such as Potvin and Trottier with new stars like Pat Lafontaine. But the franchise was no longer the same as it was in the early part of the decade. By the 1990–91 season, the Islanders were last in their division and out of the playoffs for just the second time since 1974.

The Islanders changed up the look of the team after the 1990–91 playoffs, adding Pierre Turgeon, Benoit Hogue, Steve Thomas and Ray Ferraro. By the 1992–93 season, the Islanders were once again a team that could potentially challenge in the postseason. The Islanders won their opening round against the Washington Capitals and scored a miracle win over the Penguins in a seventh-game overtime thriller, with the heroic goal coming from David Volek. But the two previous series had left the Islanders battered and bruised. Pierre Turgeon was out of the lineup because of a dirty hit by Capitals Dale Hunter in the opening round. The Islanders conference finals opponents, the Montréal Canadiens, had a relatively easy time winning the series in five games. The defeat marked the long downward spiral of the franchise.

The club had a few good years in between, with the rise of Alexei Yashin, but that ended badly for both parties. The Islanders gave up towering defenceman Zdeno Chara and the Islanders second overall pick (which the Senators used to select Jason Spezza) while only Yashin came back to New York. Then general manager Mike Milbury tried his best to build a contending team, but the experiment proved a failure by the 2003–04 season. The Islanders ended the year with an early exit from the playoffs at the hands of the Tampa Bay Lightning.

The owners of the Islanders, Charles Wang and Sanjay Kumar, tried giving their general managers the green light to build and spend money as they saw fit to make a successful franchise. But Mike Milbury and then GM Garth Snow could not find a winning combination, and after the 2004 lockout season, the Islanders had missed the playoffs six out of seven times. There are a few bright spots in the team's future, with the recent addition of Jon Tavares and Matt Moulson. However, the club may not be long for the league as there have been rumblings for years that the team was losing money and would soon move to another city. The Islanders have been losing fans with each passing season, and if the team cannot move to another building to replace the aging Nassau Coliseum, the future of the young players might be with a different team.

New York Islanders Records

Most goals in a season: Mike Bossy, 69 (1978–79)

Most assists in a season: Bryan Trottier, 87 (1978–79)

Most points in a season: Mike Bossy, 147 (1981–82)

Most points in a season, defenceman: Denis Potvin, 101 (1978–79)

Most points in a season, rookie: Bryan Trottier, 95 (1975–76)

Most penalty minutes in a season: Brian Curran, 356 (1986–87)

Most wins in a season: Rick DiPietro (2006–07), Chris Osgood (2001–02) and Billy Smith (1981–82), 32

See Nassau Veterans Memorial Coliseum

New York Rangers: The Rangers were founded in 1926 by the president of Madison Square Garden, George "Tex" Rickard, to compete with the New York Americans. Rickard had seen the Americans draw a good crowd and knew that he could use his arena for profit by adding a new team to the NHL. While the Americans struggled to build a decent franchise, the Rangers had immediate success in the league. Assembled by Conn Smythe, the Rangers had talent like Bill Cook, Frank Boucher and goaltender Lorne Chabot. Smythe, though, left the club after a falling-out with management, and Lester Patrick replaced him as manager and head coach. Patrick was able to take the team to first place in the American Division and into the playoffs in their first season in the league.

Just one year later, Patrick led his club to another strong regular-season finish and the franchise's first Stanley Cup victory over the Montréal Maroons. In the finals, Patrick was forced to play in goal for his team when Chabot was taken out with an injury. With no back-up goaltender, Patrick played the rest of the game, allowing only one goal in a 2–1 overtime win. The Rangers almost won a second straight Cup in the 1929 Stanley Cup finals, but they were edged out by the Boston Bruins. The Rangers returned to the Stanley Cup finals in 1933, with Cecil Dillion and Bill Cook leading the Rangers to another Stanley Cup with a win over the Toronto Maple Leafs.

During the late 1930s, the Rangers had some success in the regular season but were inconsistent in the playoffs. In 1939–40, the team roared back into prominence with forwards Bryan Hextall and Neil Colville and were back-stopped by Vezina Trophy–winning goaltender Dave Kerr. The Rangers beat out the Maple Leafs in the Stanley Cup final to win their third Stanley Cup since joining the NHL.

However, during the Rangers celebration, it was said that team president Colonel John Reed Kilpatrick decided it was

N

317

the perfect time to commemorate the fully paid mortgage on Madison Square Garden by setting fire to the deed in the bowl of the Lord Stanley's Cup. It was also rumoured that during their inebriated celebration, several players thought the Cup would serve as the perfect urinal. In the eyes of many, these two events began the Rangers' Cup curse. For the next 54 years, the Rangers never won another Stanley Cup.

After their 1940 Cup win, the Rangers spent the majority of the 1940s and '50s at the bottom of the league despite having talented players like Andy Bathgate, Chuck Rayner, Red Sullivan and Gump Worsley. The 1960s did not start out any better, with the Broadway Blueshirts dwelling at the bottom of the league. But the late 1960s saw the Rangers add players Phil Goyette, Jean Ratelle and Rod Gilbert. By the early 1970s, the Rangers were among the top teams in the league and finally had their fans believing in them again. The Rangers even made it into the Stanley Cup finals in 1972, but they were beaten by Bobby Orr and the Boston Bruins. However, the Rangers rise to the top did not last long as their good players retired or were traded, and the team ended up last in their division for most of the remainder of the decade.

The 1979 playoffs was a near-miracle run for the Rangers as aging superstar Phil Esposito led the Rangers in goals while goaltender John Davidson stood on his head against better teams to put his club into the Stanley Cup finals against the Montréal Canadiens. But the Rangers were cursed and once again lost to the Canadiens in five games. Through the 1980s, the Rangers were a solid club, but they played second fiddle to their rivals the New York Islanders.

The club remained competitive through the 1980s and into the '90s but lacked a certain spark. The Rangers general manager, former Oilers mastermind Glen Sather, began to reshape the team by adding many former Oilers alumni such as Adam Graves, Craig MacTavish, Esa Tikkanen and Mark Messier. When added to defensive phenomenon Brian Leetch and goaltender Mike Richter, the Rangers moved to the top of the league. By 1993–94, the Rangers had finished on top of the league standings and went into the playoffs with their best hope for success in years. After easily beating the Islanders in the opening round, the Rangers blew by the Capitals and squeaked past the New Jersey Devils with a heroic game-seven overtime goal by Stephane Matteau. Then it was on to the finals against the Canucks, where more heroic overtime wins and goals by Mark Messier spurred the team to their first victory in 54 years, breaking the curse.

N

After losing many of their Stanley Cup–winning players to retirement or free agency, the Rangers attempted to buy their way back to the championship by signing aging players to lucrative contracts, but the experiment failed, and the Rangers found themselves once again falling back to the bottom of the division despite having Wayne Gretzky and Jaromir Jagr. From 1997 to 2004, the Rangers missed out on the playoffs and looked to be once again sinking into their old losing ways.

The 2004 lockout provided the Rangers a chance to assess their franchise, and general manager Sather gave into the rebuilding process, trading off veterans for draft picks and young talent. No one expected the Rangers to bounce back once the NHL returned, but the club, bolstered by young goaltender Henrik Lundqvist, finished the season with a good record and a spot in the playoffs. Unfortunately, the Rangers were taken out in the first round by the Devils. Since the lockout, the Rangers have slowly been rebuilding their club. With all their young talent, the solid leadership of captain Ryan Callahan and the goaltending of Lundqvist, the Rangers look like a team that could win the Cup once again.

New York Rangers Records

Most goals in a season: Jaromir Jagr, 54 (2005–06)

Most goals by a rookie in a season: Tony Granato, 36 (1988–89)

Most assists in a season: Brain Leetch, 80 (1991–92)

Most points in a season: Jaromir Jagr, 123 (2005–06)

Most points by a defenceman: Brian Leetch, 102 (1991–92)

Most wins by a goaltender: Mike Richter, 42 (1993–94)

See Madison Square Garden

Newcomer: Another word for a rookie.

Nickname: Most players on hockey teams or in the NHL are given nicknames. These are either an alteration of their names or something based on their personality, looks or style of play.

Non-contact Hockey: Hockey where bodychecking is not allowed. Found in the youth and recreational leagues.

Norris Division: Division named in honour of James E. Norris. Lasted from 1974 to 1993. Originally part of the Prince of Wales Conference but was moved in 1981 to the Campbell Conference. The Norris Division underwent many fluctuations over those 19 years but has always included the Detroit Red Wings, Chicago Blackhawks, Toronto Maple Leafs and St. Louis Blues. Other teams have been the Winnipeg Jets, Minnesota North Stars and Tampa Bay Lightning.

See Central Division

Norris Trophy: *See* James Norris Memorial Trophy

Northeast Division: Formed in 1993 as part of the Eastern Conference, its predecessor was the Adams Division. The current teams in the Northeast are the Boston Bruins, Buffalo Sabres, Montréal Canadiens, Ottawa Senators and Toronto Maple Leafs.

See Adams Division

N

Northwest Division: Formed in 1998 to accommodate the arrival of new franchises around the league. Current teams are the Vancouver Canucks, Calgary Flames, Colorado Avalanche, Minnesota Wild and Edmonton Oilers.

See Smythe Division

Northlands Coliseum: Former name of the home of the Edmonton Oilers.

See Rexall Place

Nosebleeds: Seats in the upper portion of the arena, at a high-enough altitude to induce nosebleeds.

See Gallery Gods

Nosedive: When a team is leading in the standings or in a game and then begins a long losing streak, it is said that they are in a "nosedive." The term comes from aviation, when an airplane falls out of the sky nose first.

Number-one Goaltender: The goaltender who gets to play in the majority of the team's games during the regular season. Considered to be the better goaltender than the back-up goaltender.

See Back-up Goaltender

OHL (Ontario Hockey League): One of the three major junior hockey leagues—along with the QMJHL and WHL—that make up the Canadian Hockey League (CHL) for players aged 15–20. The OHL was created in 1974 out of the Major Junior A Tier I division of the Ontario Hockey Association. There are currently 20 teams in the OHL, with three teams based in the United States. The champion of the OHL receives the J. Ross Robertson Cup, and they also earn the right to play for the Memorial Cup against the other members of the CHL. The Memorial Cup has been won 14 times by teams in the OHL. Notable players to have come out of the OHL are Wayne Gretzky, Bobby Smith and Bobby Orr.

See QMJHL; WHL

Oakland Seals (also California Golden Seals): With a desire to expand into untapped markets, the NHL granted a franchise to the city of Oakland. Originally, the team was named the California Golden Seals in an attempt to appeal to wider audience than just the city of Oakland, but later they changed the name to the Oakland Seals during their first season in 1967–68.

A hockey franchise in southern California was a risk, and in the first year, the Seals were not popular. Ticket sales were slow, making the games sparsely populated. Coach and general manager Bert Olmstead tried to put together a competitive team, but they finished the 1967–68 season with just 15 wins. After the first disastrous season, a group out of Vancouver tried to purchase and relocate the club, but the NHL stopped the deal. The Seals' second season was a little better; they made the playoffs in 1969 but lost to the Los Angeles Kings in the first round. The team made the playoffs once more in 1970 but were again booted out in the first round.

In order to open up the team to a wider audience and attract more fans, owner Charles Finley changed the name of the club back to the California Golden Seals. Unfortunately, the name change did not help the team on the ice. Despite having Dennis Maruk and goaltender Gilles Meloche, the team did not make the playoffs from 1970 to 1976. After years of lacklustre fan support and no playoffs to spark the team, the club moved to Cleveland in 1976 where they became the Barons and then merged with the Minnesota North Stars in 1978.

See Cleveland Barons; Minnesota North Stars

O'Brien Cup: Established in 1910 as the championship trophy of the National Hockey Association (NHA), the trophy was named in honour of J. Ambrose O'Brien, founding member of the NHA and the Montréal Canadiens. When the NHA suspended its operations in 1917, the Cup was held by the Montréal Canadiens until 1921, when a decision was made to award the Cup annually to the champions of the NHL, as in those days, until 1927, the Stanley Cup championship was decided between the champions of the NHL, the PCHA and the WCHL.

After 1927, the Stanley Cup became the sole property of the NHL teams, so the O'Brien Cup was then awarded to the winner of the Canadian division. In 1927, the NHL had altered its divisions because of the influx of U.S. teams, so the league created the Canadian and American Divisions.

At the end of the 1937–38 NHL season, several teams had folded, requiring the league to move back to a single division, so from that point the O'Brien Cup was then awarded to the Stanley Cup runner-up. At the end of the 1950 play-offs, the league retired the O'Brien Cup, and the original now sits in the Hockey Hall of Fame. The Montréal Wanderers were the first recipients of the O'Brien Cup in 1910, and the New York Rangers were the final winners in 1950.

Obscene Language: Any sort of abusive language directed at another player or at the on-ice officials. The offending player can receive a two-minute penalty for unsportsman-like conduct or, depending on the severity, be suspended.

O

Odd-man Rush: A situation where a team enters the attacking zone and outnumbers their defending opponents. For example, an odd-man rush would be a three-player rush on two defenders, a two-on-one or a three-on-one.

Offence: One team's ability to generate goals or scoring chances against the other team's goaltender or defence.

Offender: Either the player who commits a penalty, or the player who makes an error leading to an important play by the other team.

Offensive Defenceman: A defenceman who can move the puck up the ice and join the forwards in a push into the offensive zone. The greatest offensive defenceman of all time was Bobby Orr. He set the standard for all future offensive-minded defencemen, leading the NHL in scoring at the end of the 1969–70 season (the only defenceman ever to do so) and establishing a record of 139 points in the 1970–71 season. Only Edmonton Oilers defenceman Paul Coffey came close to Bobby Orr's numbers, scoring 138 points in 1985–86.

See Stay-at-home Defenceman

Office: The area behind the net. The term was popularized by the play of Wayne Gretzky. As a player, Wayne Gretzky spent most of his time in the offensive zone behind the opposing team's net because it gave him protection from the defencemen and offered a good vantage point from which to survey the ice. He spent so much of his ice time behind the net racking up assists that the area behind the net became known as his office.

"I started when I was in Junior B," said Gretzky in Andrew Podniek's book *The Great One*. "I was too small—5-foot-5, 110 pounds—to stay in front of the goal, so Gene Popeil, my coach, told me to stake out some space for myself behind it and stay off to one side." If one defenceman was sent in after Gretzky, he could either pass the puck to a teammate in front or quickly move to the other side of the office and keep everybody guessing as to what his next move might be. Few other players in NHL history used the office as effectively as the Great One.

Official: A person who regulates the game guided by league rules from an on-ice position.

See Linesman; Referee

Off-ice Officials: Also known as minor officials. These officials are not positioned on the ice but play an important role in assisting the referees and linesmen. They include the official scorer, game timekeeper, penalty timekeeper and goal judges. In the era of video replay, the off-ice officials have become almost as important as the ones on the ice.

Offsetting Penalties: Any combination of minor or major penalties between two teams where in the end neither team is left with a power play.

Offside: The offside defines the illegal position of the player and the puck on the ice. It is used to keep one team from gaining an advantage over the other team. An offside occurs when a player or players cross the opposing team's blue line ahead of the puck. A player's stick can cross the line ahead of the puck, even one skate, but if the player's entire body crosses the blue line, then the linesman will call the offside and set up for a faceoff. Prior to 2004, an offside also occurred when a player in his own defensive zone passed the puck to a teammate who had crossed the centre red line—commonly called a two-line pass—but in order to promote a more offensive game, the NHL removed the red line from the offside equation after the 2004–05 lockout season.

Old-timer: A player who has been in a league for a long time, or a former professional who has retired.

Olympia: Home of the Detroit Red Wings from 1927 to 1979. Built specifically to house the Detroit franchise, the Detroit Cougars (as they were then called) played their first game on November 22, 1927, in a 2–1 loss to the Ottawa Senators. The Olympia was one of the larger arenas in the

NHL when it was first constructed, seating 15,000 spectators. It was also the home of the NBA's Detroit Pistons from 1957 to 1961. The Red Wings played their final game at the Olympia on December 15, 1979, ending in a 4–4 tie against the Québec Nordiques. The building was demolished in 1987.

See Joe Louis Arena

Olympic Break: Every four years, the NHL schedule pauses to allow some of its players to participate in the Winter Olympics. This trend started in 1998 (previously only amateurs could play), but for the 2014 Winter Games in Sochi, Russia, the NHL has not yet decided whether the players will be allowed back due to the distraction it causes during the course of the Olympic year.

Onside: A player is onside if he does not cross over the opposing team's blue line ahead of the puck. The linesman will usually signal a close onside call by waving his arms out to the side, called a "wash out," indicating to the players that the play was not offside.

See Wash Out

One-timer: An effective way of getting the puck into the net. A one-timer occurs when a player passes the puck to an open teammate, and the teammate takes a shot immediately without stopping the puck. A one-timer can be used anytime during the game but is most often used on the power play. Defencemen score a lot of goals in this manner.

See Slapshot

Open Wing: A part of the ice where a player expects his teammate to be, but the teammate has either neglected his duties or been caught out of position and cannot receive the pass.

Opposite Wing: When, for example, a right winger finds himself caught on the left wing, he is said to be on the opposite wing.

Original Six: Refers to the six teams in the period of NHL history from 1942 to 1967: Montréal Canadiens, Toronto Maple Leafs, Boston Bruins, New York Rangers, Detroit Red Wings and Chicago Blackhawks.

Ottawa Civic Centre: Constructed in 1967, the arena serves as the home of the OHL's Ottawa 67s. It was also the home of the Ottawa Senators from 1992 to 1995, but seating

just 10,000 fans for a game, the venue was not large enough. The Senators moved out for the start of the 1995–96 NHL season into what is now called Scotiabank Place.

See Scotiabank Place

Ottawa Senators: One of the oldest hockey franchises in the history of the game. Just a few years after students at McGill University played the first organized game of hockey in 1875, hockey had spread to other cities, and one of the first teams to form was the Ottawa Hockey Club, later dubbed the Ottawa Senators. It all began after three friends—Halder Kirby, Jack Kerr and Frank Jenkins—witnessed teams from Montréal and Québec City competing at the 1883 Montréal Winter Carnival. The trio decided that they could match the speed and skill of the Québec players, and so returned home to form the Ottawa HC.

From 1883 to 1886, the team was not affiliated with any league and mostly played "friendly" games against other teams in Ottawa and the surrounding area. The big contests were at the winter carnivals, but as more and more skilled teams began to form, the game required a structure. So in 1886, Ottawa, along with the Montréal Victorias, McGill College Club, Montréal Hockey Club and Montréal Crystals, started the Amateur Hockey Association of Canada (AHAC).

After just one season in the AHAC, the Ottawa Hockey Club was forced to shut down when its home arena, the Royal Rink, was converted into a roller-skating arena. The team did not resume action until 1891, when the Rideau Skating Rink was opened. During that time, the club helped to found two new leagues in order to raise the money needed to travel to the rival clubs of the AHAC. The two new leagues

O

331

were the Ottawa City Hockey League and the Ontario Hockey Association. The Ottawa HC dominated the clubs in Ontario and achieved its first taste of success in the AHAC by winning the championship title in 1892.

But that season, the AHAC final championship title was challenged by the runner-up. The Montréal Hockey Club had only won a single game during the season, but because they were the runner-up, they earned the right to challenge the Ottawa HC in a final playoff game to decide the winner. Montréal ended up winning that game, and Ottawa lost the championship title.

The defeat was significant because the Canadian Governor General Lord Stanley of Preston thought the decision to award the championship to Montréal in such a manner was unfair, and as a result, he offered up a solution. That solution was the Dominion Cup Challenge Cup, or the Stanley Cup, created in 1893. The Montréal Hockey Club was awarded the Stanley Cup in the first year as they were the champions of the AHAC, but on March 22, 1894, the first-ever Stanley Cup series was played between Ottawa and the Montréal Hockey Club. Ottawa lost its bid for the Stanley Cup that year, but the team soon became one of the best in all amateur hockey in Canada.

From 1893 to 1900, Montréal teams owned the Stanley Cup, and Ottawa spent that time adding some of the greatest legends in the game to their roster. Players like Harvey Pulford, Rat Westwick, Bill and Dave Gilmore and the greatest of all, "One-Eyed" Frank McGee. McGee got the nickname "One-Eyed" because he could see out of only one eye, having lost his vision during a hockey game. Joining the Ottawa

Hockey Club in 1903, McGee was the youngest and most dominant player on the team, leading the club to three straight Stanley Cup–winning seasons. In his first season with Ottawa, McGee scored 14 goals in just six games. In the Stanley Cup championship series against the Montréal Victorias, McGee was again the hero, scoring three goals in the final game of the total-goals series to give the nation's capital its first Stanley Cup. After the game as the team celebrated their win, the club manager showed up and gave each player a shiny silver nugget as a token of his appreciation. As word of the gesture hit the news media, they dubbed the team the "Silver Seven" and the name stuck.

From 1903 to 1906, the Silver Seven, led by McGee, played in 13 Stanley Cup challenges and only lost two (subsequently winning the Cup back a few weeks later from the team that beat them). The height of the team's exploits came in 1905 when a ragtag bunch of players from Dawson City, Yukon, challenged them for the Cup. They played two games to decide the winner of the Cup. Ottawa won the first game 9–2 and the second game by a monstrous score of 23–2. Frank McGee made himself a hockey legend that day by scoring 14 goals in that one game, eight of which were scored consecutively.

The Silver Seven lost a little lustre in 1906 when McGee left the team and retired after a career of just 45 games in which he scored 135 goals. McGee's last game was a loss to the Montréal Wanderers in 1906 in a Stanley Cup challenge. Many of the players who brought success to the club during the Silver Seven days left the team or retired. In 1908, the team officially changed its name to the Ottawa Senators.

Up until the creation of the NHL in 1917, the Ottawa Senators maintained their high level of play and won two more Stanley Cups titles in 1910 and 1911, with players like Percy LeSueur, Clint Benedict, Jack Darragh, Fred "Cyclone" Taylor and Harry Broadbent. When the NHL was formed, the Senators were there with alongside the Montréal Canadiens, Toronto Arenas and Montréal Wanderers. Although their first two years in the NHL were rather forgettable, by 1919 the Senators were the most dominant team in the league, winning four Stanley Cups from 1920 to 1927. Cy Denneny, Frank Nighbor, Hooley Smith and Alex Connell made the Senators into one of the best teams in the league. After 1927, many of the players who had kept the Senators at the top of the league went into retirement, and the fortunes of the team went along with them.

By the end of the 1930–31 season, the Senators were at the bottom of the league and were struggling to stay afloat. The entire NHL was struggling because of the depression, but the Senators' on-ice product was not helping to get paying fans into the seats. In order to try to save the franchise from extinction, the Senators made the tough decision to suspend operations for one season, in the hopes that the world markets would recover and the team could be brought back.

The Senators returned to action at the start of the 1932–33 season, hoping to turn their fortunes around. But, if anything, things were worse, and the Sens finished the year last in the league. The Sens lasted one more year in the league before playing their final game on March 15, 1934, a 3–2 loss to the New York Americans. The rights to the Senators' franchise were sold to St. Louis, where they became known as the Eagles. But hockey failed to catch on there as well and the franchise folded in 1935.

Senators Return

After 50 years, nine Stanley Cups and countless hockey legends who were destined for the Hockey Hall of Fame, the Ottawa Hockey Club/Silver Seven/Senators team had certainly left its mark on professional hockey. The city of Ottawa remained a hockey hub even after the Senators departed in 1935, but fans went without a professional hockey team for more than 50 years until Ottawa business-man and hockey aficionado Bruce Firestone, along with friends Randy Sexton and Cyril Leeder, revived the idea of bringing an NHL team back to Canada's capital.

It took a lot of work and financing, but the new-age Ottawa Senators returned to NHL action for the 1992–93 season. The first few years were tough going for the franchise, but loyal hockey fans in the capital stuck by their team, and the Senators slowly began to climb out of the league basement. Young players such as Daniel Alfredsson, Marian Hossa and Jason Spezza marked the beginning of a new era for the franchise. The team even had some success in the regular season between 1996 and 2004 but always seemed to fall apart in the playoffs. It wasn't until 2007 that the Senators finally made it back into the Stanley Cup finals—for the first time since 1927. Unfortunately, they met up with a determined Anaheim Ducks squad and the superb goal-tending of Jean-Sebastien Giguere.

From that loss in the finals to the present day, the Senators have struggled to find an identity, going through several goaltenders and key forwards in search of a chemistry that works. Senators fans would love the team to unearth that magic before Daniel Alfredsson retires as he has become one of the most popular members of the team.

Ottawa Senators Records

Most goals in a season: Dany Heatley, 50 (2006–07; 2005–06)

Most assists in a season: Jason Spezza, 71 (2005–06)

Most points in a season: Dany Heatley, 105 (2006–07)

Most points in a season, defenceman: Erik Karlsson 78 (2011–12)

Most wins in a season: Patrick Lalime, 39 (2002–03)

Most shutouts in a season: Patrick Lalime, 8 (2002–03)

See Scotiabank Place

Outlet Pass: A pass from behind the blue line to a streaking forward heading through the neutral zone.

Overtime: During the regular season, if two teams fail to break a tie after three periods of play, they enter into a five-minute overtime period after which, if the game is still tied, they go into a shootout. In the playoffs, the overtime periods last 20 minutes and continue until one team scores and wins the game.

See Shootout

P

PCHA (Pacific Coast Hockey Association): After playing hockey for many years in Montréal, Lester and Frank Patrick moved to British Columbia to work for their father's lumber business. After their father sold the business in 1910, the brothers pursued careers in their true passion: hockey. In January 1911, the Patrick brothers started a new professional hockey league on the West Coast called the Pacific Coast Hockey Association. Teams were designated, arenas were built, players were lured away from the East Coast leagues, and on January 3, 1912, the PCHA started with just three teams, the New Westminster Royals, Vancouver Millionaires and Victoria Senators. The league never exceeded four teams in one season. The Vancouver Millionaires, Victoria Cougars and Seattle Metropolitans were the only teams from the PCHA to win the Stanley Cup. (*See* Challenge Cup)

Over its relatively short history, the PCHA introduced many innovations and rule changes to hockey that transformed the way the overall game was played. The PCHA was the first league to use blue lines and a goal crease. They introduced forward passing, numbers on players' sweaters, the first penalty shots and a playoff system to determine a champion. They were also the first league to allow goaltenders to fall to the ice to make a save. In 1924, the Seattle

Metropolitans folded their operations, and with just two teams in the PCHA, the league decided to call it quits while the Vancouver and Victoria's teams were rolled into the Western Hockey League (WHL).

PIM (Penalties in Minutes): Designation used for marking penalty statistics.

PK: *See* Penalty Kill

PP: *See* Power Play

Pacific Coliseum: Home of the Vancouver Canucks from 1970 to 1995. Built in 1968, the Coliseum sat 16,281 spectators for hockey games. The arena hosted the first home game of the Vancouver Canucks on October 9, 1970, when the Los Angeles Kings defeated the Canucks by a score of 3–1. The Coliseum's final game was also a loss. On May 27, 1995, the Canucks played the Chicago Blackhawks and were eliminated from the playoffs by a 4–3 loss. During the 2010 Winter Olympics, the venue was used to host the figure skating and short track speed skating events.

See Rogers Arena

Pacific Division: One of the three divisions, along with the Central Division and Northwest Division, that makes up the Western Conference. It was formed in 1993 after the NHL switched to the regional divisions. Currently, the Anaheim Ducks, Dallas Stars, Los Angeles Kings, Phoenix Coyotes and San Jose Sharks make up the Pacific Division.

Pad Save: When a goaltender makes a save using his goalie pads.

Paddle Down: When the goaltender lays the widest part of his stick along the ice, usually when an opponent is coming out from the corner or from behind the net. With the goaltender committed to protecting the lower half of the net, the shooter can lift the puck into the upper part of the goal, but because the paddle-down technique is only used when the shooter is in close, it is often difficult to get the puck over the goalie.

Paint: The blue-coloured goal crease area.

Painted Mask: When Jacques Plante first wore his mask during the 1959–60 season for the Montréal Canadiens, it was a simple white fibreglass protector for his face and nothing more. It wasn't until the 1968–69 season that one goaltender put a design on his mask.

Before joining the professional ranks, Gerry Cheevers never wore a hockey mask, but once he joined the Boston Bruins, he opted for a plain white mask. Not satisfied with following the rest of the league, Cheevers tried something different. He had come to love his mask for the countless times it

P

protected him from injury, and to show the world just how many injuries it saved him from, every time he got hit in the face with the puck, he would paint stitches to indicate where the puck would have left a scar. Today, goaltender's masks are considered works of art, with a myriad of designs and colours to choose from.

See Goalie Mask

Partial Breakaway: When a player breaks into the offensive zone with a direct path to the goaltender but is closely trailed by an opponent.

Patrick Division: Formed in 1974 when the NHL realigned to accommodate the arrival of new teams. The Patrick Division was originally part of the Clarence Campbell Conference, but it was moved to the Prince of Wales Conference in 1981. The Patrick Division existed until 1993 when the league was realigned again, this time in favour of geographical designations for the divisions. This division was named in honour of the Patrick brothers, Lester and Frank, for their contributions to hockey. Before the division was altered in 1993, the New Jersey Devils, New York Islanders, New York Rangers, Philadelphia Flyers, Pittsburgh Penguins and Washington Capitals made up the division.

See Atlantic Division; Southeast Division

Pee-wee: Division of hockey for kids aged 11–12.

Penalty: A punishment for breaking the rules of the game. Originally, a single referee was responsible for handing out all penalties in the game, but now two referees are on the ice in NHL games. In some cases, the linesmen are also allowed to hand out penalties. Penalized players are put in the penalty box. The first codified penalties in hockey history was included in the "Montréal Rules," one of the first sets of published hockey rules. The penalties noted were: charging from behind, tripping, collaring, kicking or shinning the ball, and when an infraction occurred, the play was stopped and a faceoff would take place. It wasn't until around 1904 that players were removed from the ice for an infraction against the rules.

The types of penalties vary but are broken down by severity. A minor penalty is two minutes in length, whereas a major penalty is five minutes. A misconduct penalty results a player being removed from the game for 10 minutes. A player who receives a game misconduct penalty is ejected from the game and sent to the dressing room. A match penalty is when a player is banished from the game for purposely trying to injure another player. A penalty shot is awarded when one player trips or hooks another player on a breakaway or when a player covers the puck with his hand in the goal crease.

P

> *See* Bench Minor; Game Misconduct; Gross Misconduct; Minor Penalty; Major Penalty; Match Penalty

Penalty Box: Also called the "sin bin." The area directly off the ice where players serve out their penalty minutes.

Penalty Clock: The clock used to count down a player's penalty time.

Penalty Kill (PK): When one team goes on the power play, the other team must kill the penalty. The players on the PK have the difficult job of protecting their defensive zone while missing one or two players.

Penalty Shot: A free shot awarded to a player who has a clear path toward the goal but is pulled down from behind or hooked, or if a stick is thrown. Often called the "most exciting play in hockey," a penalty shot does not happen often, but when it does, it is certain to get the crowd on its feet. When a penalty shot is awarded, the referee places the puck at centre ice and the player is allowed skate in on the goalie for a free shot. The player must be in continuous forward motion with the puck, and once the shot is taken, the player cannot take a second shot in the event of a rebound. Once the puck is immobilized, it is considered dead.

When the penalty shot rule was first introduced into the NHL for the 1934–35 season, a player could not move in on the goaltender as is practiced today, but rather he had to stand behind a line 28 feet (8.5 metres) from the goal and take his

shot. Not the easiest of tasks, but one player managed to score in the penalty shot's first years of existence. The first-ever penalty shot was awarded to Montréal Canadiens forward Armand Mondou on November 10, 1934, and he was stopped by Toronto Maple Leafs goaltender Georges Hainsworth. Just three days later, Ralph "Scotty" Bowman of the St. Louis Eagles scored the first penalty shot goal in NHL history on Montréal Maroons goaltender Alex Connell.

During the 1941–42 NHL season, the league introduced two types of penalty shots, classed as major and minor penalty shots. The minor penalty shot was taken from a line 28 feet from the goal when a player was only slightly interfered with on a break to the net. A major penalty shot was awarded to a player who was tripped up from behind on a break. The major penalty shot allowed the player to skate in on the goaltender to shoot or fake from any distance. Eventually, the minor penalty shot rule was discontinued, and the NHL was left with the penalty shot that remains to the present day.

On June 5, 2006, Edmonton Oilers defenceman Chris Pronger became the first player in the history of the NHL to score on a penalty shot in the Stanley Cup finals when he beat Cam Ward of the Carolina Hurricanes.

Pengrowth Saddledome: Former name of the home arena of the Calgary Flames.

See Scotiabank Saddledome

Pepsi Center: Current home arena of the Colorado Avalanche. Built in 1999 to replace the aging McNichols Sports Arena, the Pepsi Center seats 18,007 spectators for a hockey game and plays host to the NBA's Denver Nuggets. The arena is named after chief corporate sponsor PepsiCo, and as a result, the arena is affectionately nicknamed "The Can."

See Colorado Avalanche

Period: The 20-minute span of playing time is called a period, and there are three periods in a game. The first and second periods are followed by a 15-minute intermission, though some intermissions are known to run longer due to promotional events and ice-flooding demands. In the early days of hockey, games were often separated into two, 30-minute halves.

Pest: A player who makes life difficult on the ice for his opponents by bothering or pestering them. The pest's most effective weapon is his mouth. Pests are an effective player to have on a team, because if they succeed in angering the opponent, that player will often draw a penalty.

P

Philadelphia Arena: Opened in 1920, this arena housed the short-lived Philadelphia Quakers NHL franchise during their one season in the league in 1930–31. The Arena sat just over 5000 spectators. It was closed in 1983.

Philadelphia Flyers: Ed Snider, vice-president of the Philadelphia Eagles, led a team of businessmen, including his boss Jerry Wolman, to a push for a new franchise in the NHL in 1966. The NHL granted the franchise, and a few months later, the Philadelphia Flyers were born. They joined the NHL along with Los Angeles, St. Louis, Minnesota, Oakland and Pittsburgh as the league went from the original six era to 12 teams. General manager Bud Poile was given the responsibility of setting up the club. At the expansion draft and amateur draft in 1967, the Flyers went for a young lineup that they could build into a competitive team. Alongside goaltenders Bernie Parent and Doug Favell, the Flyers added Joe Watson, Ed Van Impe and Lou Angotti.

The Flyers first game took place on October 11, 1967, against the Pittsburgh Penguins in a 5–1 loss. Despite the young lineup, the Flyers put together a decent season with a record of 31–32–11 and a place in the playoffs. The Flyers ultimately lost in the first round to the St. Louis Blues, but they were still a young team building for the future. After one season in the city, the Flyers had won over an army of fans. After their sophomore season—where they were once again beaten in the playoffs by the Blues—Flyers management increased the size of their team and selected Bobby Clarke in the 1969 draft. Over the next three seasons, the Flyers accomplished much in the regular season and nothing in the playoffs, but all along they had added players to the lineup that would soon make their mark on the team.

P

345

In 1970, Rick MacLeish joined the team, and in 1973, Bill Barber and Dave Schultz helped to bolster the offence and the physicality of the club—that year, the Flyers made it to the semifinals before losing to the Montréal Canadiens. But one of the most important acquisitions by the Flyers was the hiring of head coach Ray Shero, whose vision of the team turned them into the infamous "Broad Street Bullies."

For the 1973–74 season, the Flyers were suddenly one of the best teams in the league, competing with powerhouse clubs like the Canadiens and Boston Bruins, the reason being every Flyers game was physical and hard hitting, with the Philadelphia players trying to beat their opponents into submission. Shero's bullying philosophy worked, and the Flyers won their first Stanley Cup that year, beating the Boston Bruins in the 1974 final. They followed that up with another Cup in 1975, defeating a high-scoring, talent-laden Buffalo Sabres squad. The Flyers could have made it three Stanley Cups in a row, but they lost Bernie Parent and Rick MacLeish to injury, and knee problems had plagued Bobby Clarke for most of the season. They ultimately lost in the Stanley Cup finals to the Montréal Canadiens in four straight games.

Although the Flyers remained a competitive team, the death of assistant coach Barry Ashbee hit the team emotionally during the 1977 playoffs, losing to the Bruins in the semifinals. Then after the 1977–78 season, the Flyers lost head coach Ray Shero to the New York Rangers. Rookie head coach Pat Quinn took over and managed to led the club back into the playoffs, but the Broad Street Bullies of the mid-1970s were no more.

By the 1980s, the Flyers had lost most of the players who had been with the club for the two Stanley Cups. Despite the loss of key players like MacLeish, Barber and eventually Clarke, the Flyers remained a talented squad, always able to challenge in the playoffs. In 1980, they made it all the way to the finals once again only to lose to the New York Islanders. In 1985, with Bobby Clarke now the general manager of the team, the Flyers added gritty players Tim Kerr and Rick Tocchet and surly goaltender Ron Hextall, all of whom helped lead the club to the Stanley Cup finals against the Edmonton Oilers. But the grit of the Flyers proved to be no match for the speedy, high-scoring Oilers, and the team once more went home empty-handed. The Flyers again felt the sting of defeat at the hands of the Oilers in the 1987 Stanley Cup finals after a hard-fought, seven-game series.

From 1988 to 1994, the Flyers were a team struggling for an identity. They had skilled players on the club during those years, such as Tim Kerr, Mark Recchi and Rod Brind'Amour, but the team could not find the chemistry they needed to succeed, and as a result, they missed out on the playoffs from 1990 to 1994.

The Flyers needed a change, which came in the trade that brought Eric Lindros to Philadelphia. At the 1991 NHL Entry Draft, the Québec Nordiques selected the highly touted forward Eric Lindros first overall, but the young player refused to put on the Nordiques jersey at the ceremony, making his feelings crystal clear: he wanted nothing to do with Québec. This move forced Nordiques general manager to look for a trade. The Flyers came calling with the best offer. They traded Steve Duschesne, Peter Forsberg, Ron Hextall, Kerry Huffman, Mike Ricci, Chris Simon, two draft picks and $15 million to acquire Lindros.

347

Flyers GM Bobby Clarke was betting big on Lindros, and by the mid-1990s, it looked like his gamble would pay off with a championship. But again the Flyers disappointed in the playoffs, losing another Stanley Cup final series in 1997 to the Detroit Red Wings. All through the Lindros years, the Flyers were one of the best teams in the regular season, with the scoring talent of John Leclair, Simon Gagne, Keith Primeau and Jeremy Roenick, but the team could never seem to find consistency in goal. They even tried bringing back Ron Hextall, but that experiment failed. Roman Cechmanek, Garth Snow and John Vanbiesbrouck all tried their hand in goal for the Flyers, but none saw much success in the playoffs.

After the departure of Lindros in 2001, the Flyers continued to compete against the NHL's best teams, but the team's poor performance in the playoffs frustrated their fans. Bobby Clarke ended up resigning after the Flyers put up one of their worst performances in team history during the 2006–07 season, finishing with a 22–48–12 record.

The Flyers, now led by general manager Paul Homgren, bounced back the next season following the signing of Daniel Briere, Claude Giroux and Chris Pronger. By the 2009–10 season, they were once again looking like the Flyers of old: they played a high-intensity physical game and had the scoring prowess to back it up. After making it past the New Jersey Devils in the first round of the playoffs, the Flyers faced off against the Boston Bruins in the second round and, after the first three games, were on the edge of getting eliminated. But the Flyers managed to come back in one of the most memorable playoffs series in history, winning the next four games to move on. The Flyers then defeated the Montréal Canadiens to make it into the Stanley Cup finals. After such a memorable win against the Bruins, fans had hoped the Flyers had finally shaken off their Stanley Cup jinx, but that was not the case. The Flyers lost the Cup final again, this time to the Chicago Blackhawks. Flyers fans hope the future will be much kinder.

Philadelphia Flyers Records

Most goals in a season: Reggie Leach, 61 (1975–76)

Most power-play goals in a season: Tim Kerr, 34 (1985–86)

Most assists in a season: Bobby Clarke, 89 (1975–76; 1974–75)

Most points in a season: Mark Recchi, 123 (1992–93)

Most points in a season, defenceman: Mark Howe, 82 (1985–86)

Most points in a season, rookie: Mikael Renberg, 82 (1993–94)

Most penalty minutes in a season: Dave Schultz, 472 (1974–75)

Most wins in a season: Bernie Parent, 47 (1973–74)

Most shutouts in a season: Bernie Parent, 12 (1974–75;1973–74)

See Wells Fargo Center

Philadelphia Quakers: Long before the Flyers bashed and crashed their way into the hearts of NHL hockey fans, the city had a brief affair with the Philadelphia Quakers. After the failure of the Pittsburgh Pirates on the other side of the state, the franchise relocated to Philadelphia before the start of the 1930–31 season. The team was already in poor financial standing when they decided to relocate, and after the collapse of the stock market, the circumstances left the team in search of new funds. The ownership group hoped a change of venue would help the city flourish.

Twelve players who had played for the Pittsburgh Pirates one season earlier now donned the colours of the Quakers for the new season, players such as Harry Darragh, Hib Milks and Tex White, among others. The team also added future stars Syd Howe and goaltender Wilf Cude. Their first NHL game took place on November 11, 1930, with the New York Rangers winning the contest 3–0. The season did not get much better. It took three more games for the Quakers to score one goal, and six games for them to win a game on November 25, 1930. The Quakers did not win another game until January 10, 1931, against the Montréal Maroons. The team finished the season with a horrible record of 4–36–4. That's a winning percentage of .136, which would not be bested until the Washington Capitals in 1974–75 went 8–67–5 for a percentage of .131. After another horrible season and the continued effects of the Depression, the Quakers suspended operations. They were given until 1936 to reform the franchise, but hockey would not return to the state of Pennsylvania until 1967.

See Philadelphia Flyers

Phoenix Coyotes: Richard Burke and Steven Gluckstern brought the struggling Winnipeg Jets to the deserts of Phoenix in the hopes of turning the club around. The Jets became the Coyotes and played their first season in the desert in 1996–97. The people of Phoenix welcomed the new team to their city with open arms, and the Coyotes made it into the playoffs their first year as a show of gratitude. Unfortunately, the club went up against the league-leading Detroit Red Wings and were booted from the playoffs in six games.

With players Keith Tkachuk, Jeremy Roenick and goaltender Nikolai Khabibulin, the Coyotes were a decent team but never made it far in the playoffs. In the club's first five seasons in the league, they made it into the playoffs only to lose in the first round each and every time.

By 2001, with no progress in the playoffs and a string of mediocre seasons, the franchise began to show signs of financial weakness. Owner Richard Burke began shopping the franchise around, eventually selling it to Steve Ellman and Wayne Gretzky. After another string of losing seasons, the club placed Gretzky in the position of head coach. Gretzky's tenure as head coach of the team was a complete failure as the Great one failed to take the team to the playoffs once. Before the start of the 2009–10 season, Gretzky stepped down as coach and handed over the reins to Dave Tippett. Things seemed to turn in the right direction as the club put up a winning season and made the playoffs, but again the Detroit Red Wings took them out in the first round. The same thing happened in the 2011 playoffs, when the Red Wings swept them in four straight games.

All the while, less and less fans kept going to see the games, and in the background, the franchise was falling to pieces. In 2008, it came to light that the organization was hemorrhaging money and that the NHL was directly supporting the club. In 2009, owner Jerry Moyes, who had purchased the team in 2005, had no choice but to put the team into bankruptcy and try to sell off the club to recoup whatever money he could.

When it was discovered that Moyes was intending to sell the club to Canadian billionaire Jim Balsillie, who wanted to relocate the team to Hamilton, the NHL stepped in and

P

351

stripped Moyes of his remaining ownership authority. What followed was a long legal battle between Moyes, the NHL and Balsillie in bankruptcy court, and in the end, the NHL assumed the franchise and all its debts. The Coyotes have had temporary reprieve from relocating, but if solid investors cannot be found, then the club might move. The Coyotes' push in the 2012 playoffs has helped the future of the club, igniting a passion for the team that seemed lost in previous years, one that might save the franchise.

Phoenix Coyotes Records

Most goals in a season: Keith Tkachuk, 52 (1996–97)

Most assists in a season: Shane Doan, 50 (2007–08)

Most points in a season: Keith Tkachuk, 86 (1996–97)

Most points in a season, defenceman: Keith Yandle, 59 (2010–11)

Most points in a season, rookie: Peter Mueller, 54 (2007–08)

Most penalty minutes in a season: Daniel Carcillo, 324 (2007–08)

Most wins in a season: Ilya Bryzgalov, 42 (2009–10)

See Jobing.com Arena

Picking his Pocket: When an unsuspecting player moves up the ice with the puck and another player moves in from behind and steals the puck from him, then the first player's pocket is said to have been picked.

Pinpoint Accuracy: When a player can shoot or pass the puck directly where he wants. Point accuracy is usually a trait of the high-scoring players in the league, as they are able to find the opening in the net.

Pittsburgh Penguins: In 1965, U.S. senator Jack McGregor formed a group of local investors that included the H.J. Heinz Company, the owner of the Pittsburgh Steelers Art Rooney and Richard Mellon Scaife, and they petitioned the league to allow a new NHL franchise in Pittsburgh for the 1967 expansion. The league accepted the pitch, and the owners readied a team for the start of the 1967–68 season. The team was named the Penguins after taking inspiration from the Pittsburgh Civic Arena, more commonly known as the "Igloo."

The Penguins first general manager was Jack Riley, and head coach Red Sullivan had the daunting task of building a club that could match the talents of the more established original six teams. At the expansion draft, they took a few veteran players from the New York Rangers that had played under Sullivan when he was an assistant there, among them Earl Ingarfield and Andy Bathgate. By opening day of the season, they had put together a team of journeymen hockey players, grizzled veterans and wet-behind-the-ears rookies.

The Penguins first game was played at home on October 11, 1967, a 2–1 loss to the Montréal Canadiens. Aside from Bathgate and defenceman Leo Boivin, the Penguins did not have a good team. The Penguins' first two years in the NHL were rather forgettable, missing out on the playoffs both times. Up until the 1974–75 season, the Penguins had not even posted an above .500 season. With the help of Jean Pronovost, Syl Apps Jr. and rookie Pierre Larouche, the team climbed to a 37–28–15 record for the 1974–75 season, but in the playoffs the Penguins could not make it out of the second round.

In the following seasons, the Penguins made it to the play-offs but were frustratingly kicked out early each and every time. By the early 1980s, the Penguins were at the bottom of the league looking for any way out. However, all that losing turned out in their favour as the Penguins got to select first overall at the 1984 NHL Entry Draft, and with that selection they chose perhaps one of the greatest hockey players of all time, Mario Lemieux.

While Mario was busy lighting up the league with incredible goals and record-breaking achievements, the Penguins still struggled in the overall standings, not even making the playoffs until 1989. For the entire 1980s, Mario Lemieux's feats on the ice were overshadowed by Wayne Gretzky as he led the Oilers to several Stanley Cups while the Penguins could not even make it into the postseason. Then in 1990, the Penguins drafted a young Czech player named Jaromir

Jagr, and with that acquisition, the Penguins suddenly became one of the most dangerous teams in the league. The Penguins also managed to get Ulf Samuelsson and Ron Francis out of Hartford, and behind the bench they had hired veteran coach and legend Scotty Bowman.

The Pens were now solid up front and on defence, and with the goaltending of Tom Barrasso, they had the ingredients to go far. After finishing first in their division in the 1990–91 season, the Penguins went into the playoffs looking like a competitive team. After a tough opening seven-game series against the New Jersey Devils, the Penguins made it past the Washington Capitals and the Boston Bruins to reach the Stanley Cup finals for the first time in the team's history. Up against the Minnesota North Stars, Mario Lemieux, Kevin Stevens, Mark Recchi and Tom Barrasso helped give the city of Pittsburgh its first Stanley Cup, winning the series in six games.

The Penguins had a mediocre season in 1991–92, but in the playoffs they shined, beating the Washington Capitals, New York Rangers, Boston Bruins and Chicago Blackhawks to win their second consecutive Stanley Cup. These were high times for Pittsburgh, but in the off-season, tragedy struck the team when Mario Lemieux announced he had been diagnosed with Hodgkin's disease, a form of cancer. But after undergoing successful treatments, Lemieux returned triumphantly to the Penguins lineup; he played the remaining 60 games of the season and led the league in scoring with 160 points. It was an incredible feat, but his leadership could not help the Pens in the 1993 playoffs as they lost a heart-breaking third round series in the seventh game in overtime against the New York Islanders.

P

After a disappointing 1994 playoff campaign, Lemieux shocked the hockey world yet again when he announced that he was taking a one-year leave of absence from hockey to concentrate on his health. In the strike-shortened 1994–95 season without Mario, the Penguins had a good regular season, led by Jagr's Hart Trophy–winning season, but in the playoffs, they fell short of the Cup, losing to the New Jersey Devils in the conference semifinals. Mario returned for the 1995–96 season and led the league in scoring with 161 points, but the Penguins high-flying offence was defeated in the conference finals by the trap-defence style of the upstart Florida Panthers in a tight-checking seven-game series.

After another successful regular season in 1996–97 and a disappointing early exit from the playoffs, Mario Lemieux announced his retirement from the league because of his persistent back issues. It was a hard pill to swallow for hockey fans everywhere, and Lemieux handed over the franchise to Jagr to take to the next level. For four seasons, Jagr led the league in scoring, but the Penguins could not make any headway in the playoffs.

Off the ice, the Penguins were in financial troubles despite the successes on the ice. In 1998, the team filed for bankruptcy, and if financing could not been found, the club would be forced to move. That is when Lemieux stepped in and basically bought the team. He shocked the hockey world yet again by deciding to come back as a player, making him the first player/owner in league history. Lemieux returned to action on December 27, 2000, and helped the Penguins skate past the Capitals and the Sabres but ultimately lost to the New Jersey Devils. What followed was a series of losing seasons, but ones that helped rebuild the club and bring them back to prominence. In 2003, the team selected goaltender Marc-Andre Fleury, then in 2004, landed Evgeni Malkin, and finally in 2005, they won the draft lottery and secured their next franchise star, Sidney Crosby.

With these three players, the Penguins went from the basement of the league to the top. After a disappointing 2005–06 season in which Mario Lemieux played just 26 games alongside Crosby before announcing his permanent retirement because of heart irregularities, the Penguins completely turned the franchise around. After getting knocked out of the playoffs in 2007 in the first round by the Ottawa Senators, the Penguins returned for the 2007–08 season with Crosby firmly entrenched as the team's leader to finish the season strong and head into the playoffs looking like a top contender. The Penguins got revenge on the Senators in the first round, then beat out the Rangers and their state rivals the Flyers to make it into the Stanley Cup finals for the first time since their last Cup win in 1992. Up against the Detroit Red Wings, the Penguins fell short of their goal, losing the series in six games.

Luckily, Penguins fans did not have to wait long for the their team to achieve success because the following year the Penguins were back in the Stanley Cup final against the Red Wings, but this time Sidney Crosby and the Pens had the last laugh, hoisting the Stanley Cup after a hard-fought seven-game series. The most painful story of those two playoff series was that forward Marian Hossa played on the Penguins in 2008 when they lost, and then in the off-season, he bolted over to the Red Wings in the hopes of winning a Stanley Cup in 2009, but ended up losing to his old team.

357

The team's last season in the Mellon Arena in 2009–10 was a success, and into the playoffs, it looked as if the team would be able to repeat as Cup champions, but they were defeated in the second round by the Montréal Canadiens in seven games. Then in 2010–11, Sidney Crosby suffered a concussion that kept him off the team for the majority of the year while Evgeni Malkin suffered a season-ending knee injury. The resulting loss of their two best players was too much for the club, and they made an early exit from the playoffs. Crosby's status is still up in the air as he continues to battle concussion symptoms and neck pain, but the fans hope that their superstars can recreate the magic they used to have.

Pittsburgh Penguins Records

Most goals in a season: Mario Lemieux, 85 (1988–89)

Most assists in a season: Mario Lemieux, 114 (1988–89)

Most points in a season: Mario Lemieux, 199 (1988–89)

Most points in a season, defenceman: Paul Coffey, 113 (1988–89)

Most points in a season, rookie: Sidney Crosby, 102 (2005–06)

Most penalty minutes in a season: Paul Baxter, 409 (1981–82)

Most wins in a season: Tom Barrasso, 43 (1992–93)

See Consul Energy Center

Pittsburgh Pirates: In 1925, when the NHL decided to continue its expansion into the United States after the success of the Boston Bruins and New York Americans, Pittsburgh was chosen as the third U.S. city. Pittsburgh already had a long history of hockey, with the Pittsburgh Yellow

Jackets of the USA Hockey Association being the most popular and most successful club in the city.

The starting lineup for the Pirates boasted such future NHL stars as Lionel Conacher, Harry Darragh and goaltender Roy "Shrimp" Worters. In order to be easily identifiable, the new hockey team chose the same name as the city's pro baseball team: the Pittsburgh Pirates.

Behind the bench, the Pirates stole defensive legend Odie Cleghorn from the Montréal Canadiens. Going into their inaugural season in 1925–26, Cleghorn recognized that he did not have the offensive talent that many of the other more established clubs like the Senators and Canadiens boasted, so to maximize his top lines, Cleghorn became the first NHL coach to change his players on the fly to get the most out of them at the right moments of the game.

P

Despite having a "less talented" team, Cleghorn coached his club to a 19–16–1 record in their first year in the league and a spot in the playoffs. Unfortunately, the Pirates lost in the NHL semifinals to the Montréal Maroons in a two-game, total-goals series.

The 1926–27 season saw the NHL expand farther into the U.S., with the addition of the New York Rangers, Chicago Blackhawks and Detroit Cougars (later to become the Red Wings). The talent level of the league was also aided by the break-up of the WHL, whose players were dispersed among the NHL clubs. The Montréal Canadiens ended up with legendary goaltender George Hainsworth, defenceman Eddie Shore went to the Bruins, and the Pirates took forward Ty Arbour, who never ended up making a significant impact in the NHL. In the expanded league, the Pirates dropped behind other clubs and finished the season out of the playoffs. They made a slight rebound in the 1927–28 season, but the Pirates fell out of the playoffs in the opening round, this time to the New York Rangers. Although the club had some minor success, they could not seem to get the people of Pittsburgh to support them.

Before the start of the 1928–29 season, the Pirates began trading away their talent in order to meet their financial obligations, and as a result, the team's fortunes on the ice faltered. The 1928–29 season was an extremely painful one for the club, winning just nine games and scoring only 46 goals for the entire season. After another poor season, the owners of the club moved the team to Philadelphia in the hopes that a new city could save the franchise. It didn't.

Plastic Blade: Most often used for street or floor hockey, the plastic blade is a replaceable blade that attaches to the bottom shaft of the stick.

Play-by-play: A term used when broadcast announcers give a moment-by-moment description of the events in a game.

Play with a Broken Stick: If for any reason a player's stick breaks and he does not drop it to the ice right away and instead tries to make a play with the stick, the player is assessed a two-minute penalty. However, a goaltender is allowed to play with a broken stick.

Playoff Beard: A long-standing tradition or superstition in which players grow beards during their entire playoff run to the Stanley Cup and will only shave when their team has been eliminated or wins the Cup.

Playoffs: A game or series of games held after the regular season to determine which team advances into the next round, with the ultimate goal of winning the championship. The NHL has always determined its champions through a playoff format. Although the format has changed, from total-goals series to best-of-sevens, the objective has always been to get two teams to the final round to battle it out for the Stanley Cup.

Often, the playoffs are said to be the NHL's "second season," as the teams that make it into the postseason can disregard what occurred in the regular season and start fresh. One of the best traditions in hockey is that at the conclusion of each playoff series, the players shake each other's hands, although on a few occasions, some players have refused. Most notable was when several Detroit Red Wings players refused to shake the hand of Colorado Avalanche forward Claude Lemieux in 1996 after he delivered a dirty check that injured Red Wings forward Kris Draper.

Plexiglass: See-through acrylic panes that surround a rink and protect fans from flying pucks. The material is virtually unbreakable, although several players have managed to break them with shots or by delivering a hard body check.

Plus/minus: A player receives a "plus" if he is on the ice when his team scores an even-strength or shorthanded goal. He receives a "minus" if he is on the ice for an even-strength or shorthanded goal scored by the opposing club. The difference in these numbers is considered the player's plus-minus statistic.

See Shorthanded

PNC Arena: Current home of the Carolina Hurricanes. Opened on October 29, 1999, the arena was previously known as the Raleigh Entertainment & Sports Arena and the RBC Center. When the Carolina Hurricanes first entered the NHL in 1997, they were supposed to be based in Raleigh, North Carolina, but because there was no suitable arena for them, they were forced to move to Greensboro. Two years later, RBC Center was ready and the Hurricanes moved to Raleigh. The arena seats 18,680 spectators for a hockey game. The Canes played their first game on October 29, 1999, against the New Jersey Devils. The Hurricanes won the 2006 Stanley Cup at RBC Center in a game-seven win over the Edmonton Oilers. The building's name was changed to PNC Arena in 2012.

See Carolina Hurricanes

Point Position: The term "point" was only used in reference to the defencemen when hockey was played with a team of seven players on the ice. The point position was similar to that of the modern-day defenceman. While defencemen in the six-player game play side-by-side, the point position player was set up behind the cover point directly in front of the goalkeeper. The point player usually remained in the defensive zone while the forwards took the puck up the ice. As a result, the point player hardly ever scored.

Point Shot: Point shots are taken in the offensive zone along the blue line, usually by defencemen, but forwards take point shots as well.

P

Point-blank Range: A shot taken directly in front of a player, or more commonly a shot taken directly in front of a goaltender.

Poke Check: A technique goaltenders use to poke or push the puck off an opponent's stick as he dekes in close to the net. In making the play for the puck, the goaltender slides his hand up his stick and makes a stab at the player's stick. This is usually a dangerous move for a goaltender because if he misses the poke check, he is left to the mercy of the shooter. Two of the earliest goaltenders to employ this strategy with success were Jacques Plante of the Montréal Canadiens and Johnny Bower of the Toronto Maple Leafs.

Policeman: A player who is the protector on the team.

See Enforcer

Pond Hockey: Hockey played on a small, frozen body of water. Playing hockey on the local frozen pond is where the game began. Long before municipalities put up local rinks

and well before the advent of the indoor arena, the game was played outside on a frozen pond. There is no goaltender, and players usually shoot the puck into a net as wide as a regular goal but the crossbar is only a few inches off the ground. This form of play does not allow for slapshots in the game, placing emphasis on the players' skating abilities.

Port Arthur Bearcats: An amateur hockey team based in Port Arthur (now part of Thunder Bay) founded in 1915. The team played against the Ottawa Senators in a 1911 Stanley Cup challenge and lost the one-game championship match by a score of 13–4. Port Arthur won the Canadian Amateur Hockey Association (CAHA) championship four times, and in 1936 the team was selected to represent Canada at the Winter Olympics in Germany. They ended up losing the gold medal to Great Britain, whose team was unabashedly stocked with Canadian players. The Bearcats have had several NHL players go through their ranks, including Lorne Chabot, Art Chapman and Frank Nighbor.

Portland Rosebuds: Playing in the Pacific Coast Hockey Association (PCHA) from 1914 to 1918, the Rosebuds were the first U.S.-based hockey team to challenge for the Stanley Cup. They lost in a best-of-five series to the NHA's Montréal Canadiens, three games to two. After the 1918 season, the team folded operations. The Rosebuds were reborn for the 1925–26 WHL season when the Regina Capitals relocated to the city. The second Rosebuds did not last long, however, as the WHL ceased operations at the end of their inaugural season.

Post-concussion Syndrome (PCS): A set of symptoms an individual might experience for up to a year or more after the initial head injury. The syndrome can give the patient

P

severe headaches, difficulty concentrating, emotional instability and memory loss. There is no treatment for post-concussion syndrome, though the less severe symptoms such as headaches can be treated. Not much is known about the causes of PCS and what makes the symptoms persist in some patients and not in others who have had a similar injury. It is currently one of the most popular topics in hockey.

See Concussion

Postseason: Another term for the playoffs, which follow the 82-game regular season.

Post-to-post Save: When a goaltender has to make a save at one side of the net and then dive to the other side to make another save.

Pot a Goal: To put the puck in the net.

Power Forward: An above-average-sized player who can be physically imposing in the corners and in front of the net. Not just a physical presence on the ice, the power forward is one of the most sought-after players to have on a team.

Power Play (PP): When a player on one team is penalized, the opposing team goes on the power play. They have the advantage of having five players still on the ice while the penalized team must play for two minutes or more with only three or four players. A coach will normally send out his most offensive players on the power play to take advantage of the situation.

Preds: Nickname for the Nashville Predators.

Pre-season: The several games played before the start of the regular season.

See Exhibition Games

Presidents' Trophy: An award given out by the NHL to the team that finishes the regular season with the most points. The winning team also receives $350,000 in bonuses. The trophy was first introduced in 1985–86 by the board of governors. From 1937 to 1968, the league winner was awarded the Prince of Wales Trophy. Up until 1937, no award or banner was given to the league-leading team. From 1968 to 1986, the league-leading team at the end of the regular season received a banner that said "NHL League Champions."

The Montréal Canadiens have finished first overall a record 21 times, though the last time this was accomplished was in 1977–78, so the Canadiens have never won the Presidents' Trophy. The Detroit Red Wings have won the most Presidents' trophies since 1986 with six.

Prince of Wales Conference: Created in 1974 when the NHL realigned its teams into two conferences and four divisions. The conference was named after the Prince of Wales Trophy, which went to the winner of the conference after the third playoff round. Before the realignment, the Prince of Wales Conference (or just Wales Conference) consisted of the Adams and Patrick divisions. In 1993, the Wales Conference was changed to the Eastern Conference when it moved to geographical referencing to help new fans identify with teams.

See Eastern Conference

Prince of Wales Trophy (also Wales Trophy): An award presented by the NHL to the winner of the Eastern Conference playoff. When the award was first presented in 1926, it was given to the winner of the regular season. Throughout its history, the Wales Trophy has been awarded for eight different accomplishments, including the NHL regular-season champs, American Division champs, East Division champs, Wales Conference regular-season champs, Wales Conference playoff champs and Eastern Conference playoff champs. The Montréal Canadiens have won the trophy the most with 25 wins in its history, and the Boston Bruins are second with 16.

A common superstition surrounding the trophy is that no player should touch the trophy, along with the winners of the Clarence S. Campbell Bowl, after they have won the conference playoffs as it is deemed bad luck going into the Stanley Cup playoffs. The thought is that the players do not want to celebrate too early before getting a chance at the Stanley Cup.

See Campbell Bowl

Production Line: The Detroit Red Wings of the original six era between 1949 and 1955 were one of the greatest teams to play the game. The Wings finished first in the league several times, had some of the best players in the NHL and won the Stanley Cup four times in that period. One of the biggest reasons for their success was a trio of players who were dubbed the Production Line: Sid Abel, Gordie Howe and Ted Lindsay. The Production Line dominated every time they stepped on the ice, being three big forwards who were dangerous in all aspects of the game. Detroit manager Jack Adams and coach Tommy Ivan tried breaking up the line to spread out the talent, but the line was always put back together. The Production Line had their best year in the 1949–50 season, when the three players finished 1-2-3 in scoring, with Lindsay in first with 78 points, Abel with 69 and Howe right behind with 68. Just like the Detroit automobile assembly lines, the Production Line kept producing quality hockey until Abel was traded to the Chicago Blackhawks in 1952.

See Detroit Red Wings

Professional Hockey Writers Association (PHWA): North American association for ice hockey journalists, founded in 1967. The members assist the league in voting for the winners of several of the NHL's trophies, including the Hart Memorial Trophy and Calder Trophy.

Prospect: A young player in the minors who is looked upon as a promising future player in the NHL.

Prudential Center: Current home of the New Jersey Devils. It was opened in 2007 to replace the aging Continental Airlines Arena in East Rutherford, New Jersey. It is a state-of-the-art complex that seats 17,625 for hockey games. The Devils played their first home game on October 27, 2007, against the Ottawa Senators in a losing effort.

See New Jersey Devils

Puck: The black, vulcanized rubber disk used to score goals is probably the most essential piece of equipment in the game of hockey. NHL regulations say that the puck must be 2.54 centimetres thick, 7.62 centimetres wide and weigh 156 to 170 grams. Since a warm puck bounces more, game pucks are kept on ice throughout the game.

The little black disk has had a strange and unique history in the evolution of the game. The word "puck" has its origins in Middle English and refers to a mischievous sprite in folklore (most famously depicted in William Shakespeare's *A Midsummer Night's Dream*). The modern definition of the word comes from ice hockey's close relative, hurling. When a hurling player hit the ball, he was said to "puck it." This term was carried over to ice hockey, where players constantly hit or "pucked" the ball about. So when the hurley ball no longer suited the needs of ice hockey, players substituted a flat wooden disk, which they in turn started calling a puck.

It is hard to imagine hockey players using anything besides the black rubber pucks that we have today, but in the early days of the game, players made pucks with wood from the trees that surrounded the outdoor rinks. Cherrywood was the wood of choice for the discerning puck connoisseur because the bark stayed stuck to the wood, making the puck visible on the white of the ice and snow.

370

As the game became more organized and players got faster, the search began for another material to use for pucks. Wood was lightweight, making the disk hard to control when shooting, and after a few good smacks with the sticks, the bark began to break off. The most obvious solution was to replace wood with rubber. But the first rubber pucks were not as solidly constructed as they are today. The first ones were made up of several layers of rubber cemented together. The puck was heavier and easier to shoot, but if the cement did not hold, the puck often split into several different pieces. This proved to be a real problem during several early professional games.

For example, in 1900 during a game in Belleville, Ontario, refereed by legendary official Fred Waghorne, a player took a hard shot on goal that hit the goalpost and split the puck into two pieces. One half bounced into the corner and the other half of the puck ended up in the net. An immediate controversy arose as the attacking team claimed it was a goal, while the defending team demanded that it be disallowed. Referee Fred Waghorne immediately pulled out his rulebook and pointed to the section that said an official puck must be 2.54 centimetres thick. By his reasoning, since the puck in the net was not regulation size, the goal was disallowed.

In an NHL game, pucks often fly into the crowd, or a rookie who has just scored his first goal takes the puck, which is why there are dozens of pucks waiting on the sidelines if they are needed. Amazingly enough, on November 10, 1979, in a game between the Los Angeles Kings and the Minnesota North Stars, only one puck was used for the entire game.

See Vulcanized Rubber

Puck Bunny: A not-so-flattering reference to a woman who hovers around hockey players. Used generally as a reference to women who are only out for romantic encounters with players rather than for the love of the game. The term is analogous to the word "groupie" as it relates to music and celebrities.

Puck Has Eyes: A phrase that describes when a player shoots the puck through traffic and it somehow finds its way to the back of the net as if it had eyes and was able to avoid the mess of bodies in front of the net.

Puck Hog: A player who holds onto the puck for a long time, looking to make the play by himself without any help from his teammates. Not often used to describe a professional player, puck hog is more often used to describe a minor league player or weekend warrior who thinks he is a professional.

See Hot Dog

Puck Luck: A serendipitous puck. For example, one that hits the crossbar of the net instead of going in. This is puck luck for the defending team.

Puckhead: A fan obsessed with hockey and all that surrounds it.

Pucksters: A colloquial term for people who play hockey. "I was down at the pond with the pucksters all day."

Pull the Goalie: In hockey, each team is allowed to ice six players, usually three forwards, two defencemen and a goalie. In the closing moments of a game when a team is down by a goal or two, the coach can elect to remove the goaltender from the ice in favour of placing another attacking forward on the ice to try to score the tying goal. The first coach to pull a goalie was the Boston Bruins' Art Ross in a playoff game against the Canadiens on March 26, 1931. The Bruins failed to score with the extra attacker, but Montreal did not score either.

See Empty-net Goal; Extra Attacker

Punch Line: Of all the great lines to play for the Montréal Canadiens, one of the best had Maurice Richard on the right

P

wing, Elmer Lach at centre and Hector Blake on the left wing during the 1940s. The trio finished 1-2-3 in scoring during the 1944–45 season, with Lach in first with 80 points, Richard with his famous 50 goals and 73 points and Blake with 67 points. Lach was the set-up man to Richard's goal-scoring touch, and Blake backed them up with solid fore-checking and his instinctive, defensive style of play. The line was responsible for some of the most exciting plays in hockey and laid the foundation for one of the best teams in NHL history. After retiring from hockey in the late 1940s, Blake returned to coach Richard and the Canadiens to eight Stanley Cups in 13 seasons.

See Montréal Canadiens

Punch-up: A fight.

Pylon: A player who is not a good skater and is easy to manoeuvre around.

QMJHL (Québec Major Junior Hockey League): One of Canada's three major junior leagues along with the Ontario Hockey League (OHL) and Western Hockey League (WHL). Founded in 1969 through the merger of the best teams from the Québec Junior League and the Metropolitan Montréal Junior Hockey League, the QMJHL has always been known for its rapid, skilled hockey. Since its creation, the league has produced some of the NHL's greatest talents, such as Mike Bossy, Mario Lemieux, Guy Lafleur and Pat LaFontaine. Since its inception, the Memorial Cup has been captured nine times by a member of the QMJHL.

QMJHL Memorial Cup Winners

2011 – Saint John Sea Dogs

2006 – Québec Remparts

2000 – Rimouski Océanic

1997 – Hull Olympiques

1996 – Granby Prédateurs

1981 – Cornwall Royals

1980 – Cornwall Royals

1972 – Cornwall Royals

1971 – Québec Remparts

Qualifying Offer: A type of contract offer a team might make to one of their restricted free agents if another team makes that player a contract offer.

Quarrel: Another word for a fight or a shoving match.

Québec Bulldogs: Originally founded in 1878 as an exhibition hockey club, the team only played visiting teams to the city. An official hockey club was only formed 10 years later in 1888 when the team joined the Amateur Hockey Association of Canada (AHAC) as the Québec Hockey Club, though unofficially they were known as the Québec Bulldogs. After playing in the AHAC, Québec played in the Canadian Amateur Hockey League from 1899 to 1905 and the Eastern Canada Amateur Hockey Association (ECAHA) from 1906 to 1909.

In 1910, the Québec Bulldogs joined the National Hockey Association (NHA), but finished dead last in the league. For the 1911–12 season, the Bulldogs, with the help of Joe Malone, finished the season in first place, thus giving them the O'Brien Cup and the Stanley Cup. They were challenged once for the Stanley Cup by the Moncton Victorias but easily handled them. They finished the 1912–13 NHA season on top of the league again, therefore retaining their league title and Stanley Cup championship. Joe Malone scored an incredible 43 goals in just 20 games that season. The Bulldogs championship run ended in 1914 when they finished the NHA season in third place. But when the NHA disbanded and the NHL was formed, the Québec Bulldogs did not immediately join the new league. Being the smallest market in the league and with the strains on spectators and players because of World War I, Québec could not find the funds to join the NHL.

For the 1919–20 season, the club was revived with a fresh influx of cash from businessman Mike Quinn. Joe Malone was brought back to the club after spending one season with the Montréal Canadiens. Malone led the league that season with 39 goals, but he was the only player on the team doing anything productive. The Bulldogs won just four games the entire season, effectively signing the death warrant for the franchise.

Prior to the start of the 1920–21 season, the NHL took back the franchise and sold it to owners in the city of Hamilton, Ontario, where they became the Hamilton Tigers.

See Hamilton Tigers

Québec Nordiques: After the Québec Bulldogs left the city without an NHL team, hockey fans had to be content with junior and senior level hockey for decades until professional hockey returned to the provincial capital in 1972.

From 1972 to 1979, the Québec Nordiques (*Nordiques* means "Northmen" or "Northerners") were a part of the World Hockey Association (WHA) and played in front of hockey-mad fans at the Colisée de Québec, winning the WHA championship Avco Cup in 1977. When the WHA announced it was shutting down in 1979, hockey fans feared they would lose their team, but all was saved when the NHL announced it would be absorbing the Nordiques into the league for the start of the 1979–80 season. As a condition of joining the NHL, the Nordiques, along with the Winnipeg Jets and Edmonton Oilers, had to free up some of their players in an expansion draft. This left the Nordiques with only a few of their top players from their days in the WHA, and as a result, their first year in the NHL was

Q

a disappointment. Hope for a better future for the club came in the form of young rookies Real Cloutier and Michel Goulet, who were developing into top-tier players, but they could do little to save the first season, finishing with a record of 25–44–11. However, things turned around pretty fast for the Nordiques when they added brothers Anton and Peter Stastny to the roster and turned into a playoff contender in only their second year in the NHL.

The team improved in the 1980–81 season, making the playoffs for the first time, but they were dispatched in the first round by the Philadelphia Flyers. The Nordiques finally made waves in the playoffs during their 1981–82 run to the Stanley Cup. After beating their provincial rivals the Montréal Canadiens in the first round on a dramatic overtime goal by Dale Hunter, the Nordiques beat the Bruins in the division finals but lost in the conference finals to the eventual Stanley Cup–winning New York Islanders.

In the 1983–84 season, Peter Stastny and Michel Goulet had finished the season with a total of 119 and 121 points respectively, and with a solid team to back them up, the Nordiques moved into the upper echelons of the league. Going into the playoffs, the Nordiques easily dispensed of the Buffalo Sabres in the division semifinals, after which they met up with the Montréal Canadiens again in a series that would go down in history.

After several years in the league together, Québec and Montréal had built up a tense hatred of each other. Regular-season games were rough and violent, but they were nothing compared to the 1984 playoffs. Called the Good Friday Massacre, or *La Bataille du Vendredi Saint*, on Friday, April 20, 1984, the Nordiques walked into the Forum down in the series three games to two. The series had so far been brutally physical, and the Nordiques were not going to let up on the Canadiens for one moment. The game began like most others, but all hell broke loose at the end of the second period after a scrum started in front of the Québec goal. Both benches emptied and players began picking partners and fighting, and then Nordique Louis Slegher sucker punched Canadien Jean Hamel, knocking him unconscious with enough damage that the injury eventually ended Hamel's career. A total of 252 minutes were handed out in that one incident. The Canadiens' anger continued to brew during the intermission over their teammate's injury, and before the third period could even start, the benches cleared again as the Canadiens wanted to get back at Slegher. Sanity was eventually restored, and the Canadiens won the game by a score of 5–3 and moved on in the playoffs.

Into the late '80s and early '90s, the Nordiques fortunes began to sour. The players who led the team to success in the early '80s were getting old, and they could not settle on a goaltender to lead them through tough periods. The 1989–90 season saw the Nordiques finish with just 12 wins and a whopping 61 losses. But there was still hope amid the darkness. The poor seasons meant that year after year the team was guaranteed high draft choices. In three consecutive seasons, they selected Joe Sakic, Mats Sundin and Owen Nolan first overall, a lineup that helped turn around the franchise's fortunes on the ice.

However, like the Winnipeg Jets, the Nordiques played in too small a market to maintain a profitable franchise. Only a Stanley Cup win could have saved the Nordiques from moving, but that never came, and so, after the end of the

Q

1994–95 season when the Nordiques lost in the opening round to the New York Rangers, the team was shut down. The last NHL game played in Québec City was on May 16, 1995.

The team was packed up and shipped to Denver and renamed the Colorado Avalanche. To make the move even more painful for Nordiques fans, the Avalanche went on to win the Stanley Cup in 1996. Since their departure, there have been rumours of an NHL club's return to Québec, but as of yet the NHL has not let out any hints. The people of Québec City sit and wait.

See Colorado Avalanche

Questionable Call: A penalty call by a referee that, in the eyes of the offending player and the team, should not have been called.

Quick Up: A quick pass up the ice.

RBC Center: Former name of the home arena of the Carolina Hurricanes from 1999 to 2012.

See PNC Arena

RCAF (Royal Canadian Air Force) Flyers: The senior amateur men's hockey team that won the gold medal at the 1948 Winter Olympics in St. Moritz, Switzerland.

RW: Statistical abbreviation for Right Wing.

Ragging: A term used to describe clever stickhandling by a team's players to keep the puck away from the opposition and kill a penalty.

Rat Portage Thistles: The town of Kenora was originally known as Rat Portage, so the Kenora Thistles' original name was Rat Portage Thistles.

See Kenora Thistles

Razor Sharp: When a goaltender or player is doing really well, it is said that he is "razor sharp." A players skates are also referred to as razor sharp after being sharpened by the equipment trainer.

Read the Play: When a player on the ice can read or anticipate the movements of his opponents, teammates or the puck, he is said to be able to "read the play." This helps in setting up plays or blocking offensive rushes. By reading the play, you can skate to where the puck is going, not where the puck has been.

Rear Guard: A defenceman.

Rebound: When a shot hits the goaltender, usually on the leg pads, and bounces out. Rebounds are dangerous for a goaltender because they often bounce out to the wrong player, leaving the goalie out of position or exposing an open net. When that happens, it is referred to as a "juicy rebound."

Rebuild: It is common in the NHL today for teams to go through cycles of winning and losing seasons. When a cycle of winning for a club is coming to an end, it is usually marked by the loss of several key players who led the team to the original success or by the decline of aging veterans. It is at this point that a general manager might take the initiative to "rebuild" the team. This means trading off valuable assets in return for high-end draft picks and younger players with potential. It might take several years for a team to begin to reap the benefits of rebuilding and bring back their winning ways.

Red Light: Goal indicator behind the nets on each end of the rink. The light is triggered when the puck enters the net.

See Goal Judge

Red-light District: The area immediately in front of the net where most of the shots on goal come from.

382

Red Line: Can refer to either the narrow red lines painted on both ends of the ice that act as the goal line and as the icing line, or more commonly to the red centre line that divides the ice into two.

Referee, Ref: Ever since hockey changed from an afternoon pastime to a competitive game, there have been referees to ensure that the game is played according to the rules of the league. It is the referee's job to signal penalties, and he is the only person on the ice who can signal a goal. Referees generally shy away from breaking up fights, instead remaining at a distance ready to hand out penalties—a sucker punch or elbow might be missed if he were busy separating two players.

Because referees often call penalties that can change the outcome of a game, they are not always the best-liked people in hockey, whether in the 1800s or today. In 1895, after an Ottawa–Québec game, police had to rescue two officials when a mob of irate Québec fans dragged them to the back of the arena and tried to "persuade" the refs to change Ottawa's 3–2 victory to a draw. And a 1903 Stanley Cup game between the Ottawa Silver Seven and the Rat Portage Thistles became so violent that the referee had to wear a hard hat to protect himself from flying sticks and debris launched by fans.

One of the most influential figures in referee history was Fred Waghorne. Born in England in 1866, Waghorne moved to Canada as a young man, and although he became involved in various sports, it was hockey that piqued his interest the most. Waghorne began playing the game in the Toronto Lacrosse Hockey League, a four-team organization that played lacrosse in the summer and hockey in the

R

winter. Eventually they became simply the Toronto Hockey League as hockey overshadowed lacrosse in popularity. The league eventually disbanded completely, but Waghorne continued to be part of the city's hockey culture. In his late 20s and unable to keep up with the younger men on the ice, Waghorne became a referee in Toronto, and he continued to do his job right until his death in 1956 at the age of 90.

Before Waghorne, a designated referee to watch over league games did not exist. It was often a job given to another player, and the position wasn't treated with much respect. Waghorne changed this mentality by making refereeing his job. But refereeing in Waghorne's time was not an easy task because the ref had to perform several duties on the ice. There were no linesmen to break up fights or "face" the puck, and the lack of certain technologies made the job all the more challenging. In the book *Kings of the Ice: A History of World Hockey* by Andrew Podnieks, Pavel Barta and Dmitri Ryzkov, Waghorne said:

> *A few of the rinks were lighted by coal oil lamps, and the corners were dark pockets. It was in rinks of that type that the art of puck lifting was at its peak. The Pete Charltons (tricksters) of the day lifted the puck up to the rafters, beyond the goalkeeper's vision. Often the rubber seemed to drop from the roof, right in front of the surprised goalkeeper, then bounced crazily into the net. Some of the players could lift the puck from end-to-end.*

There was no such thing as glass partitions or arena security either, and the referees were usually the targets of irate fans' wrath, meaning they often had to fight their way out of arenas after games were over. In these early days, refereeing certainly wasn't a well-paying job, and Waghorne often found himself in remote areas of Canada, having to

wait days before moving on to the next city. But he hung on, changing the game in the process.

At first, to signal the stoppage of play or a penalty, the referees of old rang a cowbell, but a lot of the spectators worked on farms and they often brought cowbells of their own, making it difficult for players to know when the real bell was being rung. Because of this problem, Waghorne introduced the whistle.

Waghorne's innovative ways didn't stop there. During a game in Arnprior, Ontario, in 1900, he made another contribution to hockey that also changed the game forever. At the time, common practice dictated that when a referee called a faceoff, he placed the puck on the ice between the two centremen and play started immediately, usually with the ref's shins and ankles getting hacked to pieces in the process. Waghorne was tired of the bruises, so he decided during the game in Arnprior to drop the puck from about a metre above the ice, allowing him a precious second to jump out of the way. The players liked the new move—and so did referees all over Canada. Soon, Waghorne's faceoff puck-drop was a bona fide part of the game.

Waghorne refereed over 2400 hockey games in his career, and in honour of his contributions to the game, he was elected into the Hockey Hall of Fame in 1961 in the builder category. Thanks to Waghorne, the institution of the hockey official became part of the game's legitimization, which helped spread hockey's popularity across Canada.

The modern NHL referee can be distinguished by a black-and-white-striped uniform with orange armbands; it was a far cry from the first referees who dressed in heavy coats, boots, scarves and derby hats to protect themselves from the cold outdoor conditions.

Over the years, hockey and the rules that govern the game have changed, but the role of the referee has remained the same—to ensure the rules are followed and to keep the game fair and entertaining.

See Linesman

Referee's Crease: An area directly in front of the time-keeper's bench marked on the ice by a red arc. A player can be penalized for pursuing a referee into his crease to argue a call. It serves no function during play.

Rendez-vous '87: A two-game series between the NHL All-Stars and the Soviet national hockey team played on February 11 and 13, 1987, in Québec City. The series replaced the regular All-Star game.

The NHL put players Mark Messier, Dave Poulin, Chris Chelios, Mario Lemieux and Wayne Gretzky up against the Soviet Union's best players. The NHL All-Stars won the first game by a score of 4–3, and the Soviets won the second game 5–3, so everyone went home happy.

Restricted Free Agent (RFA): A player whose contract has expired but whose team retains exclusive negotiating rights. A player may only be declared an unrestricted free agent if they are over 27 years of age or have played in the league a minimum of seven years.

See Unrestricted Free Agent (UFA)

Retired Number: When a player's exploits with a specific team merits the honour of having his jersey number to be the last worn by that team, the number is considered retired. The Montréal Canadiens have the most retired numbers of any NHL club with 17. In January 2000, the NHL made the unprecedented move of retiring Wayne Gretzky's number 99 league-wide. The first team to retire a number were the Toronto Maple Leafs, who retired Ace Bailey's number 6 on February 14, 1934.

R

Reunion Arena: Former home arena of the Dallas Stars from 1993 to 2001, it seated around 17,000 spectators and was the home arena for the club during their 1999 Stanley Cup championship season. They moved into the American Airlines Centre in 2001. Reunion Arena was also the home of the NBA Dallas Mavericks. It was demolished in 2009.

See American Airlines Centre; Slush

Rexall Place: Current home of the Edmonton Oilers. Once known as Northlands Coliseum, Edmonton Coliseum and

Skyreach Centre, it became Rexall Place in 2003 when the naming rights were bought by the Rexall medicine company, a subsidiary of Katz Group, current owners of the Edmonton Oilers. It seats just under 17,000 spectators for hockey games but is still known to have some of the loudest fans in the league. Built in 1974, it is the third oldest arena in the league. The oldest is the Islanders Nassau Veterans Memorial Coliseum.

See Edmonton Oilers

Richfield Coliseum: Home arena of the Cleveland Barons. In the two short years (1976–78) that the Barons spent in the NHL, they played their home games in this 18,544-seat arena that also housed the NBA's Cleveland Cavaliers from 1974 to 1994.

See Cleveland Barons

Ricket: A cricket term that defines the goal area. There is evidence that all kinds of games were adapted to the icy conditions of Canadian winters, with cricket being one of them. The term "rickets" was also used to describe the first goalposts in hockey.

See Net

Ricochet: When the puck bounces off another player and goes into the net, leaving the goaltender with absolutely no chance of stopping the puck. A goaltender will usually give his defencemen an exasperated look and shrug his shoulders, as there is nothing they could have done on the shot.

Riding the Pine: The players' bench, also called "the pine," is the domain of the back-up goaltender (ask Martin Brodeur's former backup, Scott Clemmensen), who sits on the bench more than he plays between the pipes. "After riding the pine for five games, he finally gets the start for tonight's big game."

See Back-up Goaltender

Right in the Numbers: To cross check a player in the back (where his number is) close to the boards, usually resulting in a penalty.

See Cross-checking

Ring It Off the Iron: When a player fires a hard shot off the goalpost and it makes a distinctive "ping" sound.

Ringette: A sport similar to hockey, formerly played by young women only. Players use just the shaft of a stick and a large round soft "puck" with a hole in the middle for stick handling. The same rules and regulations of hockey apply to ringette. The sport was invented by Sam Jacks of North Bay, Ontario, in 1963.

Rink: Normally defined as an expanse of ice designated for ice skating or hockey, or an area marked off for a sport to be played. "Let's go play hockey at the rink." Most people know what a rink is, but this odd-sounding word has its roots in a more violent and bloody time that seems to mesh well with the physical nature of hockey. "Rink" originates from the Middle Ages from both Scottish and French words:

Renk: a Scottish word that means an area designed for a battle, joust or race.

Renc: an Old French word for race course.

389

The modern word "rink" most likely evolved from the Scottish *renk* since, throughout the history of hockey, the play on the ice has often resembled a medieval battle, except that today's modern rink warrior brandishes a hockey stick instead of a sword, and shoulder pads instead of armour.

The modern-day North American hockey rink is rectangular, with rounded corners surrounded by wooden or fibreglass boards about four feet (just over one metre) in height. The standard rink size as determined by the NHL is 200 feet (61 metres) by 85 feet (26 metres) with a corner radius of 28 feet (8.5 metres). The distance between the goal line and the end boards is set at 11 feet (3.3 metres). The distance from the goal line out to the blue line is set at 64 feet (19.5 metres). The distance between the blue lines, known as the neutral zone, is 50 feet (15 metres). Other areas of note on the hockey rink are the two faceoff circles found to the left and right of the net. The referee holds the faceoff at the centre of the circle.

For the start of the 2005–06 season, the NHL changed a few of the traditional areas on the ice to speed up the game. The most notable change was the area behind the goal line. A trapezoid-shaped area has been marked where the goaltenders are no longer allowed to play the puck. If they do so, they receive a two-minute minor penalty. The rule was put into place to stop puck-handling goaltenders such as Martin Brodeur from acting like a third defenceman, able to pass the puck up to the forward in the hope of starting a fast break.

See European Ice Rink

Rink Rat: A young player who scurries around the arena taking every chance he or she can get to be around hockey and to play hockey. Homework and social life come second for the rink rat.

Ripple the Mesh: This happens when a hard shot hits the back of the goal and shakes the netting.

See Tickle the Twine

Road Apples: Long before the invention of the rubber puck, children often had to use items that could be readily found around them if they wanted to play hockey. One of the most readily available source of hockey puck substitutes was frozen horse droppings. "Road apples," as they were so charmingly called, worked well for light wrist shots but would break up under the pressure of a slapshot, which would send a piece of "apple" flying into the face of the poor player standing in the goal.

See Puck

Rob (of a Goal): The act by which a goaltender makes an incredible save, effectively robbing a player of a goal.

391

"Crosby was absolutely robbed as Brodeur jumped across the crease to make a miraculous glove save!"

Rocket Richard Trophy: *See* Maurice "Rocket" Richard Trophy

Rogers Arena: Current name of the home of the Vancouver Canucks. Formerly known as General Motors (GM) Place. Opened in 1995, the arena was built to replace the aging Pacific Coliseum. The arena seats 18,890 for hockey games, has 88 luxury suites, 12 hospitality suites and 2195 club seats. It played host to the 2010 Winter Olympics and was where Sidney Crosby scored the overtime goal against the United States to give Canada the gold medal. GM Place was renamed Canada Hockey Place during the Olympics, and then was rechristened the Rogers Arena for the start of the 2011–12 season. From 1995–2001, the arena also hosted the NBA Vancouver Grizzlies.

See Vancouver Canucks

Role Player: A player on a team who is on the ice for a specific purpose, such as killing a penalty or fighting.

Rolling Puck: A puck that travels along the ice on its side and often moves unpredictably.

Roof: The top of the net between the front crossbar and the back of the goal. When a player blasts the puck into the upper part of the net, they have "roofed" the puck.

Rookie: A first-year player in any given league.

Roster: A list of the players on a team.

Roughing: A penalty given to a player who goes above and beyond the basic physical nature of the game and attempts to injure an opposing player. Referees will usually assess a two-minute penalty for a minor infraction.

When looking back to old-time hockey, many people see those days through rose-coloured glasses as a time when gentlemen played the game and fun was had by all with few instances of violence. But early hockey was anything but gentlemanly, and rough play was common.

Rover: The rover, a position that was used in the early days of the game and was often called the fourth forward, could venture anywhere on the ice and could be used as either a defensive or offensive player. On a faceoff, the rover was positioned directly to the left of the centreman. Because the rover was useful at both ends of the ice, he was usually required to be a fast and highly skilled skater. Lester Patrick, Si Griffis, Hobey Baker and Frank McGee were some of the greatest athletes to ever play the rover position.

R

The position was officially discontinued when the NHL came into existence in 1917, though other leagues such as the Pacific Coast Hockey Association (PCHA) continued to use it until the 1920s.

Rubber: A puck. During practise, a coach will often say, "All right, let's get the rubber out," meaning that he wants the pucks on the ice so that practise can start.

See Puck

S

SV%: Statistical abbreviation for Save Percentage.

Sandwich Session: The second period of a hockey game.

San Jose Arena: Former name of the San Jose Sharks arena.

See HP Pavilion

San Jose Sharks: After NHL hockey failed in Southern California when the Oakland/California Seals folded, and with the Los Angeles Kings not too far behind, it was a surprise to hear in 1990 that the NHL was trying again with the San Jose Sharks.

At the 1991 expansion draft, the Sharks took on a host of young players as well as a bunch of grizzled veterans like goaltender Brian Hayward and defenceman Doug Wilson. At the 1991 Entry Draft, the team selected Pat Fallon second overall and also picked Ray Whitney and Sandis Ozolinsh.

The Sharks played their first game on October 4, 1991, a 4–3 loss to the Vancouver Canucks. The team faced the growing pains of an expansion franchise and their first two years in the league were painful. They endured an embarrassing 13-game losing streak in 1992–93—losing one game to the Calgary Flames 13–1—and won just 11 games that season. In their third season, the Sharks moved out of the cramped Cow Palace and into their new state-of-the-art arena, now called HP Pavilion. The 1993–94 season completely reversed the fortunes of the franchise, mostly thanks to the coaching of Kevin Constantine. The Sharks ended up making the playoffs that year and upset the Detroit Red Wings in a thrilling seven-game series. San Jose was taken out in the second round after another equally thrilling seven-game series against the Toronto Maple Leafs.

Just two seasons later, however, the Sharks were back to the bottom of the league and looking for a way out. Owen Nolan was acquired in a trade to add scoring depth, and by the 1997–98 season, the Sharks returned to the top of the food chain and into the playoffs. However, success in the playoffs can be an elusive affair, and the Sharks were taken out in the first round in 1998 and 1999. The Sharks suffered for a few years from their mediocrity, never making it far into the playoffs and not being bad enough to rebuild their team with high draft picks. The team, though, still managed to look competitive each year. Patrick Marleau, Dan Boyle and the eventual signing of Joe Thornton from the Boston Bruins seemed to solidify the club as potential Stanley Cup champions, especially in the 2002 and 2004 playoffs after they finished in first place in their division, but they could not find a way to translate it to postseason success.

If there was ever a year for the Sharks to win, it would have been the 2008–09 season, when they finished the season with a 53–18–11 record and first-place overall in the entire league. They had scoring, goaltender Evgeni Nabakov was playing at the top of his game and their defence was one of the toughest and quickest in the league. But the club succumbed to the playoff pressure and were booted out by the

Anaheim Ducks in the first round. Every year since, the Sharks have finished the season strong, but their fans only hope that one day they will go all the way.

San Jose Sharks Records

Most goals in a season: Jonathan Cheechoo, 56 (2005–06)

Most goals in a season, rookie: Logan Couture, 32 (2010–11)

Most assists in a season: Joe Thornton, 92 (2006–07)

Most points in a season: Joe Thornton, 114 (2006–07)

Most points in a season, defenceman: Sandis Ozolinsh, 64 (1993–94)

Most penalty minutes in a season: Link Gaetz, 326 (1991–92)

Most games played in a season: Evgeni Nabokov, 77 (2007–08)

Most wins in a season: Evgeni Nabokov, 46 (2007–08)

Most shutouts in a season: Evgeni Nabokov, 9 (2003–04)

See HP Pavillion

Saucer Pass: A pass that seems to float slightly above the ice and lands directly on the stick of the receiving player.

Sauve les Meubles!: A colourful French term used to describe an incredible play by a goaltender or player to make a save. The literal translation is "Save the furniture!"

Scalper: A person who sells tickets outside of arenas at a higher value than the original price of the ticket. He or she stands on corners near arenas usually wearing baseball caps and screaming "Tickets!" or "Hey, Buddy, wanna buy a ticket?"

Scoreboard: The large electronic device that is suspended above the ice in the centre of the arena displaying the score of the game, instant replays on the large screens and advertisements.

Scoresheet: Official document that records the statistics of one game.

Scotiabank Place: Current home of the Ottawa Senators as of 1996, formerly known as the Palladium and the Corel Centre. Built in 1996 to house the Senators franchise, the building seats 20,000 fans for a hockey game. The first NHL game took place on January 15, 1996, when the Montréal Canadiens defeated the Sens 3–0.

See Ottawa Senators

Scotiabank Saddledome: Current home of the Calgary Flames. Formerly known as the Pengrowth Saddledome (2000–2010), Canadian Airlines Saddledome (1996–2000) and Olympic Saddledome (1983–1996). The arena seats 19,289 fans for hockey games. The Saddledome is also home to the Calgary Hitmen of the Western Hockey League (WHL) and the Calgary Roughnecks of the National Lacrosse League.

See Calgary Flames

Scottrade Center: Current home of the St. Louis Blues. Formerly known as the Kiel Center and the Savvis Center. Built to replace the aging St. Louis Arena, the arena seats 19,150 for hockey games. The Blues played their first game there on October 8, 1994.

See St. Louis Blues

Scout: Employee of a team whose job it is to travel to minor league games across North America and Europe to judge the talent of potential players for the NHL.

Scramble: When the puck is loose in front of the net and players from both teams try to get possession. In the midst of the mayhem, players attempt to get control of the puck to either shoot it into the net or to clear it away. You may hear announcers say, "There is a mad scramble in front of the net. Hasek is down and can't find the puck!"

Screen (the Goaltender): Sometimes the easiest way to get a puck past a goaltender is to make sure he cannot see it. To screen the goaltender, the shooter will either position himself between the opponent's defencemen or have one of his own teammates stand in front of the goaltender to obstruct the goalie's view of the puck.

Scribe: A hockey writer.

Scrimmage: A way of describing an informal game. Used often during a team's practice to describe a game between players on the same team.

Seattle Metropolitans: Professional hockey team from the Pacific Coast Hockey Association (PCHA) that lasted from 1915 to 1924. In 1917, when the PCHA and the NHA shared the rights to the Stanley Cup, the Seattle Metropolitans beat the NHA champion Montréal Canadiens to win the first Stanley Cup by an American team. The Metropolitans will also forever be remembered in hockey history for their 1919 Stanley Cup finals against the Canadiens when the series was cancelled because of the Spanish flu epidemic. The Metropolitans got one last shot at the Cup in 1920 but lost to the Ottawa Senators. When the PCHA folded operations in 1924, the Metropolitans closed up shop as well.

Selke Trophy: *See* Frank J. Selke Trophy

Sens: Nickname of the Ottawa Senators.

Set Play: A strategy or play that a team has practised specifically for use in a game-time situation.

Sharpshooter: Name for a player who has a quick release and is known for scoring goals.

Sher-Wood: A brand of hockey equipment.

Shin Pads: In the early days of hockey, the first and most obvious place the players protected was the shins. The shinbone was often the victim of an errant stick or puck, so players strapped on small leather pads extending from just below the knee to the skate boot that protected the leg.

Often, the type of protection used before leather pads were invented was anything a player could get his hands on, such as catalogues, books and newspapers. Modern-day shin pads are lightweight, protect both the shinbone and the knee and can withstand some of the most powerful slapshots in the NHL.

Shinny Hockey: There are many definitions for shinny hockey. The word "shinny" comes from the Scottish game of shinty, which was brought to Canada by Scottish immigrants in the early 1800s and is a cousin of modern-day hockey. Shinty is a game much like field hockey and was adapted to be played on ice. Although "hockey" became the dominant name of the game, the term "shinny" is still used to describe an informal game of hockey. There are no formal rules, but since players usually wear no equipment, the puck cannot be lifted off the ice. The game can be played on ice or concrete.

"Shinny" also refers to a game played on your knees with miniature sticks and a soft ball. Because players are on their knees, the game is played usually in a small room to keep the ball in bounds.

Shinty: Sharing an ancestry with hurling and bandy, shinty is a team sport that was mostly played in Scotland. Similar in some ways to field hockey, shinty allows far more physical contact in the course of a game than what is acceptable in hurling or bandy.

A direct cousin of hurling, shinty grew into its own sport in the Scottish Highlands. Its exact origins are impossible to decipher, but it is known that shinty has been played in Scotland for at least 2000 years. The shinty ball was originally made of wood or bone but was later made from tough leather. It's believed the name "shinty" comes from the cries uttered during the game and the physical, almost violent, nature of the sport. In fact, in Scotland, it wasn't uncommon for shinty games to be targets for government and church officials because matches often led to bouts of drinking and brutishness.

Traditionally, the Scots played shinty the entire year. The most popular time to partake in the game, however, was on New Year's Day when entire villages gathered and played in one large match. When the game was brought to Canada in the early 1800s, many Scottish immigrants continued to

S

play, but over time, the sport evolved because of the different climate and got mixed together with the sports bandy and hurling.

There are two things about shinty that are instrumental when considering the development of hockey. In shinty, players are allowed to hit the ball with both sides of their sticks, and they can also hit the ball while it is in the air. These two particular rules are important because they were incorporated into early games of hockey in Canada when Scottish immigrants brought shinty to the country. And now, as most hockey fans know, players can work the puck with both sides of the stick and are allowed to knock the puck out of the air, as long as it is hit below the level of the crossbar.

See Bandy; Hockey; Hurling

Shootout: A new format the NHL implemented at the start of the 2005–06 season. The shootout is designed to break ties at the end of a four-on-four, five-minute overtime after regulation play. Each team chooses three skaters to take penalty shots on the opposing goaltender. When the three shooters have finished, the team with the most goals wins. If the score remains tied after three shooters, the game goes into a sudden-death shootout, in which each team calls upon one shooter at a time to go head-to-head. The first team to score after an opponent's miss wins the game and earns two points. The team that loses the shootout receives one point.

Short Side: The side of the goal closest to the shooter.

Shorthanded: When one team receives a penalty and is down one or two players for the duration of the penalty, they are said to be shorthanded. A goal scored in the penalty kill is called a shorthanded goal.

See Penalty Kill (PK)

Shoulder Deke: A move used to fake-out an opponent in which the attacker makes a quick move of the shoulders one way while moving his body in the opposite direction.

Shoulder Pads: Remarkably, shoulder pads did not appear in professional hockey until the 1930s and at first were disliked by most players. The pads provided little protection, and players found that the pads restricted their movement on the ice. Many players went without shoulder pads into the late 1930s. Modern-day shoulder pads are constructed with a hard-plastic outer shell, with dense foam underneath to absorb the shock of a body check into the boards.

Shovel: To push the puck or pass in a similar motion to when a person uses a shovel.

Shutout: When a goaltender stops every shot directed at him during the game. Martin Brodeur of the New Jersey Devils owns the record for the most shutouts with 105 and counting. Georges Hainsworth of the Montréal Canadiens, who compiled an amazing 22 shutouts during the 1928–29 NHL season, holds the record for the most shutouts in one season.

Sick Bay: When a player needs to take time to recover from injury or sickness, he is said to be in the "sick bay."

Sieve: A goaltender who lets in a bunch of goals—not a name a goaltender likes having attached to his style of play. A goaltender is branded a sieve because the puck always seems to find a hole through him.

See Sunburn

Silver Seven: Nickname for the Ottawa Senators from 1903 to 1906.

Sin Bin: *See* Penalty Box.

S.J. Sharkie: Mascot of the San Jose Sharks.

Slapshot: This is the hardest shot in hockey. It is when a player winds back his stick, then violently "slaps" the ice slightly behind the puck, using his weight and momentum to propel the puck at blistering speeds. The invention of the slapshot is credited to Bernie "Boom Boom" Geoffrion, who played mainly for the Montréal Canadiens in the 1950s and early '60s. The current hardest slapshot in the NHL is courtesy of the Boston Bruins Zdeno Chara, whose shot was clocked in at 175.1 kilometres (108.8 miles) per hour during the 2012 All-Star game.

Slap Shot **(movie):** A cult classic hockey film starring Paul Newman and the infamous Hanson Brothers. The film depicts hockey as a rough-and-tumble sport with lots of fisticuffs and thuggery, but ultimately reveals the true heart of the athletes who are bonded together by a common goal and the lengths to which they will go to compete for one another. The film has one many occasions been called the greatest hockey movie of all time.

See Hanson Brothers

Slashing: When a player swings his stick at an opponent. Under the old definition, contact was necessary for the infraction to be penalized, but under the new NHL rules, simply the intent to slash can earn the player a minor penalty. Slashing is also known as "hacking" and "laying on the lumber."

Players known for slashing include Ron Hextall, who received a 12-game suspension for slashing and attacking Montréal Canadien Chris Chelios in game six of the 1989 Stanley Cup playoffs, and Billy Smith, who was well known for slashing the feet of any opposing player who came too close to his net.

One of the most famous slashing incidents happened when Boston Bruin Marty McSorley slashed Vancouver Canuck Donald Brashear in the head from behind in the 1999–2000 season. McSorley was suspended from the NHL for one year and was found guilty of assault with a weapon in a Vancouver courtroom.

Sleeper: An attacking player who slips into the centre or neutral zone behind the attacking defencemen.

Slewfoot: Dragging a skate to trip a player.

Slot: The area directly in front of the goaltender. When a player has an opportunity to score all alone close to the net, he is said to be "in the slot."

See Doorstep; In the Slot; Kitchen

Slow Whistle: When a referee or linesman waits to blow his whistle because of a delayed penalty or delayed offside.

Slush: What the ice in the old Dallas Reunion Arena was called. Maintaining an ice rink in Texas ain't easy.

See Reunion Arena

Smythe Division: Formed in 1974 as part of the Campbell Conference and named after Conn Smythe. Existed until the 1993 season when all the divisions were given geographic denominations. The Vancouver Canucks were the only constant team since the division's inauguration.

See Northwest Division; Pacific Division

Sniper: The most dangerous offensive player on the ice. The sniper can find openings in the net where others see nothing. If a goaltender moves out to cut the angle, leaving only a few inches of open net, the sniper is quite capable of quickly snapping the puck into that open part of the net. Snipers possess a blistering slapshot, a quick release and are always deadly accurate. Alexander Ovechkin and Ilya Kovalchuk are two of the deadliest modern-day snipers in the NHL.

Snow Job: Remember when the local bully would plant your face in a snowbank and you would come up with a beard of snow? Well, goaltenders across the league relive some painful childhood memories every time players stop abruptly in front of the crease and send up a wall of white ice in their face. The snow job, or snow plow, is annoying, but it is an unavoidable part of the game. Goaltenders spend a good part of the game on their knees, and it is a consequence of this position that players charging to the net must come to a complete stop rather suddenly, sending up a spray of ice into the goaltender's face. However, sometimes players purposely snow job the goaltender. A smart goaltender keeps his head down after making a save.

Snow Plow: *See* Snow Job

Soft Dump: Not what you think. A soft, lofted shot to the corner. This shot was inspired by goaltenders such as Marty Brodeur who are so good with their sticks that a normal dump-in has little chance of working.

> *See* Dump-in

Soft Hands: The innate ability that some players have to handle the puck, making difficult moves look easy. Players such as Alexei Kovalev, Sidney Crosby and Vincent Lecavalier are among the players with the softest hands in the NHL today. The opposite of a player with soft hands is one with stone hands.

Southeast Division: Formed in 1998 as part of the Eastern Conference to accommodate all the new expansion teams in the United States. Current lineup includes the Florida

S

Panthers, Washington Capitals, Tampa Bay Lightning, Winnipeg Jets and Carolina Hurricanes.

Spearing: Stabbing an opponent with the blade of the stick. An automatic major and game misconduct is given to any player caught spearing an opponent.

Spin-o-rama: When a player makes one or a series of circles or spins while keeping the puck under control to elude his opponents. The term was invented by broadcasting legend Danny Gallivan and popularized by Dennis Savard. The spin-o-rama is especially impressive when the player gets a shot off while performing this manoeuver.

Spit Splinters: What you do after you get a high stick in the mouth.

Split the Defence: When a lone player stickhandles the puck between two pinching defencemen, gets through unscathed and goes on to score a goal. Mario Lemieux was one of the most proficient players at splitting the defence, and the one time that he skated between two Minnesota North Star players to score a highlight-reel goal is still played on sports channels as one of the top goals of all time.

Splits: When a goaltender spreads his legs as far as possible in opposite directions to cover the bottom of the net. Female goaltenders have a much easier time with this manoeuver. Used mostly in desperation when the goaltender is caught out of position, though Jonathan Quick of the Los Angeles Kings has made this move an integral part of his goaltending style.

Spread Eagle: Another way of describing the butterfly style of goaltending. The goaltender spreads his legs along

the goal line, taking away the lower half of the net from the shooter.

See Butterfly Goaltending

Stacking the Pads: Generally a move of desperation by a goaltender. When there is a sudden two-on-one break, the goaltender is forced to face the puck carrier while the lone defenceman tries to block the pass across to the other player coming down the opposite side. If the player is able to pass the puck off to his teammate, the goaltender must make a desperate slide across the net to make the save. One way to do this is by "stacking the pads"—sliding feet-first with the pads stacked on top of each other in the direction of the shooter to block as much of the open net as possible.

Stand on his Head: An expression used when a goalie makes an exceptional attempt to stop a puck. Literally

409

standing on his head is most unlikely, but many goaltenders have come remarkably close to doing this in order to make a save. Radio and television personalities love to use this expression to describe an acrobatic save, but few know where the actual expression comes from.

Prior to 1918, goaltenders were not allowed to fall to the ice to stop the puck, and if they did, they received a two-minute penalty for the infraction. Goaltender Clint Benedict did everything in his power to get around this rule and have it overturned. To advance his cause, Benedict developed the unique ability to lose his balance and fall to the ice at the exact moment he needed to make a save. Referees had a difficult time deciding whether Benedict was just weak in the knees or if he was intentionally breaking the rules. For his antics, critics gave Benedict nicknames such as "Praying Benny" and "Tumbling Clint" because he spent so much time on the ice.

But Benedict's persistence finally paid off when frustrated referees complained to NHL president Frank Calder. Angered by the referees' inability to call the penalty and worried that other goaltenders might pick up Benedict's bad habits, Calder capitulated and changed the rule on January 9, 1918, allowing goaltenders to fall to the ice to make a save. Obviously annoyed at having his hand forced, Calder stated after changing the rule: "In the future, they can fall on their knees or stand on their heads if they think they can stop the puck better in that way than by standing on their feet."

Stand-up Style: In this style of goaltending, the netminder stops the puck while remaining upright. Goalies in the early days of the game were required to use the stand-up style of goaltending simply because they were not allowed to fall to the ice to stop the puck. Thanks to Clint Benedict (*See* Stand on his Head), the rule was changed in early 1918 to allow goaltenders to fall to their knees to make a save, but the stand-up style continued among the professional ranks for decades, because without the protection of face masks, goaltenders were still at the mercy of every errant puck and stick that came their way. Goaltenders using this style relied on their quick reflexes to stop pucks that skirted along the ice with a kick save or with their sticks.

Even with the advent of the butterfly style of goaltending in the 1960s and with the added protection of modern face masks, stand-up goaltending remained popular with net-minders well into the late 1980s. One of the last proponents of the style was Kirk McLean, who retired from the game in 2001. Some of the most notable goaltenders to use the stand-up with success were Jacques Plante, Terry Sawchuk, Ken Dryden, Johnny Bower, Bernie Parent and Bill Durnan.

See Butterfly Goaltending

Stanley Cup: The Holy Grail of hockey. Lord Stanley, Governor General of the Dominion of Canada, donated sports' most recognized trophy to the game he loved in 1893. Originally inscribed as the Dominion Hockey Challenge Cup, it was awarded to the top team in amateur hockey and quickly became the most coveted prize in the sport. The first team to win Lord Stanley's "Mug" (as the Cup is sometimes called) was the Montréal Hockey Club, who took home the trophy in 1893. The Montréal Canadiens have won the most Stanley Cup championships with 24, followed by the Toronto Maple Leafs with 13.

S Over the history of the Stanley Cup, it has seen and done many interesting things, like taking a shower with Steve Yzerman or getting mistaken as a pot for flowers. The Cup has also experienced its share of dirty days. After winning the Cup in 1937, Detroit Red Wings forward Gord Pettinger mistook the trophy for a toilet and urinated in the Cup. But one of the most memorable incidents happened in 1964 after the Leafs won the Cup and Red Kelly got his day with the trophy. At the Kelly home, a photographer showed up to take pictures of the family happily posing with the Cup. For one photo, Kelly thought it would make a cute picture if he placed his naked infant son in the bowl. The photo was a wonderful memory, but his son left behind a memory of his own. "He did the whole load in the Cup. He did everything," said Kelly about the incident. "That's why our family always laughs when we see players drinking champagne from the Cup."

See Challenge Cup

Stanza: A period in a hockey game.

Staples Center: Current home of the Los Angeles Kings. The Staples Center also hosts the Los Angeles Clippers and Los Angeles Lakers. After the Great Western Forum began to show its age, the Kings moved into the new Staples Center for the start of the 1999–2000 season. It is a state-of-the-art arena complex that seats 18,118 fans for hockey games.

See Los Angeles Kings

Starr Manufacturing Company: One of the earliest manufacturers of skates in Canada. Based in Dartmouth, Nova Scotia, and founded in 1861 by John Forbes and Thomas Bateman, the company came up with a design in 1865 that revolutionized leisure skating and hockey: the self-fastening spring skate. The invention allowed skaters to quickly fasten and remove the skate blades from their everyday boots with the flick of a lever. In those days, skates boots did not have the blades attached. Skaters had to spend a significant amount of time tying the blades to their boots with laces, which if not done properly made the skates unstable and prone to falling off during use. Prior to the Starr skate, most skates were made for leisure skating, with blades that were flat along the edge and very long. Starr was the first company to recognize

S

the need for a specific style of skate for the growing number of hockey players, so they made the blade shorter, with slight curves on both ends and rounded off the edges to allow for greater turning, manoeuvring and stopping.

The company then went on to develop special skate boots and then goaltender-specific skates. At the height of the company's production in the 1920s, Starr had offices world-wide, and even the Boston Bruins officially endorsed the skates.

Starting the Wrong Lineup: Probably the rarest of penalties given in the NHL. Prior to the start of the game, the coach is required to provide the referee or the official score-keeper with a list of the players who will be in the starting lineup, and if any changes are made to that lineup before the game begins, a bench minor penalty is given to the offending team, provided the referee is notified of the infraction before a second faceoff.

Stay-at-home Defenceman: Often referred to as a "defence-man's defenceman," the stay-at-home defenceman is a reliable position player who is strongly committed to defence and rarely makes an offensive rush. This type of defenceman scores few goals but is the best player to put on the ice during a penalty-killing situation.

See Offensive Defenceman

Stick: The hockey stick has come a long way from its earliest incarnation—which resembled a field hockey stick—to today's modern composite $300 (or more) stick. Most people look at a hockey stick and see a simple piece of wood that has been bent into shape. Equipment in the first several decades of the sport remained fairly simple and utilitarian. Hockey sticks (at first called "hurley" instead of "sticks") were the same sticks the players used in their summer games of hurling, but as the sport evolved, so did the sticks. Sticks lost the extreme curve at the blade and began to flatten out so that more of the blade could come into contact with the puck.

In 1850, a man named Alexander Rutherford of Lindsay, Ontario, carved a hockey stick out of a tree branch. One hundred and fifty years later, his great, great grandson had the stick evaluated as the oldest hockey stick in the world, worth $2 million.

By the early 1890s, several companies were producing hockey sticks for players across Canada and the northern United States, although in those days many players still made their own sticks from a single piece of yellow birch or hornbeam. The two most popular brands were the Mic-Mac hockey stick and the Rex hockey stick from the Starr Company. In the 1904 edition of *Eaton's Catalogue*, the Mic-Mac brand of stick sold for 39 cents. In the early days of hockey, it was not uncommon for players to call their sticks "hockeys."

S

Up until the middle of the 20th century, hockey sticks were constructed by roughly the same method, but by the 1960s, several companies had begun to experiment with fibreglass in their sticks. By placing the strong material within the shaft and the blade, sticks lasted much longer and were less likely to break under the rigours of the professional game.

St. Louis Arena: Built in 1929, the arena served as the home of the NHL's St. Louis Eagles for one short year, in 1934–35. When the NHL returned to St. Louis in 1967, the

415

building underwent a major renovation to suit the needs of a more modern NHL club. From 1967 to the day the arena closed in 1994, it sat 17,188 spectators for a hockey game. The St. Louis Blues played their final game in the old arena on April 24, 1994, losing the fourth game of the opening round of the playoffs to the Dallas Stars.

See Scottrade Center

St. Louis Blues: Added to the NHL during the 1967 expansion, the St. Louis Blues were named for the rich heritage of blues music for which the city is known. Playing in the newly created West Division along with the six other expansion clubs, the Blues were the standout team of the expansion era. During the expansion draft, the original six teams were allowed to hang onto their superstars, giving the expansion teams little chance to succeed against the tougher competition. The playoff format was also slanted in the original six teams' favour as they did not meet one of the expansion club teams until the Stanley Cup final.

However, led by Scotty Bowman, the Blues managed to make the best of the situation with their mix of veteran and rookie lineup, making the Stanley Cup playoffs in their first three years in the league. Unfortunately, each time they made it, the Blues were booted out in four straight games by one of the more talented original six teams. Despite the losses to the more powerful clubs, the players were happy in St. Louis as the new owners went out of their way to please the players, buying them cars and treating them to Florida vacations. Twilight veterans Doug Harvey, Jacques Plante and Glenn Hall all postponed retirement to play for the new franchise.

Owner Sidney Solomon Jr. was well loved, but as he got older, he passed over control of the team to his son, Sidney Solomon III, and things began to deteriorate. Taking over after the Blues third consecutive loss in the Stanley Cup finals, Solomon III began poking his nose in the affairs of the team, and the veteran players and general manager and coach Scotty Bowman did not like it one bit. From the day Bowman left in 1971 until 1977, the Blues were a team in crisis. Nine coaches came and went in that period and four general managers as well.

By 1977, the team was on the verge of a financial crisis and in need of a saviour. That year, former NHL goaltender Emile "The Cat" Francis took over as general manager and saved the team from ruin. In his first few months on the job, he convinced the Ralston Purina company to invest in the Blues. With financial backing, Francis then set out to rebuild the team on the ice. After a disastrous 1978–79 season that saw the club win just 18 games, Francis used his draft position to select future stars Bernie Federko, Brian Sutter and Mike Liut. After two years out of the playoff picture, the Blues were reborn by the 1979–80 season, and the fans were again behind the club.

Six years after their original investment, the Ralston Purina company had seen no increase in revenue, in fact losing $1.8 million in their final year of investment, so by 1983, the company decided to pull out. During the off-season, the Blues owners almost sold the franchise to a group of owners in Saskatoon, Saskatchewan, but the league blocked the deal. The Blues then faced the problem of being locked out of St. Louis Arena because it was owned by the Purina company. As a result of their tenuous position, the Blues did not even participate in the 1983 NHL Entry Draft.

On the verge of collapse, the franchise was saved when businessman Harry Ornest stepped in and bought the team. General manager Ron Caron and head coach Jacques Demers were brought on and turned the team around and back up the NHL ladder. Federko, Sutter and Doug Gilmour became the stars of the team. Gritty blue-collar type hockey spoke to the people of St. Louis and turned the franchise into a profitable one. The Blues' greatest success on the ice came in the 1986 playoffs when they were one goal away from making the Stanley Cup finals. After defeating the Minnesota North Stars and Toronto Maple Leafs, the St. Louis Blues went into the conference finals against an equally gritty Calgary Flames. The Flames and the Blues battled through seven hard-fought games, but it was the Blues that got burned in the end, losing the deciding game by a score of 2–1.

The Blues found success in the coming years with players like Brett Hull, whose incredible shot lit the lamps across the league hundreds of times in his tenure with the team. The grit and intelligence of Hull's set-up man on the ice, Adam Oates, also made the club a hard team to play on any night. Through the 1980s and 1990s, the Blues made the playoffs every year but could never seem to go far into the postseason, not once making it to the finals. Even the addition of Wayne Gretzky to the Blues for just 18 games in 1995–96 could not push them to success in the postseason.

The Blues eventually parted ways with Hull, Gretzky and Oates and found new life in players Brendan Shanahan, Chris Pronger, Roman Turek and Pavol Demitra who injected excitement into the city, but in the playoffs, the Blues still could not get any luck. The team came close again in 2001 when they made it to the conference finals but ended up losing to the Colorado Avalanche.

Since then, the Blues have changed their roster several times, changed owners, changed general managers but have yet to bring any postseason thrills to St. Louis fans. In 2006, for the first time since 1979, the Blues failed to make the playoffs. It was clear from their performance that year that they were a team in transition, and only in the 2011–12 season have the Blues managed to rebound. Led by goaltender Jaroslav Halak, Jason Arnott, Jamie Langenbrunner and the coaching of Ken Hitchcock, the Blues have transformed into the blue-collar gritty team that moved the city to cheers back in the old days.

St. Louis Blues Records

Most goals in a season: Brett Hull, 86 (1990–91)

Most assists in a season: Adam Oates, 90 (1990–91)

Most points in a season: Brett Hull, 131 (1990–91)

Most points in a season, defenceman: Jeff Brown, 78 (1992–93)

Most points in a season, rookie: Jorgen Pettersson, 73 (1980–81)

Most penalty minutes in a season: Bob Gassoff, 306 (1975–76)

Most wins in a season: Roman Turek, 42 (1999–2000)

Most shutouts in a season: Glenn Hall, 8 (1968–69)

Lowest goals-against average in a season (minimum 30 games played): Roman Turek, 1.95 (1999–2000)

See Scottrade Center

St. Louis Eagles: After the Ottawa Senators fell victim to the financial pressures of the Great Depression, the franchise picked up and moved to St. Louis to become the Eagles in 1934. Attendance on the club's opening night was around 12,000, but that steadily fell off as the season progressed. Fans could not be excited about a team that left Ottawa at the bottom of the league. By mid-season, the Eagles continued their losing ways, and the financial strain of travel, players' salaries and poor attendance had sunk the team even before the season was done. At the end of the season, the NHL bought out the franchise and distributed the players to the remaining teams. In the St. Louis Eagles' only year in the NHL, they had a record of 11–31–6 and leading scorer Syd Howe had just 14 goals and 13 assists.

See Ottawa Senators

Stone a Shooter: To stone a shooter is not to whip rocks at him, but rather it is when a goaltender makes a spectacular save on a player from in close. The shooter usually finds himself alone in front of the net with the puck, and just as he is about to put the puck in the open part of the net, the goaltender sticks out a pad, glove or any part of his body to stop the puck and thus "stones" the shooter.

Stone Hands: *See* Soft Hands

St. Petersburgh Times Forum: Former name of the home arena of the Tampa Bay Lightning.

See Tampa Bay Times Forum

Strip: To take the puck away from another player. When one player loses the puck to an opponent, he has been stripped of the puck.

Sudden Death: A term that describes the overtime or shootout period in hockey. In soccer, an overtime period continues even when a team has scored to break the tie, giving the opposition a chance to get back in the game until the time runs out. With just one goal able to clinch a win for either team in hockey, it is fitting that the overtime period has become known as sudden death. The game ends as soon as the tie-breaking goal is scored, and the opposing team does not get another chance to tie the game. The term "sudden death" can also be used for the shootout. If the first three shooters do not break the tie, the game comes down to the sudden-death shootout in which the first team to finish one round with a goal wins the game.

See Shootout

Sunburn: What a goaltender gets from the red lights behind the net when he lets in a lot of goals.

See Sieve

Superstition: A strong belief for many players. For example, many players do not shave during the playoffs, believing that this will improve their chances of winning the Stanley Cup. Other superstitions include always putting on equipment in the same order, eating the same meal before every game or not showering after a win. Goaltenders are considered to be the most superstitious. Ron Hextall used to smack his stick on the goalposts all through the game to keep himself focused, Patrick Roy used to talk to his goalposts and Glenn Hall had the strange ritual of throwing up before every game.

S

Suspension: A suspension is supplementary discipline handed out by the NHL's vice-president of hockey and business operations, which was occupied in 2011–12 by Brendan Shanahan. Suspensions are handed out when a player commits a serious infraction of the rules in the game or conducts himself in a manner outside the arena that embarrasses the league. Any athlete that is suspended must generally forfeit their pay for the duration of the suspension. Teams can also suspend players for violation of team rules. The longest suspension in NHL history was handed out to Chris Simon of the New York Islanders in 2007 for stomping on the leg of Pittsburgh's Karko Ruutu, for which he received a 30-game suspension.

S

T

TD Garden: Current home of the Boston Bruins. Formerly known as Shawmut Center, Fleet Center and TD Banknorth Garden. Built as a replacement for the legendary Boston Garden, the Boston Bruins also share the facilities with the Boston Celtics of the NBA.

See Boston Bruins

TV Timeout: A break in the flow of the game normally lasting between 60 and 120 seconds to allow television and radio stations to pause for commercials. They are called at the 6-, 10- and 14-minute mark of each period, subject to the referee stopping the play.

Taking the Man: When a player plays a one-on-one defence against an attacking opponent.

Tampa Bay Ice Palace: Former name of the Tampa Bay Lightning's home arena.

See Tampa Bay Times Forum

Tampa Bay Lightning: Founded in 1992 by former NHLers Phil and Tony Esposito, the team got its name from Tampa's status as the "Lightning Capital of North America." After installing himself as the president and general manager, Phil Esposito hired Terry Crisp as the team's head coach, and then began to flesh out his roster. In order to sell hockey to the Southern U.S. audience, Esposito tried a media stunt by allowing female goaltender Manon Rheaume to play in an exhibition game against the St. Louis Blues. The media stunt worked and garnered the Lightning a lot of attention and helped to fill the tiny 11,000-seat Expo Hall on October 7, 1992, for their first regular-season game. Tampa Bay shocked the hockey world by beating the Chicago Blackhawks 7–3, with a four-goal night by little-known player Chris Kontos. The Lightning started the 1992–93 season off well but ended out of the playoffs after a series of prolonged losing streaks.

The poor finish in the regular season allowed the team to select high in the draft, taking big forward Chris Gratton with the third overall pick. Esposito also added Petr Klima from Edmonton for additional scoring, but the Lightning needed much more help than that. The Lightning did not have a successful season until 1995–96, when Darren Puppa's goaltending and Terry Crisp's passionate coaching finally lifted the team up and into the playoffs. Unfortunately, the Lightning were ousted from the postseason by the Philadelphia Flyers. Esposito had hoped that the team's new arena, the Tampa Bay Ice Palace, would lift spirits and translate into wins for the 1996–97 season, but the team fell back into its losing ways and, until the 2002–03 season, failed to make the playoffs each year.

Even the arrival of Vincent Lecavalier in 1998 and Nikolai Khabibulin in 2001 could not pull the Lightning out of their slump. But finally, in 2002, the club added Brad Richards, Dave Andreychuk and Martin St. Louis and in the 2002–03 season completely turned the team around, making the playoffs for the second time in their history. The team even managed to win a playoff series, beating the Washington Capitals in six games. The Lightning lost to the New Jersey Devils in the next round. It was a disappointing ending, but the club was headed in the right direction.

The Lightning finished the 2003–04 season as the second best team overall, and their top players were at their best and healthy. Chugging through the playoffs, they defeated the New York Islanders, Montréal Canadiens and Philadelphia Flyers to make it to the Stanley Cup finals against the Calgary Flames. It was a tight series, going all the way to a seventh game, but in the end, the Lightning won the franchise's first Stanley Cup championship.

After waiting a year to defend their championship because of the NHL lockout, the Lightning seemed to have lost their spark, barely making the playoffs with 93 points and losing to the Ottawa Senators in the first round. After another early exit from the playoffs in 2007, the Lightning failed to make the playoffs again until 2011, where they were booted out in the opening round. Not even the addition of superstar sniper Steven Stamkos could elevate the club to postseason success, but with their star players healthy and everyone contributing, the Lightning could shock us all in the years to come.

Tampa Bay Lightning Records

Most goals in a season: Vincent Lecavalier, 52 (2006–07)

Most assists in a season: Martin St. Louis (2010–11) and Brad Richards (2005–06), 68

Most points in a season: Vincent Lecavalier, 108 (2006–07)

Tampa Bay Lightning Records (continued)

Most points in a season, defenceman: Roman Hamrlik, 65 (1995–96)

Most points in a season, rookie: Brad Richards, 62 (2000–01)

Most penalty minutes in a season: Zenon Konopka, 265 (2009–10)

Most wins in a season: Nikolai Khabibulin, 30 (2002–03)

Most shutouts in a season: Nikolai Khabibulin, 7 (2001–02)

See Tampa Bay Times Forum

Tampa Bay Times Forum: Opened in October 1996 under the name Tampa Bay Ice Palace, the now-dubbed Tampa Bay Times Forum seats around 19,200 fans for hockey games but also plays host to basketball games, concerts and wrestling matches. From 1993 to 1996, the Lightning played their home games in an older football arena.

See Tampa Bay Lighting

Tape: Adhesive fabric applied to a player's stick to help control the puck and provide grip to the upper part of the stick where the player holds it.

Tape-to-tape: An accurate pass in which the puck leaves one player's stick blade and hits a teammate's blade directly on the tape.

Ted Lindsay Award: Formerly known as the Lester B. Pearson Award. Name was changed in April 2010 to honour Hall of Fame player Ted Lindsay for his role in hockey.

See Lester B. Pearson Award

Tee Time: A golf reference used to describe a team that gets eliminated from the playoffs.

Tee Up the Puck: Describes an action in which a player receives a pass, sets up the puck in position for a shot and lets go a cannon-like blast.

Telescoping: A way for the goaltender to move forward and backward within his crease without his skates ever leaving the ice. This move is accomplished simply by bringing the feet together to slide backward and separating the feet to move forward. In a game, the goaltender will telescope to get into the right position to face the shooter, usually when the opposing team crosses into the zone.

T

Texas Hat Trick: Four goals scored by a player in a single game.

Three Blind Mice: Insulting term for the referee and the two linesmen before the days of two referees. The Disney tune "Three Blind Mice" was once played by an organist at a hockey game. It was considered offensive by the NHL, which later ruled that the tune could not be played at games.

Three Stars: A tradition in which the best three players of the game are chosen by the press, the stadium announcers or special invited guests. A hometown player who is selected as one of the three stars skates out onto the ice after the game and salutes the crowd. When a player from the away team is selected, the home crowd usually boos him severely if he has the nerve to skate out onto the ice.

When Montréal Canadiens legend Maurice Richard scored all five goals in a Stanley Cup game against the Toronto Maple Leafs in 1944, he received all three stars for the night. This didn't happen again until February 3, 2012, when Sam Gagner of the Edmonton Oilers scored four goals and had four assists against the Chicago Blackhawks, tying Gretzky and Paul Coffey's franchise record of eight points in a single game.

Throat Protector: A plastic guard that players wear to protect their necks.

Thunder Bug: Mascot of the Tampa Bay Lightning.

Tic-tac-toe: A fancy play in which an attacking team makes several quick, accurate passes before getting a final shot on net. A tic-tac-toe looks much better if it results in a goal, of course.

Tickle the Twine: When a goal is scored and the puck hits only the netting.

See Ripple the Mesh

Timekeeper: This official's job is to record the time of starting and finishing of each period in the game. The time-keeper will also stop and start the clock upon hearing the referee's whistle in the game.

Timeout: A timeout is used when a coach sees that his team needs a break and wants to go over strategy for the next play. It is normally used near the end of a game when a team is down by a goal and is in the attacking zone, sometimes with the goalie pulled.

T

Too Many Men on the Ice: A frustrating penalty that occurs when a team on a line change leaves too many players on the ice. The regulations state that having too many players on the ice is allowed as long as those leaving the ice during a line change are within five feet (1.5 metres) of the bench and do not get involved in the play. A two-minute minor is assessed to the offending team.

Toronto Maple Leafs: Toronto has been at the centre of hockey's development since the sport's beginning in Canada. But from the late 1880s up until the formation of the National Hockey Association (NHA) in 1909, Toronto didn't have a team it could call a champion.

Several athletic clubs across the city iced competitive teams, but they never seemed to gain any ground against their powerful counterparts in Ottawa and Montréal. It wasn't until the arrival of the Toronto Blueshirts in 1912 that the city's hockey fans finally witnessed a quality team. The Blueshirts had almost immediate success as part of the NHA, finishing the 1913–14 season near the top of the league and going all the way to the Stanley Cup final, where they beat the Montréal Canadiens to win the franchise's first Stanley Cup.

During World War I, however, it was difficult for teams to find players with enough skill come game time. To make matters worse in Toronto, team owner Frank Robinson joined the military and left the team without a leader. This is when Eddie Livingstone stepped in. Livingstone was a shrewd businessman and could see a good deal a mile away. In 1915, he purchased the Toronto Blueshirts from Robinson and set about building his team, which was not an easy task because many of the players had left Toronto after Robinson quit. With the promise of more money, the rival Pacific Coast Hockey Association (PCHA) had persuaded a good chunk of the Blueshirts to abandon the NHA, leaving Livingstone with the prospect of not having a team to put on the ice when the 1915–16 season began.

But Livingstone also owned another Toronto NHA franchise named the Shamrocks. He simply transferred the players from the Shamrocks to the Blueshirts and folded the former. The ease with which Livingstone always seemed to get by rubbed other team owners the wrong way, and he was left with some enemies. One classic example is when, in 1917, after trade disputes and arguments over how the Stanley Cup playoffs should be structured, the owners of the Montréal Canadiens, Québec Bulldogs, Montréal Wanderers and Ottawa Senators got together and began their plot to get rid of Livingstone.

For the 1916–17 season, the NHA added another Toronto team made up of soldiers from the Canadian military's 228th Battalion. The team was extremely popular with Toronto crowds, but its future in the league was uncertain, given that the 228th Battalion could be called to active duty at any moment and be shipped off to the war in Europe. The team, however, managed to finish the first half of the season in a respectable second place, behind the Montréal Canadiens. But the need for soldiers in the war effort grew too great for the military to allow the battalion to continue playing, and the team had to leave halfway through its first season. The owners of the rest of the teams left behind met to decide how to go ahead with the remainder of the season and so it was rather unceremoniously, without any warning or compensation, that they

T

took advantage of this opportunity to dump Livingstone and the Toronto Blueshirts from the NHA.

Livingstone immediately sought legal action against the league, but the owners were resolute in their decision to oust him from their operations. The owners of the Canadiens, Wanderers and Senators decided they needed a new league and a new team in Toronto to keep Livingstone on the outs. On November 26, 1917, all interested parties finally came to an agreement, the new National Hockey League (NHL) was formed, and Frank Calder, former NHA secretary-treasurer, was named as the NHL's first president.

The NHL had four teams: two Montréal teams, Ottawa and the new Toronto franchise the league had forced into existence, which was being helmed by a group of approved Toronto businessmen from the Toronto Arena Company. All the players from the Blueshirts were assigned to the new team, and Calder gave Livingstone the order to sell his team to the Toronto Arena Company. Livingstone refused, and so without an official name, the Toronto press simply continued to call the team the Blueshirts, or the Torontos.

 Despite the battle that was going on behind the scenes, the new Toronto team still managed to sign its players and hire its first coach, Dick Carroll. The team that eventually came to be known as the Toronto Maple Leafs officially began operations on December 19, 1917. The team played all their home games at the Toronto Arena Company's building, Arena Gardens (also known as Mutual Street Arena).

Losing their first game against the Montréal Wanderers by a score of 10–9, the Toronto team got off to a bad start, but

432

they soon found chemistry on the ice and, despite the opening loss, finished the season first overall, just ahead of the Montréal Canadiens. For Toronto's first playoff in franchise history, there was not a more fitting opponent than the Canadiens. The eventual rivalry between the two teams began in a two-game, total-goals series, the winner of which was to go on to face the PCHA champion for the Stanley Cup. Toronto won the series by a total score of 10–7 and then went on to win the NHL's first Stanley Cup championship against the Vancouver Millionaires. Toronto goaltender Hap Holmes and forward Howard Meeking were the stars for Toronto in the playoffs.

Ready for a fresh start at the beginning of the 1918–19 season, the now-dubbed Toronto Arenas came back with many of the same players, save for goaltender Holmes who was lured west to join the PCHA's Seattle Metropolitans. As it turned out, without their stellar goalie, the Toronto Arenas were unable to beat teams like the Montréal Canadiens or the Ottawa Senators, and the Arenas finished last in the league and out of the playoffs.

After that season, the franchise was sold to a group of Toronto businessmen, and to re-energize the fans and the players, they changed the name of the team to the Toronto St. Patricks in recognition of the large Irish population in Toronto at the time. Under new management and the addition of Cecil "Babe" Dye and goaltender John Ross Roach, the St. Pats were soon on top of the league and became Stanley Cup champions again in 1922. After the Stanley Cup wins, the franchise took a turn for the worse. Veterans Reg Noble and Jack Adams no longer had the same scoring punch they once had, and the addition of the American

T

franchises meant more competition. By early 1927, the owners of the St. Pats were looking for a buyer, and in February of that year, they sold the franchise to Conn Smythe for $160,000.

On February 15, 1927, not wasting any time making his mark, Smythe renamed his team the Toronto Maple Leafs after the World War I Canadian Maple Leaf regiment and changed the team's uniform to the iconic blue-and-white jersey with the maple leaf crest. In the team's first game as the Maple Leafs on February 17, 1927, Toronto won 4–1 over the New York Americans. But the product on the ice was still slumping in the standings, and it wasn't until the addition of three young players named Charlie Conacher, Joe Primeau and Busher Jackson that the Leafs looked like champions again.

T

With Toronto winning more games, fans packed into Mutual Street Arena. It was then that Smythe realized that if he was going to own a world-class team, he needed to build a world-class arena. Before the start of the 1931–32 season, Smythe began construction of Maple Leaf Gardens. On November 12, 1931, the Toronto Maple Leafs played their first game in Maple Leaf Gardens before a crowd of 14,000 fans. Unfortunately, they lost the inaugural game to the Chicago Blackhawks by a score of 2–1, but the season was going to get a lot better for Leafs fans. The line of Conacher, Primeau and Jackson lit up the league that regular season, but it was in the playoffs that they really shined, beating the Blackhawks, the Montréal Maroons and finally the New York Rangers to win the franchise's third Stanley Cup and their first Cup as the Maple Leafs.

Although the Leafs continued to put together winning seasons, they did not have any luck in the playoffs for the next 10 years. It wasn't until the 1941–42 season that the team turned things around with a new lineup of players that included Sweeney Schriner, Syl Apps and goaltender Turk Broda. Toronto finished the season just three points out of first place overall going into the playoffs. After defeating the New York Rangers in the opening round, Toronto faced the Detroit Red Wings in a best-of-seven series that went down in history. After losing the first three games of the series to the Red Wings, the Toronto Maple Leafs became the only team in NHL history to this day to come back from 3–0 series deficit to win the Stanley Cup.

Toronto won another Cup in 1945, and led by the brilliance of forward Ted Kennedy, the Leafs became the first team in NHL history to win three Stanley Cups in a row, taking the prize from 1947 to 1949 and again in 1951. These were some of the best years for Leafs Nation: the rivalry with Montréal was at its peak, and in addition to Kennedy, Toronto had players such as Howie Meeker and Max Bentley who electrified the crowds on a nightly basis.

Then there was Bill Barilko, arguably one of the most famous Toronto Maple Leafs ever. Barilko was the home-town hero who scored the Stanley Cup–winning goal in overtime that beat out the Montréal Canadiens in the 1951 finals. A week after the massive celebrations died down, Barilko and a friend flew up north on a fishing trip. They never reached their destination, and it wasn't until 11 years later in 1962 that someone spotted the wreckage of Barilko's small plane. Because of his overtime game-winner, his mysterious disappearance immediately afterward and the Leafs' 10-year Cup drought until his body was found, Barilko's story has become the stuff that myths are made of. The band The Tragically Hip immortalized Barilko's story in their 1992 hit song "Fifty-Misson Cap," bringing the young defenceman's story to a whole new audience.

The 1960s brought on the greatest generation of Toronto Maple Leafs. With players Frank Mahovlich, Dave Keon, Red Kelly, goaltender Johnny Bower, George Armstrong and Bob Pulford, the Maple Leafs won three straight Cups from 1962 to 1964, not to mention the last Cup of the original six era in 1967 with a dramatic win over the Montréal Canadiens.

Since 1967, the Toronto Maple Leafs have experienced a few highs and many lows. Harold Ballard, owner, general manager and dictator of the Leafs from 1972 until his death in 1990, plagued the team with bad trades and horrible draft choices, and the team had a terrible unlucky streak in their playoff draws that saw them meet the strongest teams in the early rounds. The 1970s and 1980s were not happy times for Leafs fans.

Even the 1990s were questionable, with the brightest spot coming in the 1992–93 season. Doug Gilmour and the brilliance of goaltender Felix Potvin took the Leafs to within a hair of making it into the Stanley Cup finals for the first time since 1967, and the series would have been against the Canadiens, had the Leafs not run into Wayne Gretzky at the helm of a determined Los Angeles Kings team that eliminated the Leafs.

The team has undergone some drastic changes in recent years through the workings of current general manager Brian Burke, but it remains to be seen if the club can ever return to the top. Fans are religiously dedicated to the boys in blue, however, and they keep the hope alive that one day the Cup will return to Toronto.

Toronto Maple Leafs Records

Most goals in a season: Rick Vaive, 54 (1981–82)

Most goals in a season, rookie: Wendel Clark, 34 (1985–86)

Most assists in a season: Doug Gilmour, 95 (1992–93)

Most points in a season: Doug Gilmour, 127 (1992–93)

Most penalty minutes in a season: Tie Domi, 365 (1997–98)

Most wins in a season: Andrew Raycroft (2006–07) and Ed Belfour (2002–03), 37

See Air Canada Centre (ACC); Maple Leaf Gardens

Tour du Chapeau: French for "hat trick."

See Hat Trick

Trade: When one or more players from a team are exchanged for another player or combination of players from another team. A trade can include draft picks and money as well.

Traffic: As annoying as the five o'clock rush hour can be, goaltenders hate it even more when they find a traffic jam of large hockey players in front of their net. If one of the better goaltenders in the league is manning the goal, the opposing team will always try to put as many bodies as possible in front of him to obstruct his view of the puck. Trying to find a little black disk through a mess of sticks, legs and skates makes the goaltender's job all the more difficult, and even if the goaltender does spot the puck through the traffic, it is more likely to be deflected.

Trailer: A player who follows the action of the play seemingly from a short distance but is actually at the ready for a drop or blind pass.

Trap: While "firewagon hockey" best describes a style of hockey centred purely on scoring as many goals as possible, the "trap" is a style of hockey that is focused on keeping the puck out of a team's zone and out of the net. With the trap, defence is the key. While a good defence has always been part of the game since the sport began, the trap system was not widely used until the mid-1990s.

Players hate the trap and fans are bored by it, but using the style has proven to be an effective way to win hockey games. In the late 1990s, with the proliferation of new franchises in the NHL, it became competitive for general managers to sign the most talented players, leaving some teams such as the Detroit Red Wings with an All-Star lineup, while new teams such as the Florida Panthers languished in the basement of the league. To compensate for the unevenness, coaches with the "less-talented" teams had to work around the system, and soon the neutral zone trap was born.

The trap is easily explained. Take two teams, for example, the Detroit Red Wings versus the New Jersey Devils. When the Devils take the early lead on a goal by Claude Lemieux, that's when head coach Jacques Lemaire puts the neutral zone trap into effect. Sergei Fedorov and Steve Yzerman break out of their zone on the rush but are stopped by a formidable wall of Devils players in the neutral zone, led by master defencemen Scott Stevens and Scott Niedermayer. Every time Detroit tries to break into the Devils' zone, the puck carrier faces a wall of players blocking his way. The odd time the Red Wings do get into the zone to set up for a shot, they are met by the stellar goaltending of Martin Brodeur. The Devils end up winning this game by a score of 2–1 and most of their other games by similar close margins. When

T

the Devils defeated the Detroit Red Wings in the 1995 playoffs to win the Stanley Cup for the first time in their history, weaker teams saw that the trap provided less offensive-minded teams a way to remain competitive.

Another team that based their play around the trap, the Florida Panthers, used the style to get all the way to the Stanley Cup finals in 1996, only to lose in four straight to the Colorado Avalanche.

Veteran defenceman Gary Suter started his career during the high-scoring days of the 1980s and ended it during the heydays of the trap and was never shy in hiding his disdain for it. "You started to see it more and more as expansion grew," he said of the trap. "With the talent level being watered down, teams had to figure out a way to shut down the opposition. When a team is successful at something, it becomes a trend, and that's exactly what happened. It started with New Jersey and then moved around the rest of the league. Now everyone does it."

Always good for an interview, Jeremy Roenick once said of the trap in a post-game interview after a particularly defensive game in which he was held scoreless: "Whoever invented the trap should be shot!"

While the league has tried to make changes to the rules of the game and have referees apply the rules to the letter, defensive systems will always be a part of the game, and no matter what the league does to increase scoring, coaches will always work around the rule changes if they need to.

See Firewagon Hockey

1985–1986 (before the trap became popular)

Thirteen players finished the season with over 100 points, with Wayne Gretzky leading the way with 215 (a league record). Five players finished with 50 goals or more, with the Oilers Jari Kurri at the top with 68 goals. Goaltender Bob Froese of the Philadelphia Flyers led the league with the lowest goals-against average of 2.55, followed by Al Jensen of the Washington Capitals at 3.18.

1998–1999 (the height of the trap's popularity)

Only three players finished the regular season with over 100 points, with Jaromir Jagr at the top with 127 points.

T

Paul Kariya got the most goals that season with 47. Goaltender Ron Tugnutt won the lowest goals-against average race, finishing the regular season at 1.79, while Dominik Hasek of the Buffalo Sabres was not far behind with a 1.87 goals-against average.

Trapper: A goaltender's catching glove. When hockey was just getting its start and people played for no other reason than for the love of the game, the goaltenders' equipment looked almost exactly like the other players. They wore the same skates, donned the same gloves and had nothing but prayers protecting their faces. Sure, there was a little extra padding around the legs, but the only protection against injury that goaltenders had in those days was their instincts. The modern goaltender has all kinds of protection from the puck, but in the past, goalies did not even have anything to catch the puck with; his gloves were identical to those worn by other players. Some goaltenders modified their gloves by adding extra padding, but the objective was protection, not catching pucks. There was little advancement beyond this until 1947, when Chicago Blackhawks goaltender Emile "The Cat" Francis altered his equipment and changed the position forever.

While some goaltenders had altered their gloves to make catching pucks easier, Francis took the idea one step further by designing a glove that copied the style of a first baseman's glove in baseball. He extended the protective wrapping down to his wrists and reinforced the webbing to catch or to trap hockey pucks. He first used the trapper in a game against the Detroit Red Wings; however, when Wings head coach Jack Adams saw the new piece of equipment, he protested to officials that the glove did not belong in a hockey game and was tantamount to cheating. Despite the protests, Francis was allowed to keep his glove on, but the issue was later brought up before NHL president Clarence Campbell for review. After some consideration, he approved the new innovation, and it was written into the rulebook that goal-tenders could now "trap" the puck.

See Blocker

Tripping: An infraction in which a player uses a part of his body or stick to knock the feet out from under another player. It carries a sentence of two minutes in the penalty box.

Turnover: When the team in possession of the puck inadvertently gives the puck to their opponents. This usually occurs when one player makes a mistake, such as a bad pass, losing the puck on a check or a soft dump.

See Soft Dump

Turtle: In the wild, when a turtle is threatened or attacked by a larger, more aggressive predator, it will quickly retreat into its own shell for protection, thus saving itself from harm. This describes a type of hockey player who, when challenged to a fight by an opponent, immediately falls to the ice in the fetal position and covers his head to protect it from the punches of the aggressor. "Turtling" is rather uncommon in the NHL because it is considered a cowardly act.

While there have been many turtles in the NHL, none are more famous than Claude Lemieux. During his long career, Lemieux put his hands to his head and tucked his knees close to his chin on many occasions, but none more famous than his mix-up with Darren McCarty of the Detroit Red

Wings. The story starts during the 1996 conference finals between Lemieux's Colorado Avalanche and the Red Wings on May 29. Lemieux became Detroit's public enemy number one when he checked the Wings Kris Draper from behind, sending him face-first into the boards. Draper suffered a broken jaw and a bloody face in the incident, while Lemieux only received a two-game suspension. The Avalanche went on to win the Stanley Cup, but the Red Wings never forgot what Lemieux did to their teammate.

On March 26, 1997, after waiting for just the right moment, Red Wing Darren McCarty sought out his retribution for the vicious hit on Draper in the first period of the game in front of the partisan crowd at Detroit's Joe Louis Arena. But McCarty would be denied a satisfying revenge because, at the moment he dropped his glove to attack, Lemieux fell to his knees and assumed the turtle position. The opinion is widely held that according to the unwritten code of conduct in the NHL, Lemieux should have stood up and fought McCarty for what he did to Draper.

Twig: Another term for a hockey stick.

See Branch; Stick

Twine Minder: A goaltender.

Two-line Pass: With the new rule that removed the centre red line from play, the two-line pass is no longer part of the game, but before the 2005–06 season, when the rule was introduced, a two-line pass was when a player in his defensive zone passed the puck over his own blue line to a teammate who had already crossed the centre red line. The play was whistled down by the referee, and a faceoff was taken in the offending team's zone.

See Red Line

Two-platoon Goalkeeping: Before the 1960s, most teams used to dress just one goaltender in their starting lineup. But as the league expanded and the number of games increased, the demands on the lone goaltender in the lineup proved to be too much, so teams started dressing two goaltenders for each game. The two-goaltender system became known as two-platoon goalkeeping, though the term is never used today.

T

USA Hockey: The governing body for all amateur ice hockey in the United States. The association is also a member of the International Ice Hockey Federation (IIHF). USA Hockey was founded on March 16, 1920, as a way to organize and promote the development of hockey programs. USA Hockey now operates out of Ann Arbour, Michigan.

Umpire: In the early days of hockey, referees were often called umpires, but the term is no longer used.

See Referee; Ref

Unbeaten Streak: A stretch of consecutive wins used in reference to a team's or a goaltender's performance. The longest team unbeaten streak in the NHL goes to the 1979–80 Philadelphia Flyers, who started their streak on October 14, 1979, with a 4–3 over the Toronto Maple Leafs and ended the streak with a 7–1 loss to the Minnesota North Stars, for a total of 35 games (25 wins, 10 ties).

Unconscious: When a player is struck in the head and losses consciousness. One of the more common words used in hockey these days as such injuries are garnering more media attention.

See Concussion; Post-concussion Syndrome (PCS)

Uncork: Colloquial term for when a player shoots the puck, as in "He really uncorked that shot on the goaltender."

Undefeated: *See* Unbeaten Streak

Underdog: Any particular team that is not expected to win a game or playoff series. People generally like to cheer for the underdog.

Undisclosed Injury: When a player is injured and the team does not release the nature of the injury to the media so as not to give opponents an edge, especially in the playoffs.

Undressed: When a player or goaltender is completely fooled by another player's sweet stickhandling moves, he has been undressed. As the word naturally suggests to the

U

447

imagination, it can be embarrassing for a player to be caught undressed in front of thousands of screaming fans.

United Center: Home of the Chicago Blackhawks. It is also home to the Chicago Bulls. Built in 1994, it replaced Chicago Stadium, which was demolished after the United Center opened in August 1994. It seats 19,717 for a hockey game, although the Blackhawks set an attendance record in 2011 when 22,195 fans packed in (including standing room) to see the Hawks play against the San Jose Sharks in the playoffs.

Instead of putting in a new state-of-the-art sound system blaring the latest music, the United Center retained the old organ from Chicago Stadium, giving the new building a connection to its history. Its nicknames are "The UC" and "The Madhouse on Madison."

See Chicago Blackhawks

Unrestricted Free Agent (UFA): A hockey player over the age of 27 who has earned the right, if he so chooses, to walk away from his current team when his contract has expired and "test the waters" of free agency. Any team in the NHL can make a UFA player an offer to try and lure them to play for their team. UFAs usually cash-in with high-paying contracts and lucrative bonuses.

See Restricted Free Agent (RFA)

V

Vancouver Canucks: Vancouver is no stranger to hockey. Back in 1912, the city was booming—it had a population of over 100,000, and money was rolling in from its busy ports. The Patrick family, who had amassed a great deal of wealth in the lumber industry during this time, decided that the West needed to have its own professional hockey league. Brothers Lester and Frank Patrick had reputations as astute hockey men because they had played in Montréal for teams such as the Wanderers and Victorias, so there was no question that they knew their way around the system. The pair successfully worked out the formation of the Pacific Coast Hockey Association (PCHA), and in 1912, the league had its first season. The Vancouver Millionaires (1915) and the Victoria Cougars (1925) brought the Stanley Cup to the West Coast, but professional hockey eventually failed when the Western Canada Hockey League (WCHL) folded in 1926. After the loss of the professional clubs, amateur and junior hockey took its place, but the people of British Columbia always longed to see the return of NHL-style hockey.

From 1945 to 1970, the minor league Vancouver Canucks toiled in the PCHA and Western Hockey League (WHL). In 1966, the Canucks were sold to a group of local executives who began to lay the groundwork for the team's admittance into the NHL. Thus, when the NHL expanded from the original six teams, Vancouver was one of the cities that put in a bid to start the 1967–68 season with a new franchise. The NHL turned it down. It wasn't until 1969 that the Canucks' bid was finally accepted, and the new Vancouver team was allowed to join the big leagues along with the Buffalo Sabres.

The team's first decade wasn't easy. The lone bright spot in those dark years was the 1974–75 season, when the team finished atop the Smythe Division and earned their first playoff berth. Unfortunately, that first playoff round was against the Montréal Canadiens, who had finished the season with 30 more points than the Canucks and who had three players in the top 20 in league scoring. The Canucks did manage one win in the series but were out in five games.

While wearing some of the most horrible uniforms in NHL history (remember the yellow, orange and black V-neck jerseys?), the Canucks managed to sneak into the playoffs with a losing record of 30 wins and 33 losses during the 1981–82 season—they were second in their division, so lucky for them, it guaranteed the team a spot in the postseason. Unlike the rest of the league, the Canucks weren't afraid

to stock their lineup with European players, and when it came time for the playoffs, the team pulled together and surprised the entire NHL. Players such as Thomas Gradin, Stan Smyl, Ivan Boldirev, Ivan Hlinka and Lars Lindgren formed the scoring backbone of this 1981–82 team, while Dave "Tiger" Williams was their resident tough guy.

The Canucks might not have had Wayne Gretzky or Mike Bossy, but they played solid hockey led by the brilliant coaching of Roger Neilson. And so in the playoffs, Vancouver charged past the Calgary Flames, Los Angeles Kings and Chicago Blackhawks to make it into the franchise's first Stanley Cup final. Unfortunately, it was against the powerful, high-scoring, tough New York Islanders, and the Canucks couldn't do anything to beat them and were swept in four games straight.

Over the next several seasons in the NHL, Canucks fans established a deep rivalry with Edmonton and Calgary because it seemed like every year that Vancouver made it into the playoffs, they were greeted by either the Oilers or Flames and thus promptly eliminated in the first round. And when Gretzky moved from Edmonton to Los Angeles, he still continued to frustrate Canucks fans, eliminating Vancouver from Cup contention on more than one occasion.

Finally, in the 1994 playoffs, the Vancouver Canucks shook off all their competitors to make it to the Stanley Cup final for the second time. On May 31, 1994, the Canucks, led by Trevor Linden and Pavel Bure, faced off against the New York Rangers at Madison Square Garden. Sure, Vancouver had put aside a disappointing season to reach the finals, but the Rangers were also hungry, ready to battle the demons of a 54-year Cup drought. The Canucks jumped out to a 3–1 series lead and were ready to bring the Cup to Vancouver for the first time since 1915, but the Rangers rallied and handed the Canucks a game-seven loss that was difficult to swallow. Vancouver fans were, to be blunt, angry. They rioted on the streets of their city, and by the time order was restored, 200 people were arrested, damage was estimated in the millions and a 19-year-old man became severely disabled after being shot in the head with a rubber bullet.

Since 1994, the Vancouver Canucks have had a few successes and seen some amazing players go through their lineup, but it wasn't until the arrival of the twins Daniel and Hendrik Sedin, centre Ryan Kesler and goaltender Roberto Luongo that the Canucks fans felt once again that their team could challenge for the Cup. The moment finally came in the 2011 Stanley Cup finals, when Vancouver met the Boston Bruins. It was the tale of two different teams: while Boston played a hard-hitting, rough, crash-the-net style of hockey, the Canucks relied on the skills of the Sedins and Kesler. The series went to a deciding seventh game in Vancouver, but the Canucks again lost in the final. The loss was painful for the city, but what turned out to be harder to accept was that after the game, the fans descended into the streets around the arena and rioted, destroying anything in their paths. The one consolation for the city is that in this day and age everyone has cellphone cameras, and a good number of the rioters were arrested.

The Canucks returned to the playoffs in 2012 after that tough loss but were unceremoniously beaten in the first round by the Los Angeles Kings. The city will have to wait another year for another run at the Cup.

Vancouver Canucks Records

Most goals in a season: Pavel Bure, 60 (1993–94; 1992–93)

Most assists in a season: Henrik Sedin, 83 (2009–10)

Most points in a season: Henrik Sedin, 112 (2009–10)

Most points in a season, defenceman: Doug Lidster, 63 (1986–87)

Most points in a season, rookie: Pavel Bure (1991–92) and Ivan Hlinka (1981–82), 60

Most penalty minutes in a season: Donald Brashear, 372 (1997–98)

Most wins in a season: Roberto Luongo, 47 (2006–07)

Most shutouts in a season: Roberto Luongo, 9 (2008–09)

Lowest goals-against average in a season (minimum 30 games played): Roberto Luongo, 2.11 (2010–11)

Best save percentage in a season (minimum 30 games played): Roberto Luongo, .928 (2010–11)

See Rogers Arena

Vancouver Millionaires: Founded in 1911, the Vancouver Millionaires were part of the Pacific Coast Hockey Association (PCHA), and the team was owned, coached and managed by Frank Patrick (he even played for them for a bit). At the time, the PCHA was in tough competition for quality players with the East Coast leagues and often stole players away. For example, the Ottawa Senators lost superstar Frederick "Cyclone" Taylor to the Millionaires in 1912.

At the start of the 1914–15 season, the PCHA and the National Hockey Association (NHA) came to an agreement that each league's respective champion would play for the rights to the Stanley Cup. In that first year, the Millionaires won their league title and then defeated the Ottawa Senators to earn their first and only Stanley Cup win. The Millionaires once again challenged for the Stanley Cup in 1918 but lost to the NHL's Toronto Arenas, and in 1921 and 1922 lost out to the Ottawa Senators both times.

In 1923, the Millionaires moved over to the Western Canadian Hockey League (WCHL) but never again achieved the success they had in previous years. In 1926, the WCHL folded because of financial problems and with them went the Millionaires. Vancouver did not see professional level hockey again until the arrival of the Canucks in 1969.

Vaughn: Hockey equipment maker, specializing in goalie gear.

V

Velvet Touch: A player who is said to have the "velvet touch" is one who can score goals and make plays with seemingly little effort and maximum artistry.

Verizon Center: Formerly known as the MCI Center, the home arena of the Washington Capitals, the Verizon Center was constructed in 1997 to replace the Capital Center, which played host to the Capitals from 1974 to 1997. The Verizon Center is located in downtown Washington, DC, and seats 18,506 fans for hockey games. It is also the home of the Washington Wizards of the NBA and the Washington Power of the National Lacrosse League.

See Washington Capitals

Vezina Trophy: Trophy awarded annually to the NHL's best goaltender, voted upon by the 30 general managers at the end of the regular season. The trophy is named in honour of Georges Vezina of the Montréal Canadiens, who played from 1910 to 1925. The Canadiens donated the trophy one year after Vezina died from complications relating to tuberculosis. The trophy was first handed out at the end of the 1926–27 season and was given to Vezina's successor on the Canadiens, Georges Hainsworth.

When the trophy was originally handed out, it was given to the most valuable goaltender in the league. In 1946, the criteria were amended to go to the goaltender(s) who allowed the fewest goals during the regular season. This criteria was again changed in at the end of the 1981–82 season with the creation of the William Jennings Trophy that was given to the goaltender(s) who allowed the fewest goals. The Vezina Trophy then returned to be an award for the best goaltender in the league. The system of giving the Vezina Trophy to the goaltender with the fewest goals was flawed as it did not necessarily recognize the best goaltender; rather, it reflected the goaltender(s) who just happened to be on the best (or most defensive-minded) teams.

Georges Hainsworth of the Montréal Canadiens won the first three Vezina trophies, while Jacques Plante holds the most Vezinas with seven (six with the Canadiens and one with the St. Louis Blues).

See William M. Jennings Trophy

Victoria Cougars: Founded in 1911 and run by Lester Patrick, the Cougars were the last non-NHL team to win the Stanley Cup in 1925. They began life in the Pacific Coast Hockey Association (PCHA) as the Victoria Senators, but then in the 1916–17 season, the team was forced to move to Spokane, Washington, when the Canadian military took over their arena during World War I. In Spokane, they were known as the Spokane Canaries. The team folded at the end of the season and only started back up in Victoria in 1918, but this time named the Aristocrats. From 1918 to 1922, they were known as the Aristocrats, then they changed their name one final time to the Victoria Cougars. In 1924, they joined the Western Canada Hockey League (WCHL) along with other teams from the PCHA. In 1925, the Cougars won their league championship and then went on to defeat the Montréal Canadiens in the Stanley Cup finals.

Victoria Cougars 1925 Stanley Cup Roster: John Jocko Anderson, Wally Elmer, Frank Foyston, Gord Fraser, Frank Fredrickson, Harold Halderson, Harold Hart, Clem Loughlin, Harry Meeking, Jack Walker and Harry Holmes.

Victoria Rink: An indoor skating rink located in Montréal that played host to some of the most historic moments in hockey history. When it opened in 1862, the rink was lauded as one of the finest in the world. In winter, the rink's natural ice surface was used for skating, hockey games and skating races, and in summer, the building hosted live concerts and other events. It was also the first building in Canada to have electricity, allowing patrons to skate into the night.

On March 3, 1875, the rink played host to the first recorded organized indoor hockey game. Hockey at the time was often an unorganized mash-up of numerous players with no rules and no time limits. The difference in this March game was that Victoria Skating Club member James Creighton had played hockey most of his life in Halifax and brought with him to Montréal the rules he used to play under. Creighton gathered a few of his club friends and a few from McGill and divided his friends into two teams of nine players. Creighton did not just want this to be a game between friends—he wanted the public to know about this new game—so he sent notice to the *Montréal Gazette,* and on March 3, 1875, they published a notice in the paper about the game.

About 40 people showed up to watch the two teams skate around the ice, chasing a flat block of wood (most hockey at the time was played with a rubber ball) around the ice. The game ended with Creighton's team winning 2–1. The *Gazette* reporter the next day wrote of the event as an "interesting and well-contested affair, the efforts of the players exciting much merriment." This game provided a set of guidelines around which players could organize future games and took hockey from the frozen ponds and pick-up games to a proper organized sport.

Video Goal Judge: The off-ice official who reviews disputed goals by watching television replays of the play in question from various camera angles to render the decision.

Visiting Team: The team that has travelled from their home city to the home arena of their opponents.

See Home Team

Visor: Name for the plastic shield attached to the front of a player's helmet to protect the face and the eyes from injury. The first player to wear a visor, or shield as it is sometimes called, was Greg Neeld, who lost an eye after being high-sticked in a junior game in 1973. Neeld never made it to the NHL. Today, over 60 percent of NHL players wear a visor.

Vulcanized Rubber: Vulcanization is a chemical process that converts rubber into a more durable material via the addition of curing chemicals. Vulcanization of rubber changed the way hockey was played. When the first rubber pucks were used, they often broke after being slapped about on the ice. Vulcanization of the pucks made them more durable and able to withstand the abuse that professional hockey players put their equipment through.

See Puck

WCHL (Western Canada Hockey League): A major professional hockey league originally based in the Prairies. Founded in 1921, the league comprised four teams: the Calgary Tigers, Edmonton Eskimos, Regina Capitals and Moose Jaw Sheiks. The Regina Capitals won the league title in the first year. The WCHL lasted until the end of the 1924–25 season. During the offseason, the league merged with the also-defunct Pacific Coast Hockey Association (PCHA) and added the Vancouver Maroons and Victoria Cougars to its ranks. The new league changed its name to the Western Hockey League (WHL).

See PCHA; WHL

WHA (World Hockey Association): Professional hockey league that operated in North America from 1972 to 1979. Sold as an alternative to the NHL, the WHA opened up franchises in many cities that did not have NHL teams, including (but not limited to) Hartford, Winnipeg, Edmonton and Québec City. When the league began, the average NHL salary was $25,000, so the WHA was able to lure many NHL players over to their league with higher salaries and less restrictive contracts. The biggest name to sign a deal with the WHA was Bobby Hull, who agreed to a 10-year, $2.7-million contract with the Winnipeg Jets in 1972.

Despite the promise of quality hockey and new markets, financial problems plagued the franchises, with many teams folding after one season or even mid-season. Teams simply could not afford the higher player salaries and the cost of renting the arenas in many of the cities from the NHL team owners. After several years of failed teams and waning interest from fans, the WHA agreed to sell off some of its players and some of the franchises to the NHL. In 1979, the World Hockey Association closed its doors.

The championship trophy in the WHA was called the Avco Cup, and it was won by the Winnipeg Jets three times in seven years.

See Avco Cup

WHL (Western Hockey League): In the history of hockey, there have been three important incarnations of the WHL. Formerly known as the Western Canada Hockey League, the WCHL lasted only for the 1925–26 season. It became the WHL after the Pacific Coast Hockey Association (PCHA) disbanded and two of its teams joined the WCHL. The Victoria Cougars of the WHL were the last non-NHL team to win the Stanley Cup. In 1926, the league folded because of financial difficulties. The WHL was then a minor pro league from 1952 to 1972.

The Western Hockey League (previously known as the Western Canada Hockey League until American teams joined) was founded in 1978 as a major junior league with teams competing throughout Western Canada and north-western United States. The Memorial Cup has been won by a WHL team 18 times since the league's founding. Some

notable NHL players to come out of the WHL are Ray Ferraro, Carey Price, Shane Doan and Cam Neely.

Waffle Pad: Also known as the goaltender's blocker. It is the large, rectangular pad attached to the goaltender's stick hand.

See Blocker

Wales Conference: Created in 1974 when the NHL realigned its teams into two conferences and four divisions. The conference was named after the Prince of Wales Trophy, which is handed out to the winner of the conference in the playoffs before the Stanley Cup final. The divisions in the conference were initially named the Adams and Patrick divisions because their alignment had nothing to do with geography. In 1993, when the NHL did another realignment, the Wales Conference along with all other conference and division names were tossed out in favour of geographical names in order to reflect the locations and to help new fans identify with the league on a regional basis.

See Eastern Conference

Wales Trophy: *See* Prince of Wales Trophy

Wandering Goalie: A goaltender who likes to stray from his crease in order to play the puck. This type of goaltender gives coaches grey hair.

Wash Out: A goal that is ruled invalid or when an infraction such as icing is waved off by the referee. The ref will usually swing his arms outward to his sides in a "washing-out" motion to signal to the players that the play was ruled invalid.

Washington Capitals: Construction company owner Abe Pollin lobbied hard to bring an NHL team to the American capital and was rewarded in 1972 with the rights to a franchise. But building a quality team at the time was difficult as the WHA and the NHL player requirements had stretched the talent pool very thin. The result was that the Washington Capitals did not have a good team when they hit the ice for their inaugural season in 1974–75. Head coach Jimmy Anderson and general manager Milt Schmidt could do little to salvage the season. They finished with an abysmal record of 8–67–5. There was nothing to be proud of after that season, but the Capitals fans stuck with the team through the rough patches.

The Capitals made a slight improvement the following season, winning 11 games and losing 59, but behind the scenes, the Capitals were slowly building the franchise, and while a team like the Kansas City Scouts struggled to get fans in the stands, the Caps managed to survive. The 1976–77 season gave the city a reason to hope when the team finished with a record of 24–42–14, thanks to the acquisition of players Guy Charron and Gerry Meehan, but the Caps faltered again, finishing with a record of 17–49–14 in 1977–78. Until 1981–82, the Capitals could not find a way out of the basement of the league. They tried new coaches, new general managers and new players, but the Caps did not have the right combination for success.

Right before the 1982–83 season, the Capitals acquired Montréal defenceman Rod Langway, Brian Engblom, Doug Jarvis and Craig Laughlin. This infusion of new blood finally pulled the team out of the cellar and into their first winning season. Finishing third in their division, the Capitals made it into the playoffs for the first time but were taken out in the first round by eventual repeat Stanley Cup champions New York Islanders. It was a tough loss, but the Capitals only got better. The following season, the entire team was working well, with Rod Langway winning the James Norris Memorial Trophy, Doug Jarvis taking the Frank J. Selke Trophy and the goaltending pair of Al Jensen and Pat Riggin winning the Williams M. Jennings Trophy. The Caps finished the 1983–84 season with their best-ever record of 48–27–5. After beating the Philadelphia Flyers in the opening round of the playoffs, the Capitals were foiled in their pursuit of the Cup once again by the New York Islanders.

Disappointment in the playoffs would become a familiar refrain in Washington as the Caps put up good numbers in the regular season but could never make any impact in the playoffs. Despite having such good players as Mike Gartner, Mike Ridley and Larry Murphy, the Capitals only made it as far as the conference finals once in 1990, losing the series to Boston in four straight. It was the same story for most of the 1990s, and despite elite players like Adam Oates and Peter Bondra, the Capitals just could not formulate a Stanley Cup winner. What they needed was a franchise goaltender. They thought they had found that in rookie Jim Carey in the early 1990s, but he fizzled fast. Then along came German Olaf Kolzig who found a hot hand in the 1998 playoffs, leading the team past Boston in the first round, Ottawa in the conference semifinals and beating Buffalo in the conference finals before losing tragically in the Stanley Cup finals to the Detroit Red Wings in four straight games.

The Capitals had hoped that the arrival of Russian phenom Alexander Ovechkin in 2004 would help the team progress, but the club has still not found its rhythm in the postseason. Ovechkin led the league in points and in his flair for the dramatic, but the team's playoff hopes never materialized into anything. From 2007 to 2010, the Capitals were one of the best teams in the league, with young players like Ovechkin, Nicklas Backstrom and Alexander Semin, but they have not made any in roads in the playoffs. Even in 2009–10, after finishing with a record of 54–15–13, the Caps lost in the first round of the playoffs to the eighth-seeded Montréal Canadiens. The Capitals led the series three games to one and allowed the Canadiens to make a comeback before losing the series in the seventh game. All along, the Capitals have recognized the need for a franchise goaltender, and during the 2010–11 offseason, they acquired Tomas Vokoun from the Florida Panthers, but only time will tell if the Capitals will ever live up to expectations.

Washington Capitals Records

Most goals in a season: Alexander Ovechkin, 65 (2007–08)

Most goals in a season, defencemen: Kevin Hatcher, 34 (1992–93)

Most power-play goals in a season: Alexander Ovechkin (2007–08) and Peter Bondra (2000–01), 22

Most power-play goals in a season, defencemen: Mike Green, 18 (2008–09)

Most shorthanded goals in a season: Peter Bondra (1994–95) and Mike Gartner (1986–87), 6

Most shorthanded goals in a career: Peter Bondra, 32

Most game-winning goals in a season: Peter Bondra, 13 (1997–98)

See Verizon Center

Weak Side: Used in reference to a goaltender's ability to make a save. Most goaltenders will be better either on their left or right side, leaving one side as the "weak side."

Wells Fargo Center: Formerly known as the CoreStates Center, First Union Center and Wachovia Center. Wells Fargo Center is the current home of the Philadelphia Flyers. The Center replaced the aging Spectrum in 1996. It is also the home of the NBA's Philadelphia 76ers and the Philadelphia Wings of the National Lacrosse League. The arena seats 19,537 for a hockey game and is known for being one of the louder arenas in the league.

See Philadelphia Flyers

Western Conference: Previously known as the Clarence Campbell Conference, the Western Conference was born when the NHL realigned its teams in 1993 moving for a more geographically divided league. Currently, there are three divisions in the Western Conference made up of 15 teams: the Central, Northwest and Pacific.

See Campbell Conference

Wheels: Legs. An excellent skater is said to have great wheels.

Whiteout: A name given to the playoff tradition started in Winnipeg and later in Phoenix, where all the fans wear white T-shirts and wave white towels during the game. With the return of the Winnipeg Jets in 2011, the tradition continues.

Wicket: A term borrowed from cricket. In cricket, it describes the three posts and two bails that are positioned behind the batter. When hockey first began, the game was a hybrid of many sports and did not really have its own name. So in the absence of any concrete name for the new sport, the word "wicket" was used to describe what would come to be known as hockey.

William M. Jennings Trophy: Annual NHL award given to the goaltender(s) with the fewest goals scored against in the regular season. From 1946 to 1981, the Vezina Trophy was awarded under that criteria but was later dropped in favour of the Jennings Trophy. Donated by the NHL board of governors, the trophy is named in honour of William M. Jennings, who was a long-time NHL governor and president of the New York Rangers. It was first donated in 1982 to Rick Wamsley and Denis Heron of the Montréal Canadiens. Patrick Roy and Martin Brodeur have both won the trophy a record five times.

See Vezina Trophy

Wings: The left and right wings are the two players that flank the centre on the forward attacking line.

See Centreman

Winning Percentage: The ratio of points a team gains over a season to the total possible points available.

Winnipeg Jets: When the NHL expanded in the 1970s, Vancouver was the only Canadian team lucky enough to receive a franchise. For all the other professional hockey teams in Canada, the WHA was where it was at. The WHA brought pro hockey to Ottawa, Québec City, Winnipeg, Edmonton and Calgary, but when the association folded in 1979, it left behind five empty, hockey-hungry markets. The Winnipeg Jets were one of the best teams in the WHA, with three Avco Cup championships to their name, but when the league dissolved and the Jets were incorporated into the NHL, they had to give up their top players to the Expansion Draft, losing the key ingredients that had made them a successful team in the first place. In the Jets' debut year in the NHL in 1979, they were at the bottom of the league for the entire season. In fact, the Jets only got worse, and the following season, the team won just nine games and finished with only 32 points—one of the worst 70-plus-game seasons on record.

One perk about these terrible seasons, however, was that the Jets were able to pick at the top of the pack during the NHL Entry Drafts that followed their dismal years. And so, by the mid-1980s, the Jets had signed a solid lineup of players that included top draft picks Dale Hawerchuk and Kent Nilsson. Adding grit were players Dave Babych, Randy Carlyle and David Ellett, and just one year after posting one of the worst winning records in NHL history, the Jets finished the 1981–82 season second place in the Norris division and earned their first appearance in the playoffs. The St. Louis Blues eliminated Winnipeg in the first round, but the Jets had experienced a significant turnaround that, at the very least, kept them away from last place.

The Jets' Prairie rivals were strong, however, and despite the firepower of Hawerchuk and Paul MacLean, the team spent nearly the entire 1980s under the thumbs of the Edmonton Oilers and Calgary Flames. Winnipeg was good, but the Oilers and Flames were simply better. The Jets' faithful always hoped that their club would make it to the Stanley Cup finals, but Winnipeg never advanced past the second round of the playoffs during the team's entire history.

As the team's fortunes took a downward turn in the late 1980s and mid-1990s, and the team's losing records and early playoff exits began to mount, the Jets' expenses, inconveniently, started to increase. They were one of the league's smallest markets, and continuing a franchise in the city guaranteed a financial loss for the team's owners. Unable to compete with the large-market teams and retain quality players, the Jets were forced to fold. It was a devastating blow for the fans in Winnipeg, who had fully embraced their team despite its losing ways. The Winnipeg Jets played their last game on April 28, 1996, in game six of the opening round of the playoffs against the Detroit Red Wings. The Jets lost the game 4–1 and, thus, the series. Norm MacIver scored the final goal in the franchise's history, and after the season was over, the team was moved to Phoenix, where they became the Coyotes.

Fast forward about 15 years and talk began to swirl around the league and in Winnipeg that True North Sports & Entertainment were looking at bringing NHL hockey back to Manitoba. Since the idea of expanding the league to accommodate another team seemed unlikely, the True North company began looking at other struggling NHL franchises. Early reports indicated that the Phoenix Coyotes were looking for a buyer, but that avenue never panned out. Then True North's sights were set on the Atlanta Thrashers, who made the playoffs only once in their 12-year existence and had been losing money for years. After much speculation and behind-the-curtain negotiations, it was finally announced on May 20, 2011, that the Atlanta Thrashers would relocate to Winnipeg. On May 31, 2011, league commissioner Gary Bettman officially confirmed the news.

The True North company had stated that the name of the team would be announced at a later date, but everyone in Winnipeg knew the team name had to be the Jets. Kevin Cheveldayoff was selected by True North as the new Winnipeg Jets general manager. Unlike playing in an empty arena in Atlanta, the new Jets players were welcomed to their first home game on October 9, 2011, by a sold out crowd, where fans paid almost $750 a ticket just to see their old team. The new Winnipeg Jets lost their home opener to the Montréal Canadiens by a score of 5–1, but the fans didn't seemed to care. All that mattered were that the Jets were back in town. To date, the team has put together a decent season and is looking to build on the future with young stars like Mark Scheifele, Evander Kane and Zach Bogosian.

Winnipeg Jets Records

Most goals in a season: Teemu Selanne, 76 (1992–93)

Most assists in a season: Phil Housley, 79 (1992–93)

Most points in a season: Teemu Selanne, 132 (1992–93)

Most points in a season, defenceman: Phil Housley, 97 (1992–93)

Most points in a season, rookie: Teemu Selanne, 132 (1992–93)

Winnipeg Jets Records (continued)

Most penalty minutes in a season: Tie Domi, 347 (1993–94)

Most wins in a season: Brian Hayward (1992–93) and Bob Essensa (1984–85), 33

See Atlanta Thrashers; MTS Centre; Phoenix Coyotes

Winnipeg Victorias: Originally organized in 1899, the team mainly played other teams in Manitoba and later helped in the formation of the Manitoba Hockey Association. In the era of the Challenge Cup, the Victorias challenged the champion Montréal Victorias in February 1896 and won the Cup. They held onto the Cup for only a few months, when Montréal won the Cup back in December. The Victorias then won the Cup again from the Montréal Shamrocks in January 1901 and held onto the prize until March 1902, losing to the Montréal Hockey Club. After 1908, when the Stanley Cup was only awarded to professional clubs, the Victorias remained an amateur club, competing for the Allan Cup.

Wire: Another euphemism for shooting the puck hard. "He wired that puck at the net."

World Cup of Hockey: In 1996, the Canada Cup officially became the World Cup of Hockey. Unlike the World Championships of Hockey, organized by the IIHF, the World Cup is organized by the NHL. Since changing over to the World Cup of Hockey, there have only been two tournaments. The United States won in 1996 and Canada won in 2004.

Wrap-around: One of the most annoying goals for a goaltender to let in. A wrap-around occurs when a player takes the puck behind the net and tries to come around quickly from the side to slide the puck into the net. The move is effective because it forces the goaltender to quickly move laterally from one side to another, and if the player can confuse the goaltender as to which side he will attempt to put the puck in, then he will have a better chance on the wrap-around.

Wrist Shot, Wrister: A type of shot in which the player uses a strong flick of the wrist and the forearm to shoot the puck. A wrist shot is much slower but far more accurate than a slapshot.

See Slapshot

X Y

Z

Xcel Energy Center: Current home of the Minnesota Wild. It was constructed to house the return of the NHL to St. Paul–Minnesota after the departure of the Minnesota North Stars in the mid-90s. Opened in September 2000, the arena seats over 18,000 fans for hockey games and also plays host to the Minnesota Swarm of the National Lacrosse League and various concerts and events. The arena sold out over 400 straight Minnesota Wild home games between September 29, 2000, and October 16, 2010.

See Minnesota Wild

X-ray Vision: A goaltender who is able to see the puck through the traffic in front of his net and make the save is said to have X-ray vision.

Yawning Cage: A wide-open net. This can occur when a goaltender is caught out of position or when the net is empty after a goaltender pull. "Jagr shot the puck into the yawning cage."

Youppi: The mascot once only seen at the Olympic Stadium, running up and down the aisles cheering on Major League Baseball's Montréal Expos, is now wearing a Habs jersey cheering on the Canadiens.

It is hard to imagine the great Montréal Canadiens, winners of 24 Stanley Cups and boasting the most distinguished lineup of former players and Hall of Famers, would be represented by a large, hairy and orange mascot named Youppi, but in 2005, the Montréal Canadiens adopted the former Montréal Expos mascot as their own.

With the impending demise of the Montréal Expos in 2004, the fate of the team's beloved mascot hung in the balance. It was suggested that Youppi move along with the team to their new home with the Washington Nationals, but the Nationals opted for a new mascot, leaving poor Youppi in limbo. It was suggested that Youppi be placed with one of Montréal's other professional teams, either the Canadiens or the Alouettes.

Finally, on September 16, 2005, the Montréal Canadiens announced they were adopting Youppi as the first official mascot of the organization. Youppi thus established himself as the first league-switching mascot in professional sports history.

Zamboni: This wonderful machine that fans see at hockey games between periods magically scrapes off a layer of ice

and replaces it with a shiny, wet, new surface. The Zamboni was invented by Frank Zamboni and has become an integral part of hockey culture since it first appeared in 1949. Other companies produce ice resurfacers, but it is the Zamboni machine that has worked its way into the hearts and minds of hockey fans everywhere.

Zambonis: The name of an American musical quartet founded by Dave Schneider and billed as "the greatest, and only, hockey rock band."

Zebra: Because of their black-and-white-striped uniforms, referees are often referred to as zebras.

Zone: A team's end of the ice.

Notes on Sources

Book Sources

Basu, Arpon. *Hockey's Hottest Players.* Montreal: Overtime Books, 2005.

Batten, Jack. *The Leafs: An Anecdotal History of the Toronto Maple Leafs.* Toronto: Key Porter Books, 1994.

Cole, Stephen. *The Canadian Hockey Atlas.* Toronto: Doubleday Canada, 2006.

Coleman, Charles L. *The Trail of the Stanley Cup.* Volumes 1,2,3. Sherbrooke: Progressive Publications, 1969.

Diamond, Dan, ed. *Total NHL.* Toronto: Dan Diamond and Associates, 2003.

Diamond, Dan and Eric Zweig. *Hockey's Glory Days: The 1950s and '60s.* Kansas City: Andrews McMeel Publishing, 2003.

Dowbiggin, Bruce. *The Meaning Of Puck.* Toronto: Key Porter Books, 2008.

Dryden, Ken. *The Game.* Toronto: Wiley Press, 1983.

Hornby, Lance. *Hockey's Greatest Moments.* Toronto: Key Porter Books, 2004.

Jones, Martin. *Hockey's Home: Halifax–Dartmouth.* Halifax: Nimbus Publishing, 2002.

McDonnell, Chris. *Hockey's Greatest Stars: Legends and Young Lions.* Willowdale: Firefly Books, 1999.

McKinley, Michael. *Putting a Roof On Winter*. Vancouver: Greystone Books, 2000.

Podnieks, Andrew, et al. *Kings of the Ice: A History of World Hockey*. Richmond Hill: NDE Publishing, 2002.

Turowetz, Allan and Chrys Goyens. *Lions In Winter*. Scarborough: Prentice Hall, 1986.

Vaughan, Garth. *The Puck Starts Here*. Fredericton: Four East Publications, 1996.

Web Sources

www.hockeydb.com The Internet Hockey Database (n.d.) Retrieved January to May 15, 2012.

en.wikipedia.org Wikipedia, the free encyclopedia (n.d.) Retrieved January to May 15, 2012.

All teams statistics taken from Wikipedia.org

J. Alexander Poulton is a writer, photographer and genuine enthusiast of Canada's national pastime. A resident of Montreal all his life, he has developed a healthy passion for hockey ever since he saw his first Montreal Canadiens game. His favorite memory was meeting the legendary gentleman hockey player Jean Beliveau, who in 1988 towered over the young awe-struck author.

He earned his B.A in English Literature from McGill University and his graduate diploma in Journalism from Concordia University. He has more than 20 books to his credit, including *Canadian Hockey Record Breakers, Greatest Moments in Canadian Hockey, Greatest Games of the Stanley Cup, Canadian Hockey Trivia, Hockey's Hottest Defensemen, The Montréal Canadiens, The Toronto Maple Leafs, Sidney Crosby, Does This Make Me Look Fat? Canadian Sport Humour* and *A History of Hockey in Canada,*